MAP LEGEND

▬	Expressway	Ⓢ	Shop/Shopping	⬛	Embassy/Consulate
▬	Major Street	Ⓑ	Bank	🎭	Theater
	Secondary Street	⊠	Post office	★	Police
	Large Minor Street	🏫	School	✚	Hospital
	Small Minor Street	■	University	▬	Stadium
	Footpath	Ⓐ	Apartment	❶	Tourist Information
	Parks/Gardens	⛩	Shinto Shrine	Ⓗ	Hotel
→	One-way arrow	卍	Buddhist temple	Ⓡ	Restaurant
🚌	Bus terminal	†	Church	★	Place of interest
✈	Travel Agent/Airline Office			🏛	Museum

Published by Tuttle Publishing, an imprint of Periplus Editions (HK) Ltd

www.tuttlepublishing.com

Copyright © 2017 by Periplus Editions (HK) Ltd
Cover photo © TommiL, iStockphoto

LCC No.: 2010938391

ISBN 978-4-8053-0965-0

Distributed by

North America, Latin America & Europe
Tuttle Publishing
364 Innovation Drive
North Clarendon, VT 05759-9436 U.S.A.
Tel: 1 (802) 773-8930;Fax: 1 (802) 773-6993
info@tuttlepublishing.com
www.tuttlepublishing.com

Japan
Tuttle Publishing
Yaekari Building, 3rd Floor
5-4-12 Osaki, Shinagawa-ku, Tokyo 141 0032
Tel: (81) 3 5437-0171;Fax: (81) 3 5437-0755
sales@ tuttle.co.jp
www.tuttle.co.jp

Asia Pacific
Berkeley Books Pte. Ltd.
61 Tai Seng Avenue #02-12, Singapore 534167
Tel: (65) 6280-1330; Fax: (65) 6280-6290
inquiries@periplus.com.sg
www.periplus.com

20 19 18 17   1709CM
10 9 8 7 6 5

Printed in China

Getting Around

TOKYO

POCKET ATLAS
AND TRANSPORTATION GUIDE

Includes Yokohama, Kamakura, Yokota,
Yokosuka, Hakone and Mt. Fuji

Boyé Lafayette De Mente

TUTTLE Publishing

Tokyo │ Rutland, Vermont │ Singapore

CONTENTS

Left: *Tokyo Tower —the symbol of Tokyo*

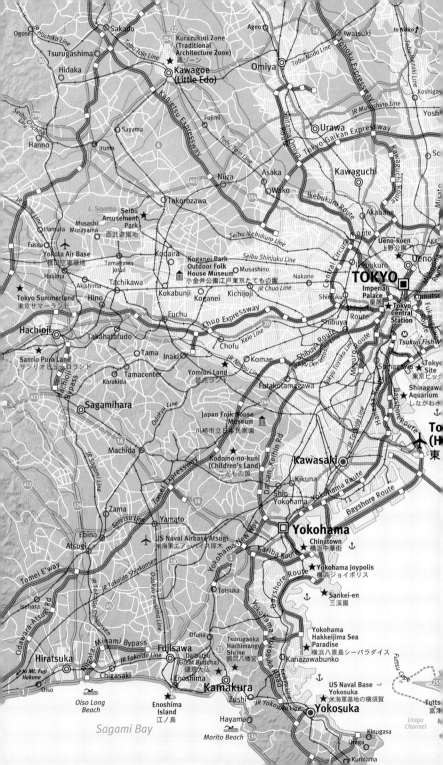

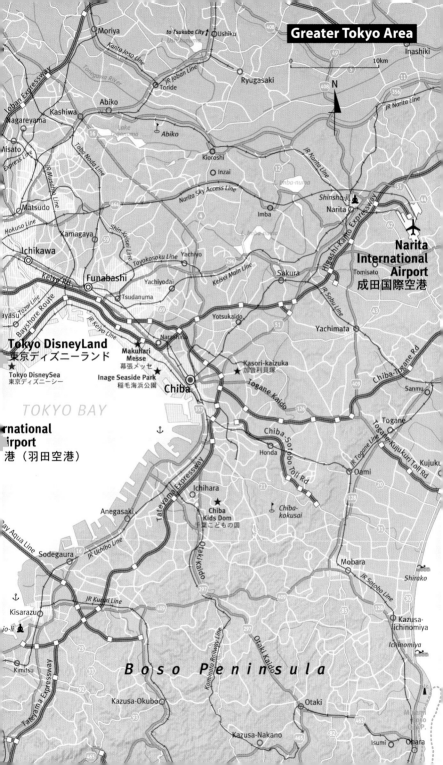

Navigating Tokyo's Byzantine Transportation Network

Tokyo has the largest and most efficient public transportation system in the world, but using it effectively requires some detailed information. The system consists of commuter train lines, subway lines and bus lines integrated into a vast network that makes it possible to transfer or change from one line to the other and reach over a thousand destinations within the city, in suburban areas, and to go to adjoining towns and cities.

These transfer points are centered in several dozen hub stations, where as many as five subway lines and seven commuter railway lines intersect. All of these hub stations have platform signs indicating the locations of the connecting lines and directions to go from one line to the others.

There are two subway companies serving Tokyo with 13 lines and several commuter train lines, both public and private. In most cases, these lines share the same hub stations so all you have to do is follow the platform directions to go from one line to another. At some stations the boarding platforms are up to 400 or more meters apart via long corridors.

Tokyo's Train and Subway System

Once you are in Tokyo, there are several very real challenges in using the city's surface railway and subway systems. First is determining which of the systems offers the best choice of transportation. Second is determining which line or which combination of lines to use. Third is buying your ticket (see page 12). Fourth is identifying the station that is nearest your destination (there are over 250 subway stations and upwards of 100 train stations in Tokyo), and finally, determining which exit to use after you have disembarked at the right station.

The first four challenges are fairly easy to meet. The fifth one—using the exit that is closest to your destination—is often the most difficult of all.

Tokyo's subway stations generally have two or more exits. Many have over a dozen exits. If you cannot read or speak Japanese, the problem presented by multiple exits can be very serious. Even if you do know the language, your destination is often not on any of the station and platform signs, and unless you are going to a well-known place, station attendants (who generally do not speak English) usually can give you only general directions based on the area address of your destination.

If you do not know which exit to take and "guess" wrong, you can "come up" blocks away from where you want to be. In fact, there are many stations where you can be on the opposite side of huge building complexes or other barriers that block your passage, making it a major trek to your destination. This regularly results not only in visitors and newcomers but long-time residents as well getting hopelessly lost.

Asking Japanese or long-time foreign residents of Tokyo to tell you what exit to take for a particular destination is not a satisfactory option. Few of them have memorized more than three or four exit numbers—if that many. They normally learn their own regular routes by turns and other signs, and pay no attention to the exit numbers.

Commuter train stations in Tokyo generally have from two to four or five primary exits, and some of the larger stations have a variety of other exits—some leading to subway and other train connections, and others leading into the basements of office buildings and department stores.

Shibuya Station, one of the primary transportation hub stations on the Yamanote Line, is in fact on an upper level of a huge department store, with multiple exits to a variety of connections and destinations, including two adjoining city bus terminals, two subway lines, two commuter train lines and famous entertainment and shopping districts.

Multiple Subway and Railway Operators

Many of the key destinations in Tokyo are served by more than one subway line, making them more accessible from a wider variety of starting points. Many of them are also served by Japan Railway (JR) lines and other private lines as an additional option for users who are closer to a train station than a subway station.

Most subway and JR stations have automatic ticket wickets as well as live attendants. Most of the stations accept both printed paper tickets and electronic passes that you just swipe or pass over a reader (very much like checkout counters in stores).

At these high-tech gates you insert your ticket into an entry slot and it pops up from an exit slot about 60 centimeters away. In the process, it is punched and causes the low batwing doors to open—all in less than a second. You retrieve your ticket from the exit slot as you pass through the turnstile doors.

When exiting via an automatic wicket, it keeps your ticket. Again, if the amount of the ticket is incorrect, the doors will not open and a buzzer sounds. (You must retrieve the ticket and go to the Ticket Adjustment Window or a Ticket Adjustment vending machine and pay the required balance.) Automatic entry and exit wickets that are in operation are marked by green and red lights indicating whether they are entry or exit turnstiles. Green lights on entry gates include arrows pointing forward.

There are Information Offices, with some English-speaking attendants, at a number of subway stations, including Ginza, Nihonbashi, Otemachi and Shinjuku. There is also a Toei Information Office in the passageway connecting the Toei Mita and Yurakucho Lines at Hibiya Station. Larger JR stations have Information Offices.

City Bus Services & Bus Stations

The larger of Tokyo's transportation hub stations are also the starting points of an extensive public bus system that covers the interior residential areas of the several hundred districts making up the city, and are mostly used by residents going to and from their homes.

There are two large bus companies: Toei, which operates buses on the east side of the city, and Keio, which operates buses on the west side of the city. Buses are generally more expensive than commuter trains and subways.

There are bus terminals at most of the main railway transportation hubs in Tokyo. These include: Tokyo Station, Ikebukuro Station, Shinjuku Station, Shibuya Station, Asakusa Station, Ueno Station, Ryogoku Station and Nihonbashi Station, where their routes—some of them to distant outlying areas—begin and end.

If you are going to a private residence or some other relatively isolated destination it is very important that you have someone call the destination for you and get precise instructions on which bus line or other transportation service to use, and where you should get off.

At bus terminals there are lines of *Noriba* [No-ree-bah] or Boarding Areas that are marked by individual sign posts that give their route numbers. Some of the city buses have their routes displayed in Roman letters as well as Japanese ideograms. Drivers generally speak only Japanese. So if you choose to ride a bus, be sure you know the number of the route you want to take and have the name of the stop where you want to get off written in Japanese to show to the driver when you board.

ADDRESSES & STREET NAMES IN JAPAN

In Japanese cities only major streets have names, and addresses of buildings are not based on the streets where they are located. The addressing system is based on wards, larger districts within wards, smaller districts within the larger districts, and finally a set of numbers that designate the larger and smaller districts and the building or house itself.

For example, the full address of the Ginza branch of the famous Mitsukoshi Department Store chain is: Tokyo, Chuo Ward, Ginza 4-chome, 6-16. [4-chome is the 4th area in the Ginza district; 6 is a smaller block-like section within 4-chome, and16 is the number of the department store itself.]

If you are going to a destination that is not a well-known landmark virtually within sight of a subway or train station it is very important for you to have the name and address of the destination written in Japanese [to show to a policeman or to passers-by], and if possible a map of the immediate area showing the precise location of your destination—which your hotel Information Desk can usually print out for you.

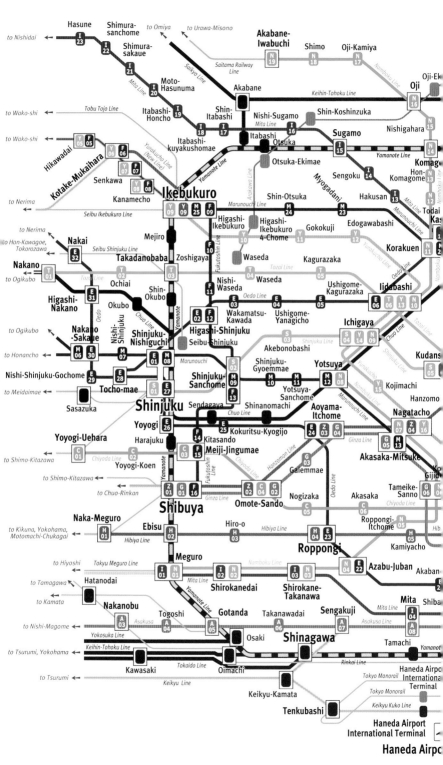

Central Tokyo's Rail & Subway Network

On buses with front-door boarding you pay when boarding. On buses with boarding doors in the center of the bus you pay when exiting. There are payment slot machines adjoining the driver and the front door. All of the payment slots will accept coins and some will also accept bills, and will return any change due to you.

Most buses have automated scrolling read-out signs above the driver's head that give the name of the next stop. When the name of your stop shows up on the read-out sign push one of the buzzer buttons lining the sides of the bus.

TOEI buses [as well as the subway and JR railway lines] accept One-Day Tokyo Combination Passes. When you insert the one-day pass into the payment slot it deducts the charge from the prepaid amount. Other payment options include the Suica Card and the Pasmo Rail Card. You swipe these on the panel next to the cash payment slot and the machine automatically deducts your fare from your balance.

In the center of Tokyo buses major stops in both English letters and in Japanese characters are usually indicated.

Bus service usually stops at around 10 pm. Maps and timetables are available at main bus terminals. People who live in relatively isolated areas and are out after 10 pm generally take taxis home from the nearest subway or train station.

Sightseeing Bus Services

Several of Japan's large travel companies, including Japan Travel Bureau, provide bus service to major tourist attractions. Most of these services pick passengers up at their hotels. Reservations can be made either by hotel Information Desk clerks or at offices of the travel agents, some of which have branch offices in major hotels. Your hotel staff can also advise you on which bus company serves the destination you want to go to.

Taxi Service in Tokyo

Taxis are a vital part of Tokyo's transportation system, with several companies concentrating on different parts of the huge city. They can be expensive, however.

As of this writing, the starting charge is ¥710, which covers 2km. Thereafter an additional charge of ¥80 is added for every 274m traveled. ¥80 is also added for each two minutes the cab is stuck in traffic. There is a surcharge, usually around 30%, between the hours of 11 pm and 5 am. A green light shows up on the meter when the surcharge goes into effect.

At night a lighted "flag arm" on the meter is visible through the front window of the taxi. If it is red it means the cab is occupied. If it is green it means the cab is available. If it is yellow it means the cab is on-call or is off-duty.

The left-side entry doors of Japanese taxis open and close automatically, by the driver turning a switch, and it is important that you **do not** try to open or close the doors manually. Taxi fares are set and there is no haggling.

If you have large bags or suitcases, the driver will automatically open the trunk of the cab for you. At airports and other designated taxi stands there may be sidewalk attendants who load baggage for passengers. On other occasions, with the exception of busy streets, most taxi drivers will get out of their cabs and help women and older people load their luggage into the trunk.

Tipping taxi drivers is not common in Japan. But if the cab driver gets out and helps you load your baggage or gets out of the cab one or more times to ask directions at local police boxes, shops or passers-by, tipping is a courteous and kind thing to do. Most taxis are equipped with navigational devices, so they can locate virtually any address by pushing buttons.

Unlike taxis in some countries, Japanese cabs do not charge by the person, so the same base fare applies to several passengers.

Finding Train Stations

Train stations on the commuter lines in Tokyo are generally anywhere from 0.8 km (half a

Shinjuku Station, South Exit

mile) to 3.2–4.8 km (2–3 miles) apart, depending on the area of the city. The further away you get from the central area of the city (which is encircled by the JR Yamanote Line), the further apart the stations tend to be.

This is not as inconvenient as it might appear. Every train station within the city and in the suburbs is surrounded by a combination business, entertainment, shopping and/or heavily populated residential area, meaning that a significant number of all of the key destinations in the city are right next to or quite near a train station.

Tokyo Station, for example, which is served by a dozen transportation lines, is within a one to five- or ten-minute walk of several hundred of the most important destinations in the city, including office buildings, shops of all kinds, department stores, restaurants, major organization offices, etc.

The railway maps in this book show you the location of commuter train stations throughout

TOKYO STATION

For most visitors to Tokyo, the most important station in the city is the venerable Tokyo Station (referred to as just "Tokyo" by locals), which consists of the original main area and "wing" areas on both sides.

The main station consists of 10 platforms, serving 20 tracks that are raised above street level running in a north-south direction. The main concourse passengers use to reach the platforms and tracks runs east-west below the platforms. The following nine train lines begin and/or converge at the station:

Chuo Line (中央線)
Keihin-Tohoku Line (京浜東北線)
Keiyo Line (京葉線)
Sobu Line (総武線)
Tokaido Main Line (東海道本線)
Tokaido Shinkansen (東海道新幹線)
Tohoku Shinkansen (東北新幹線)
Ueno-Tokyo Line (上野東京ライン)
Yamanote Line (山手線)
Yokosuka-Sobu Line (横須賀線・総武線快速)

The "Bullet Train" Shinkansen lines are on the east side of the station on the ground level. The Yokosuka-Sobu line platforms serving four tracks to the west of the main portion of the station are five stories underground. Narita Express airport trains from Ikebukuro, Shinjuku and Yokohama use the Yokosuka-Sobu line platforms.

The two Keiyo line platforms serving four tracks are four stories below ground and several hundreds of meters to the south of the main portion of the station with moving sidewalks to serve connecting passengers. The Keiyo line serves passengers going to Tokyo Disneyland and Makuhari Messe.

Tokyo Station is also served by the Marunouchi subway line, and is linked by a series of underground passageways to the Otemachi underground subway station complex served by the Tozai, Chiyoda, Hanzomon and Mita lines. The whole station complex is linked by an extensive system of underground passageways which merge with surrounding commercial buildings and shopping centers. There are coin lockers at several places in the station.

Within the Tokyo transportation network transfers to the lines of other companies may require that you exit from one station and enter the adjoining station of the other company. Transferring from one subway line to the other line may require a special ticket. If you do not have the right ticket at the end of your destination or if you have not paid the proper amount, the automated turnstiles will not accept the ticket, requiring you to go to the window adjoining the turnstiles and pay the extra amount. If you know the amount you paid is incorrect, just go directly to the window and hand your ticket to the attendant who will tell you the additional amount you owe. That is the easiest thing to do.

All of the Tokyo's major hotels, business districts, shopping districts and tourist attractions are served by subways and/or trains. Most of the major hotels in the city are within short walks of subway stations and/or subway/train hub stations.

Before departing for any destination requiring the use of subways or trains it is highly recommended that you ask your hotel staff to write down precise guidelines for you, including the number of the Boarding Platform, which side of the platform you should board from, where you must transfer if necessary, and the name of your final stop.

If your destination is some distance from your last subway or train stop you may want to take a taxi from the station, especially if the weather is bad. In this case you should have the name and address of your destination written in Japanese to show to the taxi driver. All larger transportation hubs in Tokyo are major taxi pick-up points.

the city—most of which are on the Yamanote, Chuo-Sobu, and Keihin-Tohoku lines.

Finding Subway Stations

The stations of Tokyo's two subway operators are designated by their company symbols, plus the word SUBWAY in both Japanese ideograms and in English.

Tokyo Metro's Toei symbol usually includes the name of the station in both Japanese and English.

Tokyo Metro's Omotesando Station

Most small subway station entrances/exits are inconspicuously sandwiched in between buildings, or are just openings in regular buildings, with stairs leading downward. The signs for some of these stations are set back from the sidewalks, and cannot be seen until you are abreast of them.

Entrances/Exits to larger stations are often on the sidewalks, and can be spotted from a distance of two or three blocks.

The distance between subway stations on the same line varies from three or four blocks to 1.6 km (1 mile) or more, depending on whether they are in the central area of Tokyo or on the outskirts of the city.

In the central wards of Tokyo many subway stations are beneath major office buildings,

Ticket vending machines of Tokyo Metro

making access to the buildings especially convenient.

The Hanzomon Line Suitengumae Station that serves the Tokyo City Air Terminal (TCAT) in Hakozaki-cho has a short underground passage that leads to the ground-floor level of the terminal, where limousine bus passengers arrive from and depart for Narita Airport.

Buying Train and Subway Tickets

Tokyo Metro & Toei Ticket

The first challenge is buying subway and train tickets. In addition to two different subway companies whose tickets are often available from the same vending machines (you have to know which buttons to push), in some major terminals, subway and commuter train ticket vending machines are side-by-side or in the same vicinity.

Feeder train lines branching out from their transportation hubs in Tokyo have their own tickets and banks of vending machines.

The price of tickets is based on the distance to be traveled. Pricing charts are on display, usually above the banks of ticket machines, giving the amount for each station on the lines. Many of the charts are in Japanese only. If you cannot read the charts or cannot find the listing for your destination, just buy the lowest priced ticket.

Be sure to push the price button giving the cost of your ticket before you put money into the vending machine. The machines will accept ¥1,000, ¥5,000 and ¥10,000 notes and return the correct change. There are buttons on the left side of the machines for buying multiple tickets [2 or 3 adults, or 1 child + 1 adult, etc.]

If you go beyond the distance covered by the lowest fare, the automatic batwing "doors" of the exit turnstiles will not open when you insert the ticket. Retrieve the ticket and take it to the attendant at the exit gate (on the left or right of the turnstiles). He or she will tell you how much more you must pay.

It is so common for passengers not to buy the right ticket that virtually all stations also have Fare Adjustment vending machines which tell passengers how much more they must pay, and issue them new tickets. Station attendants routinely allow foreign passengers who do not read or speak Japanese to just add the extra amount in cash and hand it to them.

Special Passes and Tickets
Railway and Subway Passes
Visitors going to Japan may purchase Japan Rail Pass "Exchange Orders" from authorized sellers before arriving in Japan and exchange them for the actual rail passes at offices in the underground railway stations at Narita Airport's two terminals.

Exchange Orders can be purchased from the following JR authorized sales offices and agents: JTB Corp., Nippon Travel Agency, Kintetsu International, Toptour Corporation, Japan Airlines offices, All Nippon Airways offices, JALPAK, and their associated agencies. [If you buy the Exchange Order from JAL you must book a JAL group flight.]

Your Exchange Order must be turned in for a Japan Rail Pass within three months of the date the Order was issued. When you make the exchange you will be asked to fill in a simple application form (you can fill in the form after you arrive in Japan, but it can be downloaded from the JR Pass home page on the Internet and filled out in advance), and also to show the Temporary Visitor visa that was stamped in your passport when you entered Japan. You must show your passport with the Temporary Visitor stamp in it in order for your Rail Pass exchange order to be screened.

Without your passport, the pass exchange cannot be made. A photocopy of your passport is also not acceptable because you must show the "Temporary Visitor" stamp in it.

JR Passes are available only for those who are going to Japan as "Temporary Visitors." Please note that under Japanese Immigration Law, "Temporary Visitor" status differs from other types of stays that are also for short time periods.

If you enter Japan under any other official status, such as "Trainee," "Entertainer," or "Re-entry Permit," you are not eligible for a JR Pass.

JR Passes are good for unlimited travel on virtually all JR trains in Japan, including the famous Shinkansen (Bullet Trains) for specific periods of time.

There are two types of JR Passes: Green (for superior-class Green cars), and Ordinary.

Each of these types is available for 7-day, 14-day, or 21-day periods. For current prices, access the JR Pass website. http://www.japanrailpass.net/eng/en001.html

PASMO Cards
The PASMO card is a convenient card for rail and bus services in the Metro Tokyo area. It is a rechargeable card that enables the user to simply sweep the card over a PASMO reader at the ticket gates in train stations. When the transaction is successful, the screen of the reader will flash blue and gives a "pi" or "pi pi" at the end of the scanning.

PASMO Card

The card can also be used in Sendai's and Niigata's metropolitan areas. It doubles up for electronic payments at all stores displaying the Suica sign.

Buy a PASMO card (¥1,000, ¥2,000, ¥3,000, ¥4,000, ¥5,000, ¥10,000) from a station vending station or from any private railways, subways or bus stations that accept PASMO. The cost of the card includes a ¥500 deposit.

Suica Cards
The Suica is a prepaid transport pass, issued by JR. It can be used for traveling on almost all railways, subways and buses, and for shopping in the Tokyo area. It cannot be used for Shinkansen travel but is good for the Tokyo Monorail at Haneda Airport.

Suica Card

When using the card for rail travel, just touch it to the ticket gate and the fare is automatically deducted at the end of a journey. Both adult's card and children's card cost ¥2,000 each but children (under 11 years old) travel at a 50% discount. There is a ¥500 deposit per card. When the balance in the Suica card is low, just top up and continue using the card.

The Suica card can be used to pay for purchases at stores that display the Suica sign.

Local Commuter Passes

Tokyo's commuter train and subway lines also sell a number of passes that are good for one or more days, obtainable from station offices and vending machines. The various choices include unlimited use on subways and trains. JR's one-day Holiday Pass can be used on local trains in Tokyo and for trips to surrounding cities such as Yokohama and Kamakura.

Prepaid cards are also available for use on subway and train lines. This eliminates the need to buy tickets each time you board, making frequent travel around the city a lot more convenient. [The popular JR Pass cannot be used on subways and non-JR trains.]

JR Tokyo and Subway One-day Tickets

This is a prepaid card issued by JR for one-day travel on local and rapid JR East trains (non-reserved seats) in Tokyo's 23 Wards, the Tokyo Metro and Toei subways, Nippori-Toneri Liner and Toden Arawaka Line. It can also be used on the Toei Bus routes (non-reserved seat and not late night buses).

An adult card costs ¥1,580 while a child's costs ¥790, and these are available from JR ticket offices at major JR East Tokyo stations and Travel Service Centers. It can be purchased one month ahead of the day of use.

JR Tokyo One-day Passes

This card is issued by JR and costs ¥730 (adult) or ¥360 (child). It allows unlimited rides within Tokyo's 23 Special Wards on the local and rapid JR East trains (non-reserved seats) for one day.

JR Holiday Passes

This one-day pass by JR enables the user to travel unlimited on local and rapid JR East trains (non-reserved seats), on the Rinkai Line (TWR) and on the Tokyo Monorail in and around designated zones of Tokyo. It costs ¥2,300 (adult) and ¥1,500 (child).

The Holiday Pass can be used on the Shinkansen and other express trains within designated open seating zones if an additional Super (Limited) Express Seat Ticket is bought. It cannot be used for the Tokaido Shinkansen. It is also invalid for use on a weekend or any day within these periods: April 29 to May 5, July 20 to August 31, December 29 to January 3.

JR Weekend Passes

JR's Weekend Pass—a limited time-offer, discounted fare—allows unlimited rides on local and rapid JR East trains (non-reserved seats) as well as on Izu Kyuko Line, Hokuetsu Kyuko Railway Hokuhoku Line, Aizu Railway Aizu Line within the designated open seating zone—covering Nagano, Niigata, Sendai and Yamagata. It can be used with a Super (Limited) Express Seat Ticket for travelling on the Shinkansen and express trains (including Green Cars), but not for the Tokaido Shinkansen.

The adult card costs ¥8,700 and the child's ¥2,600. The card can be used for two consecutive days.

JR Kanto Area Passes

This discounted three-day pass enables one to travel unlimited on local and JR East trains (non-reserved seats) and on five other railway lines in the Kanto area (for more information, refer to www.jreast.co.jp/e/kantoareapass/).

This pass enables one to visit popular places such as Mt. Fuji, Izu and Nikko. It can be used to travel to Tokyo metropolitan area from Narita and Haneda Airports. With an express ticket, it can be used on Shinkansen (not for Tokaido Shinkansen though) and express trains. It costs ¥8,300 (adult) and ¥4,200 (child).

Tokyo Metro Subway One-Day Tickets

This one-day open ticket by Metro Rail can

Tokyo Metro One-Day Open Ticket

be bought in advance from certain commuter pass offices, and on the same day from all ticket vending machines at Tokyo Metro stations. It costs ¥600 (adult) and ¥300 (child) per ticket. The advanced ticket has a validity of 6 months from the date of purchase; the same-day ticket is good only for the date of purchase. The ticket can be used on all Tokyo Metro Lines.

One-day Tickets for Tokyo Metro and Toei Subway Lines

Special One-Day Open Ticket

This open-day ticket is for a single-day travel on Tokyo Metro and Toei Subway lines. It costs ¥1,000 (adult) and ¥500 (child) per ticket, and can be bought from vending machines at Tokyo Metro and Toei Subway stations.

Information (given in Japanese) on passes, tickets and other rail-related matters can be obtained from:

- **Tokyo Metro Information Desks**—these are located at Ginza, Shinjuku, and Omote-sando stations, operating from 10 am to 6 pm.

- **Service Managers** stationed near ticket gates and ticket vendors at major stations (such as Ginza, Shinjuku, Ikebukuro or Ueno) from 10 am to 5 pm.

- **Customer Relations Center:** 03-3941-2004 from 9 am to 8 pm.

Call the Lost and Found office on 03-3834-5577 for any lost/found items. This office is open from 9:30 am to 7 pm (Mondays to Fridays), 9:30 am to 4 pm (Saturdays and public holidays) and closed on Sundays.

PLATFORM EXIT SIGNBOARDS

All of Tokyo's subway stations have "Exit Signboards" on the walls in smaller stations and on the boarding platforms in larger stations. The signboards list a number of the more important destinations in the immediate vicinity of the stations, particularly major office buildings, banks, government buildings, and important cultural attractions, with their exit numbers or letters.

Destinations on the signboards are divided into left and right groups, indicating that one should proceed either to the left or to the right after disembarking from the subway. In some of the larger stations where two or more subway lines intersect, some of the designated exits are the equivalent of two, three or more blocks away, and some require going up and down several flights of stairs or escalators.

Where the boarding platforms of the intersecting subway lines are some distance apart, there are numerous wall, overhead and/or floor signs for passengers to follow when transferring from one line to another, and when proceeding to exits located in that area of the station.

JR Railway stations, some of which are huge in size, have a variety of platform signs and

overhead signs that give directions to specific areas within short distances of the stations. Some of these signs indicate North, South, East and/or West directions. Others display the names of specific areas accessible from that exit—such as Ginza, Hibiya, Shio-dome, etc., while still others point to address designations, such as 1-chome, 2-chome, which refer to a section that may be two or three "blocks" in size (in a variety of shapes), with dozens of individual buildings in each chome.

A typical signboard in a subway station

Part 2: ARRIVING IN TOKYO

Arriving at Tokyo's Narita Airport

Narita Airport is located approximately 66 kilometers (41 miles) from downtown Tokyo, on the outskirts of Narita City in Chiba Prefecture, near the coast.

Narita handles the majority of international passenger traffic to and from Japan, and is also a major connecting hub for air traffic between Asia and the Americas. It is the second-busiest passenger airport in Japan, the busiest air freight hub in Japan, and third busiest air freight hub in the world.

Narita has two terminals: Terminal 1 (which is the original terminal) and Terminal 2. The two terminals are about 0.4 km (a quarter of a mile) apart, with a regular shuttle bus service between them if you need to go from one to the other. The shuttle buses run at intervals of 8-20 minutes, between 6:30 am and 10:30 pm. Each trip takes about ten minutes.

Which terminal you arrive at (and depart from) depends on your choice of airlines, and from both terminals you have several choices of transportation to destinations in Tokyo and beyond, including trains, limousine buses, subway, taxis, and mini-buses.

If you have not been to Narita before and are uncertain about which mode of transportation to use to go into Tokyo or any other destination you can start by asking the in-flight staff of your airplane before arriving. After you exit from the baggage claim and customs areas into the Arrival Lobby you can also go to any of the limousine bus ticket counters on the opposite side of the lobby and ask the counter staff.

If you are not going to one of the major hotels—all of which are served by limousine buses from the front doors of the terminals— and are best served by train or subway you can proceed down to the next level by escalator where the train and subway boarding platforms are and ask at one of the Information Desks or ticket counters.

Limousine bus service from the front doors of the two Arrival Lobbies is more expensive than train service and a bit slower, but it is especially convenient and practical for visitors with more than one suitcase who are going directly to one of the major hotels in Tokyo. Visitors not booked at a major hotel often take a limousine bus to the hotel nearest their destination, and then take a taxi to their final destination.

When taking a limousine bus from your hotel back to Narita Airport you should make a reservation at the Bell Desk at least one day in advance, for a bus that leaves for the airport at least 4 hours before the departure time of your plane. If you are going to be out of the hotel on that day prior to your departure for the airport you should check your baggage at the Bell Desk before leaving the hotel, or plan on returning to the hotel early enough so that you can get your baggage checked at least 15 minutes before your bus is scheduled to leave.

Bell Desk staff will also accept limousine bus reservations for passengers not staying at that particular hotel.

When you check your baggage at the Bell Desk you will receive check stubs for each piece of luggage. The hotel staff and limousine bus driver will load your bags on the bus when it arrives in front of the hotel. When you arrive at the airport limousine staff at the airport will take your bags off the bus and set them on the sidewalk. You reclaim your bags by presenting your claim stubs to the baggage handlers.

Train Services from Narita Airport

There are two railway companies serving Narita Airport, with a total of eight lines. **JR East Railway Company** has two lines serving the airport: the JR East Narita Express, and JR East Sobu Line Rapid Service. The **Keisei Railway Company** also has five lines serving the airport: Narita Sky Access (the New Sky Liner began operating on 17 July 2010), the City Liner, Morning Liner, Evening Liner and Keisei Limited Express Line.

JR East Narita Express, with stations at both Terminal 1 and Terminal 2, provides direct service to JR Tokyo Station, JR Shinjuku

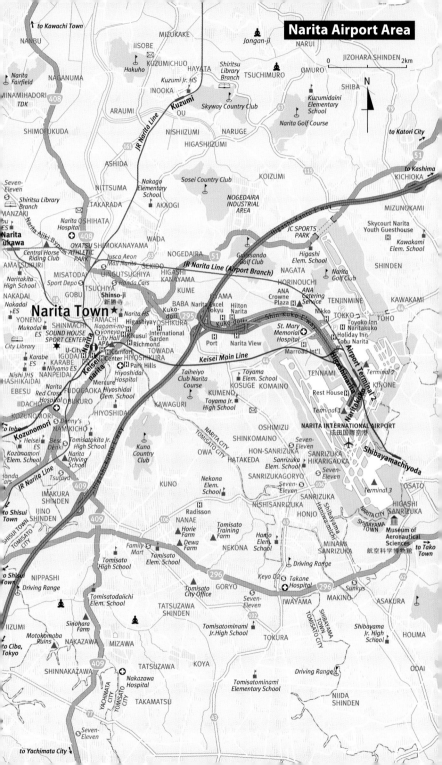

JR EXPRESS TRAINS TO AND FROM NARITA

The JR Narita Express and the JR Sobu-Yokosuka Line connect Narita Airport to local JR commuter lines in central Tokyo. The JR Narita Express runs from Narita Terminals 1 and 2 to Ikebukuro Station, with stops shown below. You can change at any of the stations along the Yamanote Loop Line for local trains to other stations along this line.

To get to Shinagawa and Yokohama Stations, visitors can take the Narita Express or the JR Sobu-Yokosuka train. From either one of these Stations, they can transfer to get to other stations on the Yamanote Loop Line.

You can travel to Narita Airport by using the reverse route: take JR Narita Express from Tokyo Station or Yokohama Station to go to Narita. Or take the JR Sobu-Yosokuka Line train from any of its designated stops along the Yamonote Loop Line. This approach is not practical if you have more than lightweight luggage that is on wheels or that cannot be hand-carried.

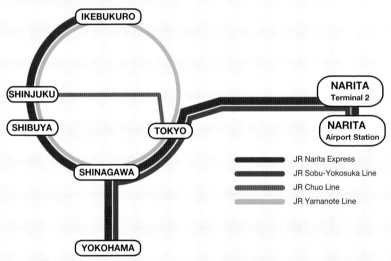

IKEBUKURO

SHINJUKU

SHIBUYA

TOKYO

NARITA Terminal 2

NARITA Airport Station

SHINAGAWA

YOKOHAMA

JR Narita Express
JR Sobu-Yokosuka Line
JR Chuo Line
JR Yamanote Line

JR NARITA EXPRESS TRAIN TO/FROM:
TOKYO STATION
60 minutes Adult : ¥3,020 Child: ¥1,510
SHINAGAWA STATION
70 minutes Adult : ¥3,190 Child: ¥1,600
SHIBUYA STATION
85 minutes Adult : ¥3,190 Child: ¥1,600
SHINJUKU STATION
90 minutes Adult : ¥3,190 Child: ¥1,600
IKEBUKURO STATION
95 minutes Adult : ¥3,190 Child: ¥1,600
YOKOHAMA STATION
90 minutes Adult : ¥4,290 Child: ¥2,150

JR SOBU-YOKOSUKA LINE RAPID SERVICE
TOKYO STATION
85 minutes Adult : ¥1,320 Child: ¥660
SHINAGAWA STATION
95 minutes Adult : ¥1,490 Child: ¥750
SHINJUKU STATION
90 minutes Adult : ¥1,490 Child: ¥750
(Transfer to JR Chuo Line at Tokyo Station)
SHIBUYA STATION
85 minutes Adult : ¥1,490 Child: ¥750
(Transfer to JR Yamanote Line at Shinagawa Station)
IKEBUKURO STATION
110 minutes Adult : ¥1,490 Child: ¥750
(Transfer to JR Yamanote Line at Tokyo Station)
YOKOHAMA STATION
120 minutes Adult : ¥1,940 Child: ¥970
HANEDA TERMINALS 1 AND 2
125-130 minutes Adult : ¥1,900 Child: ¥950
(Transfer to Keikyu Line at Shinagawa Station)

The ticket windows and boarding platforms of all of these train lines are located underground directly in front of both Terminals 1 and 2, and are accessible via escalators from the middle of the Arrival Lobbies if you are arriving, and from the middle of the Departure Lobbies if you are leaving. The entrances to the escalators are easy to spot. Travel to central Tokyo destinations by train ranges from one hour to one hour and forty minutes.

Airport Limousine Buses from Narita

There are two bus lines providing limousine and shuttle bus service from Narita to central Tokyo destinations, including direct door-to-door service to leading hotels — with return service from these destinations to Narita.

The largest of these companies is Airport Transport Service Co. (ATS), which provides direct limousine bus service to over 75 hotels and other major access routes connecting Narita Airport with linked centers in Metro Tokyo. ATS has approximately 700 departures daily from the airport.

Buses operated by ATS serve hotels in Shinjuku, Ikebukuro, Akasaka, Shiba, Ginza and Shinagawa; as well as Haneda Airport; Tokyo City Air Terminal; Yokohama City Air Terminal; JR Tokyo Station; Tokyo Disney Resort; and Keio Hachioji highway bus terminal. Its buses have large "Airport Limousine" signs on their sides.

When you have retrieved your baggage, cleared Customs, and entered the Arrival Lobby, you will see orange-colored **Airport Limousine Bus** ticket service counters on the opposite side of the lobby. Give the service counter attendants the name of the hotel or other destination you want to go to.

The printed tickets you receive will list the scheduled departure time of your bus and the number of the Bus Stand it will leave from just outside of the Arrival Lobby doors. There are several Bus Stands in a line along the front entrance of the lobby.

Be sure you look at your ticket to see which Stand your bus leaves from, and its departure time. The Stands have large numbers on them and are easy to spot. They also have digital read-outs, indicating the destination of the next bus and its departure time.

Each stand is manned by several ATS attendants who will tag your baggage and give you a Claim Check just before your bus is scheduled to arrive, line it up on the sidewalk, and load onto the bus when it arrives. Another

The Narita Sky Access Train

Station, JR Ikebukuro Station and JR Shinagawa Station.

JR East Sobu Line Rapid Service [with service from both terminals] provides transportation to JR Tokyo Station, where passengers can change to the JR Chuo Line for Shinjuku Station and to the JR Yamanote Line for Ikebukuro Station; and to Shinagawa Station; and to the Keihin Tohoku Line, which runs through Tokyo on a north-south axis and goes beyond Yokohama on the south side and to Saitama Prefecture on the north side.

[The Yamanote Line encircles central Tokyo, providing service to over a dozen of the city's leading business, dining, hotel and shopping districts, including Kanda, Akihabara, Ueno, Nippori, Ikebukuro, Shinjuku, Shibuya, Meguro, Shinagawa, Hamamatsucho, Shimbashi and Yurakucho.]

The Keisei Narita Sky Access (New Skyliner) goes from Narita Airport directly to JR Nippori Station, where passengers can change to the Yamanote Line, which serves over a dozen hub stations, including Tokyo, Shinjuku, Shibuya, and Shinagawa Stations, as well as to the Keihin Tohoku Line, which runs north and south through Tokyo to outlying suburbs and cities.

The Keisei Limited Express line also runs between Narita Airport and JR Nippori Station, where it connects with the Yamanote and Keihin Tohoku Lines.

KEISEI EXPRESS TRAINS TO AND FROM NARITA

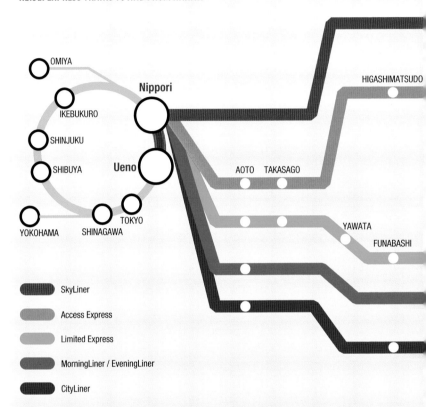

OMIYA

HIGASHIMATSUDO

Nippori

IKEBUKURO

SHINJUKU

SHIBUYA

Ueno

AOTO   TAKASAGO

YAWATA

FUNABASHI

YOKOHAMA   SHINAGAWA   TOKYO

SkyLiner

Access Express

Limited Express

MorningLiner / EveningLiner

CityLiner

PRIVATE EXPRESS TRAINS TO NARITA

Keisei Honsen [Keisei Main Line Co.] operates five categories of service from Keisei-Ueno Station and Nippori Station in central Tokyo: the Skyliner, Access Express, Limited Express, Morningliner/ Eveningliner and Cityliner.

The **SkyLiner** leaves from Nippori Station and goes directly to Terminals 2 and 1 at Narita.

The **Access Express** starts at Nippori, with stops at Higashi-Matsudo, Shin-Kamagawa, Chiba Newtown Chuo, Imba Nihonidai, Narita Yukawa, and Terminals 2 and 1, in that order.

Keisei's Limited Express trains leave from Nippori with stops at Aoto, Takasago, Yawata Funabashi, Tsudanuma, Yachiyodai, Katsutadai, Sakura, Narita and Terminals 2 and 1.

The **MorningLiner and EveningLiner** trains depart from Nippori and stop at Aoto, Yachiyodai, Sakura, Narita, and Terminals 2 and 1.

The **CityLiner** starts at Keisei-Ueno Station, with stops at Aoto, Yawata Funabashi, Narita and Terminals 2 and 1.

Both Keisei-Ueno and Nippori Stations are on the Yamanote Loop Line and are therefore accessible from other hub stations in Tokyo, including Yokohama, Omiya and other outlying cities as well as Ikebukuro, Shinjuku, Shibuya, Shinagawa and Tokyo Central stations.

Keisei train passengers go through two ticket barriers/gates upon arriving at Narita, so you should retain your ticket to pass through these gates. If you are using PASMO or Suica passes you must run the passes through reader-slots at both barriers.

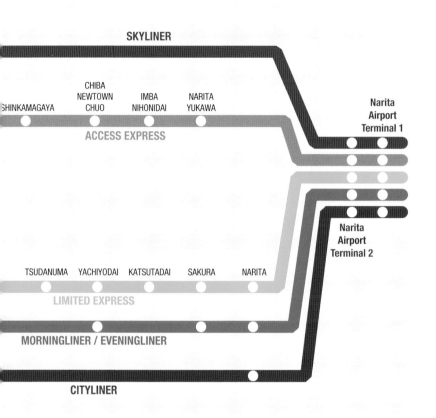

SKYLINER

CHIBA
NEWTOWN
CHUO

IMBA
NIHONIDAI

NARITA
YUKAWA

SHINKAMAGAYA

Narita
Airport
Terminal 1

ACCESS EXPRESS

Narita
Airport
Terminal 2

TSUDANUMA   YACHIYODAI   KATSUTADAI   SAKURA   NARITA

LIMITED EXPRESS

MORNINGLINER / EVENINGLINER

CITYLINER

NARITA SKY ACCESS LINE
(New Skyliner)
UENO STATION
44 minutes   Adult : ¥2,470 Child: ¥1,240
NIPPORI STATION
39 minutes   Adult : ¥2,470 Child: ¥1,240

MORNINGLINER, EVENINGLINER
There are two different names for this service.
Morning route = MorningLiner
Evening route = EveningLiner
UENO STATION
62 minutes   Adult : ¥1,440 Child: ¥770
NIPPORI STATION
57 minutes   Adult : ¥1,440 Child: ¥770

KEISEI LIMITED EXPRESS
NIPPORI STATION
70 minutes   Adult : ¥1,030 Child: ¥520
TOKYO STATION
90 minutes   Adult : ¥1,190 Child: ¥600
(Transfer to JR Line at Nippori Station)
SHINAGAWA STATION
110 minutes   Adult : ¥1,300 Child: ¥650
SHINJUKU STATION
115 minutes   Adult : ¥1,230 Child: ¥620
(Transfer to JR Line at Nippori Station)
IKEBUKURO STATION
95 minutes   Adult : ¥1,200 Child: ¥600

NARITA AIRPORT LIMOUSINE BUS ROUTES

This is the most convenient method for foreigners with luggage to get into the city. Tickets purchased at an Airport Limousine Bus service counter in the Arrival Lobbies are required for bus service from Narita to Tokyo hotels, to Haneda Airport, and to other destinations. The fare from Narita to most hotels and other destinations in Tokyo is ¥3,000 for adults and ¥1,500 for children. For return trips to Narita and Haneda advance reservations are strongly advised. They can be made and confirmed at the Bell Desk of your hotel.

Narita Airport Limousine Bus Routes to Central Tokyo

T-CAT (TOKYO CITY AIR TERMINAL)
(東京シティエアターミナル)

HANEDA AIRPORT (羽田空港)

TOKYO STATION, NIHONBASHI
(東京駅、日本橋方面)
- Tokyo Station Yaesu South Exit
- Tokyo Station Marunouchi North Exit, Marunouchi Hotel
- Yaesu Fujiya Hotel
- Mandarin Oriental Tokyo

IKEBUKURO (池袋方面)
- Hotel Metropolitan
- Sunshine City Prince

SHIBUYA (渋谷方面)
- Cerulean Tower Tokyu
- Shibuya Excel Hotel Tokyu

MEJIRO, KORAKUEN, KUDAN
(目白、後楽園、九段方面)
- Four Seasons Hotel Tokyo at Chinzan-so
- Hotel Grand Palace
- Tokyo Dome Hotel

HIBIYA (日比谷方面)
- The Peninsula Tokyo
- Imperial Hotel
- Dai-Ichi Hotel Tokyo

GINZA, SHIODOME (銀座、汐留方面)
- Mitsui Garden Hotel Ginza Premier
- Courtyard by Marriott Tokyo
- Conrad Tokyo
- Park Hotel Tokyo
- Royal Park Shiodome Tower
- Sukiyabshi

SHIBA (芝方面)
- Celestine Hotel
- The Prince Park Tower Tokyo
- Tokyo Prince Hotel
- Shiba Park Hotel

TAKESHIBA, ODAIBA, ARIAKE
(竹芝、お台場、有明方面)
- Inter-Continental Tokyo Bay
- Tennozu Isle (Dai–Ichi Hotel Tokyo Seafort)
- Tokyo Bay Ariake Washington
- Nikko Tokyo
- Sunroute Ariake
- Grand Pacific LE DAIBA*

SHINJUKU (新宿方面)
- Shinjuku Station West Exit No.23
- Century Southern Tower
- Sunroute Plaza Shinjuku
- Keio Plaza Hotel Tokyo
- Hyatt Regency Tokyo
- Shinjuku Washington
- Park Hyatt Tokyo   ■ Hilton Tokyo

AKASAKA (赤坂方面)
- Hotel New Otani, Hotel Okura
- Grand Prince Hotel Akasaka
- Akasaka Excel Hotel Tokyu
- ANA Intercontinental Tokyo

ROPPONGI (六本木方面)
- The Ritz Carlton Tokyo
- Grand Hyatt Tokyo

KINSHICHO, TOYOCHO, SHIN-KIBA
(錦糸町、東陽町、新木場方面)
- Tobu Hotel Levant Tokyo
- Hotel East 21 Tokyo   ■ Shin-Kiba Station

EBISU, SHINAGAWA (恵比寿、品川方面)
- The Westin Tokyo
- Sheraton Miyako Hotel Tokyo
- The New Sanno Hotel
- Hotel Laforet Tokyo
- Shinagawa Prince Hotel
- The Prince Sakura Tower Tokyo
- Grand Prince Hotel Takanawa
- Grand Prince Hotel New Takanawa
- Shinagawa Station East Exit No. 7 The Strings
- Hotel Tokyo Intercontinental

Narita Airport Limousine Buses to Outer Tokyo Areas

Adult fares range from ¥3,000 to ¥3,800. Fares for children range from ¥1,500 to ¥1,900. Travel time from Narita to the various hotels ranges from 60 to 190 minutes, depending on the distance and traffic conditions.

KICHIJOJI STATION (吉祥寺駅)

*Reservations are required for limousine buses from Kichijoji to Narita Airport and should be made the day before your departure. Tel. 03-5438-8511

TACHIKAWA (立川方面)
- Tachikawa Bus Josui Branch
- Tachikawa Station North Exit No.27 (Tachikawa Grand Hotel)
- Palace Hotel Tachikawa

*Reservations are required for limousine bus service from this hotel to Narita Airport, and should be made at least a day in advance. Tel. 042-500-0301

CHOFU STATION (調布駅)

*Reservations are required for limousine bus service from Chofu Station to Narita Airport and should be made at least a day in advance. Tel. 03-5376-2222

HACHIOJI STATION (八王子駅)
- JR Hachioji Station

Keio Hachioji Station

*Reservations are required for limousine buses from Hachioji Station to Narita Airport and should be made at least a day in advance. Tel. 042-648-6522

MACHIDA STATION (町田駅)

SAGAMI-ONO STATION (相模大野駅)

KEIO TAMA-CENTER STATION (京王多摩センター駅)

SEISEKI SAKURAGAOKA STATION (聖蹟桜ヶ丘駅)

*Reservations are required for limousine bus service from this station to Narita Airport and should be made at least a day in advance. Tel. 03-5376-2222

MINAMI-OSAWA STATION (南大沢駅)

*Reservations are required and should be made at least a day in advance. Tel. 03-5376-2222

Narita Airport Limousine Buses to Chiba Destinations

On average, adults pay ¥2,400–3,000; child's fare is ¥1,200–1,500; and each trip takes 85–140 minutes, depending on the distance traveled.

SHIN-URAYASU (新浦安方面)
- Oriental Hotel Tokyo Bay
- Emion Tokyo Bay
- Palm Terrace Hotel
- Fountain Terrace Hotel
- Mitsui Garden PRANA Tokyo Bay

TOKYO DISNEY RESORT, MAIHAMA
(東京ディズニーリゾート、舞浜方面)
- Disney Ambassador Hotel
- Tokyo Disney Sea

- Tokyo Disney Sea Hotel
- Mira Costa
- Sheraton Grande Tokyo Bay Hotel
- Hotel Okura Tokyo Bay
- Hilton Tokyo Bay
- Sunroute Plaza Tokyo
- Tokyo Bay Maihama Hotel
- Tokyo Bay Hotel Tokyu
- Tokyo Disneyland
- Tokyo Disneyland Hotel

Narita Airport Limousine Buses to Yokohama

On average, adults pay ¥3,500; child's fare is ¥1,750; and each trip takes 85–130 minutes, depending on the distance traveled.

Y-CAT (Yokohama City Air Terminal)
(横浜シティエアターミナル)

YOKOHAMA MINATOMIRAI
(横浜みなとみらい方面)
- Yokohama Royal Park Hotel
- The Pan Pacific Yokohama Bay Hotel Tokyu

- Yokohama Grand Inter-Continental (Pacifico Yokohama)
- Hotel New Grand

SHIN-YOKOHAMA (新横浜方面)
- Shin-Yokohama Sta. (Associa Shin-Yokohama)
- Shin-Yokohama Prince Hotel

Narita Airport

attendant will take your ticket as you board the bus.

Depending on the destination, the wait for the right bus ranges from five or ten minutes to half an hour or more for those going to less popular places. The buses are equipped with toilets.

Advance reservations are not required for airport limousine buses from Narita Airport to hotels, but they may be required for passage to Haneda Airport since there are fewer buses on that route. Return reservations to Narita are advised and can be made at the Bell Desk of your hotel and should be made at least a day in advance. As of this writing the fare for adults is ¥3,000; child's fare is ¥1,500. A one-way trip takes 60-140 minutes, depending on the distance traveled and the amount of traffic

Mini-bus Taxi Service

There are hourly nine-passenger mini-bus taxi services from Narita Airport to destinations in Tokyo and Chiba Prefecture. Passengers buy omnibus tickets at the Green Port Agency (GPA) counters in the Arrival Lobbies. This service is convenient for people with heavy baggage, since omnibus taxis offer door-to-door service, unlike regular buses which stop only at bus depots.

These mini-bus taxis leave from the designated taxi lane in front of the Arrival Lobbies of both terminals.

These mini-bus services go to and from the 23 Wards of Tokyo to Narita Airport. The fare is ¥25,000 per person (excluding extra charges for highway toll charges, etc) and it can have a maximum passenger load of 13 persons. Confirmation is required for each booking, one day in advance of the trip.

Normal Taxi Service

Several taxi companies offer services at Narita Airport. The taxi stands are located across the street from the main exits of the Arrival Lobbies — beyond the Limousine Bus Stands. Fares include the taxi fare plus expressway tolls. Some taxi companies use a zone fare system, with each zone having a uniform fare.

Free Airport Hotel Shuttle Bus Service

The following hotels in Narita near the airport provide free shuttle bus service to and from Narita airport terminals and scheduled shuttle service daily to JR Narita Station.

- Garden Hotel Narita
- Hilton Narita
- Hotel Nikko Narita
- Holiday Inn Narita
- Narita Port Hotel
- Marriott International Hotel Narita
- Narita Airport Rest House
- Narita U-City Hotel
- Mercure Hotel Narita
- Narita Excel Hotel
- ANA Crowne Plaza Hotel Narita
- Radisson Hotel Narita
- Kikusui Hotel.

Limousine Buses to Tokyo City Air Terminal & Yokohama City Air Terminal

The **Tokyo City Air Terminal** [TCAT], located in the Hakozaki district of central Tokyo, provides limousine bus service from and to Narita Airport for passengers not staying at hotels and/or those departing from or going to other points in the city where airport train service is not convenient. TCAT is on the Hanzomon Subway Line at the east end of Suitengu-mae Station, and is linked to several other subway lines in the city. There is an escalator at the end of the entry and exit platform that connects to the lobby of TCAT. The Yokohama City Air Terminal provides the same service.

Limousine buses leave from the front of the Narita Arrival Lobbies for Tokyo City Air Terminal (TCAT) every 10-15 minutes, and for Yokohama City Air Terminal (YCAT) about every 30 minutes. The trip to TCAT takes about 60-75 minutes and to YCAT about 85-130 minutes.

Both TCAT and YCAT are linked to the two cities' subway networks, providing convenient transportation to many business, hotel and residential areas in the two cities. There are restaurants, gift shops and other service facilities at the two city air terminals.

One of the most useful of these services is next-day shipping services for extra baggage or heavy baggage to your hotel or other destination in the Tokyo area. Check with the Information Desk in the Arrival Lounge for directions to the shipping facility. Also see: **Baggage Delivery Service** entry (page 29).

USEFUL RESOURCES FOR NARITA AIRPORT

Narita Airport Official Website

Website: http://www.narita-airport.jp/en/
Mobile phone site: http://www.narita-airport.jp/mobile/
Narita Airport Flight Information: +81 (0)476-34-8000

Timetable and Route

HYPERDIA-timetable:
http://www.hyperdia.com/en/
"Hyperdia" is a service which offers the route and the timetable of the railway and the aviation of Japan.

E Airport Narita [e-information]

Website: http://naa.ivcreation.com/pc_us/
Mobile phone Site: http://naa.ivcreation.com/
"E Airport Narita" is a quick search engine for access information on Narita Airport.

Fixed Fare Taxis

Narita International Airport Taxi Council:
+81 (0)476-34-8755

Limousine Bus

AIRPORT LIMOUSINE:
http://www.limousinebus.co.jp/en/
TEL. 03-3665-7200 (Reservation Center)
KEISEI BUS: TEL. 043-433-3800

Mini-bus Taxi

Tokyo Kanko.com: +81 (0)3-3599-6737/
http://www.tokyokanko.com
Hitachi Jidosha Kotsu: +81(0)3-5682-1112

Taxi Service

Airport Taxi Service: +81 (0)476-34-8755
Tokyo MK Sky Gate Shuttle: +81 (0)3-5547-5667
http://www.tokyomk.com/eng/index.html
Teito Jidosha Kotsu Limousine Liner (Narita Airport Office): +81 (0)3-5621-3651

Arriving at Tokyo's Haneda Airport

Tokyo's **Haneda Airport**, now renamed **Tokyo International Airport** (but still commonly referred to as Haneda), is located on the south side of Tokyo about 20–25 minutes from the downtown area. It is the main domestic airport for Tokyo, the busiest airport in Japan and the fourth busiest airport in the world, and now also handles quite a few international flights through its new International Terminal.

There are three terminals at Haneda: **Terminal 1** is the domestic hub for Japan Airlines (JAL) and **Terminal 2** is the domestic hub for All Nippon Airways (ANA) and its subsidiaries. The New International Terminal [which opened in October 2010] has flights to and from Shanghai, Beijing, Hong Kong, Seoul, Singapore and several other destinations.

Haneda Airport is accessible from Narita Airport and from locations around Tokyo by five interconnecting train and monorail lines. These lines are the Tokyo Monorail, the Toei Asakusa Line, the Keikyu Line, the JR Line, and the JR Yamanote Line.

The Tokyo Monorail starts at Hamamatsucho Station on the Yamanote Loop Line, with stops at Tennozu Isle, Oi Keibajo-mae, Ryutsu Center, Showa Jima, Seibijo, Tenkubashi, Haneda Airport International Terminal, Shin Seibijo, Terminal 1 and Terminal 2. [See page 32.]

The only other line that goes to Haneda Airport directly is the Keikyu Line, which starts in Yokohama, with stops at Kamata and Tenkubashi before reaching the airport.

All of the feeder lines require transfers either at Hamamatsucho for boarding the Tokyo Monorail, or at Shinagawa to board the Keikyu Line.

For many visitors staying at one of the several hotels in Shinagawa taking a taxi to Haneda is a viable choice, especially if there are two or three in a group to share the cost.

Transferring from Narita Airport to Haneda

International passengers arriving at **Narita Airport** with connections on domestic flights may go directly from Narita to **Haneda Airport** by AST Limousine Bus or the Keihin Kyuko Electric Railway. [See page 33.]

Haneda Airport

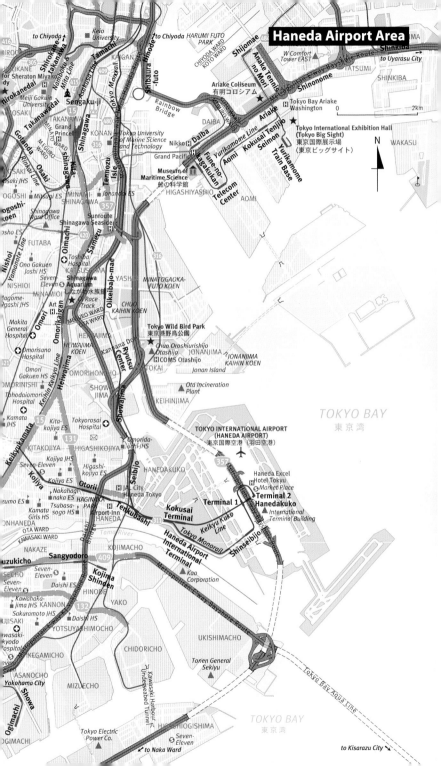

Haneda Airport Area

Train and Subway Lines to Haneda Airport

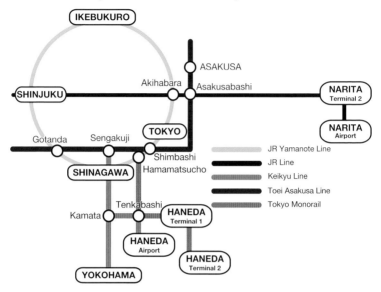

TRAIN AND SUBWAY LINES TO HANEDA

There are a combination of train, subway and monorail lines that connect to Haneda Airport from Narita Airport and from Tokyo and Yokohama. These lines include the JR Line that connects Narita first to the Toei Asakusa Subway Line at Asakusabashi and then to the Yamanote Loop Line at Akihabara Station. The Toei Asakusa Subway Line goes to Shimbashi Station where you can transfer to the Yamanote Line, go to Hamamatsucho and there transfer to the Tokyo

Monorail that goes to Haneda. You can avoid transferring at Asakusabashi and Shimbashi by staying on the JR Line train to Akihabara and there transferring to the Yamanote Line which will take you to Hamamatsucho where you transfer to Tokyo Monorail. If you are going to Yokohama you stay on the Yamanote Line until you reach Shinagawa and there transfer to the Keikyu Line. To go to Haneda from Yokohama you can take a limousine bus from Yokohama City Air Terminal [YCAT] or a Keikyu Line train that goes to Tenkabashi, and there transfer to the Tokyo Monorail.

KEIKYU LINE
SHINAGAWA STATION
20 minutes   Adult : ¥410 Child: ¥210
TOKYO STATION
40 minutes   Adult : ¥580 Child: ¥290
(Transfer to JR Line at Shinagawa Station)
ASAKUSA STATION
45 minutes   Adult : ¥660 Child: ¥330
(Transfer to Asakusa Line at Sengakuji Station)

FROM AND TO YOKOHAMA STATION
30 minutes   Adult : ¥480 Child: ¥240
(Transfer to Keikyu Line at Kamata Station)

TOKYO MONORAIL
TOKYO STATION
35 minutes   Adult : ¥650 Child: ¥330
(Transfer to JR Line at Hamamatsucho Station)
SHINAGAWA STATION
30 minutes   Adult : ¥650 Child: ¥330
(Transfer to JR Line at Hamamatsucho Station)

Limousine buses depart from the front of the Narita Arrival Lobbies for Haneda every 20–30 minutes. [See pages 30-31 for a list of routes.] Tickets are available at the Limousine Bus service counters in the lobbies. Travel time from Narita to Haneda is about 75 minutes.

Direct train service from Narita Airport to Haneda Airport is provided by the Keikyu Airport Line, which also runs between Haneda Airport and Shinagawa Station, connecting with the Yamanote and Keihin Tohoku Lines, and the Shinkansen Line.

Keikyu Line tickets are available in the underground departure areas of Terminals 1, 2 and the New International Terminal via escalator from the center of the Arrival Lobbies.

When going to Haneda Airport from within Tokyo one of the most popular transportation modes is the **Tokyo Monorail**, which departs from Hamamatsucho Station on the Yamanote Line every 10 minutes. It is about 15 minutes from the station to the airport.

A new train station—Kokusai (International) Terminal Station (which opened in 2010)—is served by the Keihin Kyuko Electric Railway (Keikyu) and the Tokyo Monorail.

From Haneda Airport to Tokyo & Beyond

If you arrive in Tokyo at Haneda Airport, there are two rail transportation systems connecting Haneda Airport with central Tokyo and points beyond: the Tokyo Monorail and the Keikyu Airport Line.

The Tokyo Monorail runs between Haneda Airport and JR Hamamatsucho Station, where it connects with the Yamanote and Keihin Tohoku Lines. The Yamanote Line encircles the central wards of the city; the Keihin Tohoku Line runs north and south through the city to adjoining cities and towns.

The Keikyu Airport Line goes from Haneda Airport to Narita Airport as well as to JR Shinagawa Station, where it connects with the Yamanote and Keihin Tohoku Lines as well as the Shinkansen "Bullet Train" Line. When boarding a Keikyu train at Haneda make sure that particular train goes to the destination you want to reach—either Narita Airport or JR Shinagawa Station.

Baggage Delivery Service

Keeping all of your baggage with you is quite simple if you are going into Tokyo or to other destinations by limousine bus, mini-bus or taxi, but if you are going by subway or train you may choose to have your baggage delivered to your destination the following day by special delivery services. These have service counters at the far end of the Arrival Lobbies of Terminals 1, 2 and the New International Terminal.

Companies providing next-day baggage delivery services include ABC Co. Ltd. and Green Port Agency (GPA). This can be a lifesaver for those with large, heavy bags.

Haneda Airport Shuttle Bus Service

A free shuttle bus runs between all terminals.

Mini-bus Taxi Service

Passenger load: 13 people maximum
To and from Tokyo's 23 wards: ¥15,000~
Availability: all year
* Reservation required one day in advance.
Note: The above charges include expressway tolls. Contact Human Vehicle +81 (0)3-6880-1475 or https://www.humanvehicle.co.jp/en/inquiry/quote.php for reservations.

Jumbo Taxi Service

Fixed fares that are based on destination zones apply to services from Haneda Airport.
Passenger load: 9 people maximum
To and from Tokyo 23 Wards: ¥16,800
To and from Tokyo Disney Resort and Hotels: ¥16,800
To and from Narita Airport: ¥22,700
Note: The above charges include expressway tolls. Contact New Lines Transys Taxi Group: +81 (0)3-6427-6767 for reservations.

Medium-size Taxi Service

Passenger load: 4 people maximum
To and from Tokyo's 23 Wards: ¥6,800-¥10,700
Availability: all year
* Reservation required one day in advance.
Note: The above charges include expressway tolls. Contact Limousine Hire [http://www.rakurakutaxi.jp/customer/static/hire01.html] for reservations.

Normal Taxi Service

Passenger load: 4 people maximum
To Tokyo's 23 Wards: ¥9,200
To Tokyo Disney Resort and Hotels: ¥9,700
To Narita Airport: ¥20,800
Note: The above charges do not include expressway tolls. Contact New Lines Transys Taxi Group: +81 (0)3-6427-6767 for reservations.

HANEDA AIRPORT LIMOUSINE BUS ROUTES

Haneda Airport Limousine Buses to Central Tokyo (23 Wards)
On average, adults pay ¥620–1,230; child's fare is ¥310–620; and each trip takes 15–85 minutes, depending on the distance traveled.

T-CAT (TOKYO CITY AIR TERMINAL)
(東京シティエアターミナル)

TOKYO STATION, Nihonbashi
(東京駅,日本橋方面)
- Tokyo Station Yaesu South exit

IKEBUKURO (池袋方面)
- Hotel Metropolitan
- Sunshine City Prince
- Ikebukuro station East exit #1

SHIBUYA (渋谷方面)
- Cerulean Tower Tokyu
- Shibuya Excel Hotel Tokyu
- Shibuya Station West exit

MEJIRO, KORAKUEN, KUDAN
(目白,後楽園,九段方面)
- Four Seasons Hotel Tokyo at Chinzan-so
- Hotel Grand Palace
- Tokyo Dome Hotel
- Akihabara Station (Yodobashi Camera)

SHINJUKU (新宿方面)
- Shinjuku Station West Exit No.23
- Century Southern Tower
- Sunroute Plaza Shinjuku
- Keio Plaza Hotel Tokyo
- Hyatt Regency Tokyo
- Shinjuku Washington
- Park Hyatt Tokyo
- Hilton Tokyo

AKASAKA (赤坂方面)
- Hotel New Otani
- Grand Prince Hotel Akasaka

- Akasaka Excel Hotel Tokyu
- ANA Intercontinental Tokyo

ODAIBA, ARIAKE (お台場,有明方面)
- Tokyo Bay Ariake Washington
- Nikko Tokyo
- Sunroute Ariake
- Grand Pacific LE DAIBA
- Kokusai Tenjijo Station
- Palette Town

KINSHICHO, TOYOCHO, TOYOSU
(錦糸町,東陽町,豊洲方面)
- Tobu Hotel Levant Tokyo
- Hotel East 21 Tokyo
- Toyosu Station
- Toyocho Station

SHINAGAWA (品川方面)
- Shinagawa Prince Hotel
- The Prince Sakura Tower Tokyo
- Grand Prince Hotel Takanawa
- Grand Prince Hotel New Takanawa

GINZA (銀座)
- Imperial Hotel
- Dai-ichi Hotel Tokyo
- Courtyard By Marriott Tokyo Ginza

OTHER AREAS
- Nerima Station
- Nogata Station
- Nakano Station North exit (Sunplaza)
- Kameari Station South exit
- Koiwa Station South exit
- Ichinoe Station
- Kasai Station

Haneda Airport Limousine Buses to Outer Tokyo
On average, adults pay ¥1,230–1,750; child's fare is ¥620–880; and each trip takes 45–135 minutes, depending on the distance traveled.

KICHIJOJI STATION (吉祥寺駅)

TACHIKAWA (立川方面)
- Tachikawa Station North exit No. 27 (Tachikawa Grand Hotel)
- Palace Hotel Tachikawa

CHOFU STATION (調布駅)

KOKUBUNJI STATION (国分寺駅)

FUCHU STATION (府中駅)

TAKAO, HACHIOJI, HINO STATION
(高尾,八王子,日野駅)
- JR Hachioji Station
- Keio Hachioji Station
- Takao Station South exit
- Choodo Hino

MACHIDA BUS CENTER (町田センター駅)
SAGAMI-ONO STATION (相模大野駅)
KEIO TAMA-CENTER STATION
(京王多摩センター駅)
MINAMI-OSAWA STATION (南大沢駅)
SEISEKI SAKURAGAOKA STATION (聖蹟桜ヶ丘駅)

Haneda Airport Limousine Buses to Chiba Destinations

On average, adults pay ¥830–3,100; child's fare is ¥420–1,550; and each trip takes 25–85 minutes, depending on the distance traveled.

NARITA AIRPORT (成田空港)
- Terminal 1
- Terminal 2

SHIN-URAYASU (新浦安方面)
- Oriental Hotel Tokyo Bay
- Emion Tokyo Bay
- Palm Terrace Hotel
- Fountain Terrace Hotel
- Mitsui Garden Hotel PRANA Tokyo Bay

MAKUHARI (幕張)
- Hotel Francs
- Hotel New Otani Makuhari
- Kaihin Makuhari Station North exit
- Hotel Springs Makuhari
- Makuhari Bay Town
- Hotel Green Tower Makuhari
- Apa Hotel & Resort
- Hotel The Manhattan

CHIBA (千葉)
- Chiba Chuo Station West exit
- JR Chiba Station

TOKYO DISNEY RESORT, MAIHAMA
(東京ディズニーリゾート、舞浜方面)
- Disney Ambassador Hotel
- Tokyo Disney Sea
- Tokyo Disney Sea Hotel Mira Costa
- Sheraton Grande Tokyo Bay Hotel
- Hotel Okura Tokyo Bay
- Hilton Tokyo Bay
- Sunroute Plaza Tokyo
- Tokyo Bay Maihama Hotel
- Tokyo Bay Hotel Tokyu
- Tokyo Disneyland
- Tokyo Disneyland Hotel

Haneda Airport Limousine Buses to Yokohama

On average, adults pay ¥580–840; child's fare is ¥290–420; and each trip takes 30–40 minutes, depending on the distance traveled.

Y-CAT (Yokohama City Air Terminal)
(横浜シティエアターミナル)

YOKOHAMA STATION WEST EXIT (横浜駅西口)
- Yokohama Bay Sheraton

YAMASHITAKOEN, MINATOMIRAI, RED BRICK WAREHOUSE
(山下公園、みなとみらい、赤レンガ倉庫)
- Yamashitakoen

- Red Brick Warehouse
- Yokohama Royal Park Hotel
- The Pan Pacific Yokohama Bay Hotel Tokyu
- Yokohama Grand Inter-Continental
  (Pacifico Yokohama)

SHIN-YOKOHAMA (新横浜方面)
- Shin-Yokohama Station
  (Associa Shin-Yokohama)
- Shin-Yokohama Prince Hotel

Haneda Airport Limousine Buses to Saitama

On average, adults pay ¥1,340–1,750; child's fare is ¥670–880; and each trip takes 70–120 minutes, depending on the distance traveled.

Seibu Bus Omiya Terminal
- Omiya Station West exit
- Saitama Fukutoshin Station

- Tokorozawa Station East exit
- Hon-Kawagoe Station
- Kawagoe Station West exit

Tokyo Haneda Airport Monorail 東京モノレール

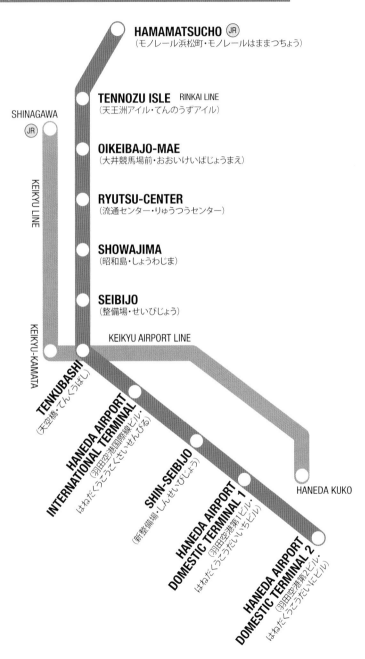

HAMAMATSUCHO (JR)
（モノレール浜松町・モノレールはままつちょう）

TENNOZU ISLE RINKAI LINE
（天王洲アイル・てんのうずアイル）

SHINAGAWA
(JR)

OIKEIBAJO-MAE
（大井競馬場前・おおいけいばじょうまえ）

RYUTSU-CENTER
（流通センター・りゅうつうセンター）

KEIKYU LINE

SHOWAJIMA
（昭和島・しょうわじま）

SEIBIJO
（整備場・せいびじょう）

KEIKYU-KAMATA

KEIKYU AIRPORT LINE

TENKUBASHI
（天空橋・てんくうばし）

HANEDA AIRPORT INTERNATIONAL TERMINAL
（羽田空港国際線ビル・はねだくうこうこくさいせんびる）

SHIN-SEIBIJO
（新整備場・しんせいびじょう）

HANEDA KUKO

HANEDA AIRPORT DOMESTIC TERMINAL 1
（羽田空港第1ビル・はねだくうこうだいいちビル）

HANEDA AIRPORT DOMESTIC TERMINAL 2
（羽田空港第2ビル・はねだくうこうだいにビル）

Keihin-Kyuko [Keikyu] Electric Railway 京浜急行電鉄[京急]

TO TOEI ASAKUSA LINE
OSHIAGE

TO TOEI ASAKUSA LINE
NISHI-MAGOME

SENGAKUJI TOEI ASAKUSA LINE
（泉岳寺・せんがくじ）

SHINAGAWA (JR)
（品川・しながわ）

KITA-SHINAGAWA

SHIN-BABA

AOMONOYOKOCHO
（青物横丁・あおものよこちょう）

SAMEZU

TACHIAIGAWA

OMORI-KAIGAN

HEIWAJIMA
（平和島・へいわじま）

OMORIMACHI

UMEYASHIKI

KEIKYU-KAMATA
（京急蒲田・けいきゅうかまた）

KOJIYA
（糀谷・こうじや）

OTORII
（大鳥居・おおとりい）

ANAMORI-INARI
（穴守稲荷・あなもりいなり）

TENKUBASHI
（天空橋・てんくうばし）
TOKYO MONORAIL

TOKYU TOYOKO LINE
SOTETSU LINE
YOKOHAMA MUNICIPAL
SUBWAY LINE
MINATOMIRAI LINE

YOKOHAMA （横浜・よこはま）(JR)

KEIKYU TSURUMI
（京急鶴見・けいきゅうつるみ）

KEIKYU KAWASAKI
（京急川崎・けいきゅうかわさき）

KAWASAKIDAISHI
（川崎大師・
かわさきだいし）

KOJIMA SHINDEN
小島新田
（こじましんでん）

DAISHI LINE
大師線

AIRPORT LINE
空港線

YOKOSUKA-CHUO
（横須賀中央・よこすかちゅうおう）

**HANEDA AIRPORT
INTERNATIONAL TERMINAL**
（羽田空港国際線ターミナル・
はねだくうこうこくさいせんたーみなる）

**HANEDA AIRPORT
DOMESTIC TERMINAL**
（羽田空港国内線ターミナル・
はねだくうこうこくないせんたーみなる）

TO MISAKIGUCHI,
URAGA

Part 3: Maps of Tokyo

Introducing Tokyo's Main Districts

Tokyo is made up of several hundred distinct communities, many of which date back to the early 1600s when the famed Tokugawa Shogunate began. Here are brief profiles of the most important of these districts.

Map 1 TOKYO STATION, MARUNOUCHI & NIHONBASHI

■ **Imperial Palace** (皇居)
■ **Tokyo Station** (東京駅)
■ **Marunouchi & Otemachi Business Districts** (丸の内、大手町ビジネス街)
■ **Bridgestone Museum of Art** (ブリヂストン美術館)

These three districts encompass the original center of Tokyo, including the huge Tokyo Central Station transportation hub which is a short distance from the Imperial Palace Grounds. The areas are the primary business and financial centers of Japan, marked by high-rise buildings that contain offices, shops and restaurant rows that make them major destinations for both residents and visitors. The Marunouchi district also has a colorful cafe nightlife, and is a popular strolling area in the evenings.

Map 2 GINZA, YURAKUCHO, HIBIYA & TSUKIJI

■ **Ginza-dori High-Fashion Shopping District** (銀座通り)
■ **Ginza Yon-chome Intersection** (銀座四丁目交差点)
■ **Sony Buidling** (ソニービル)
■ **Hibiya Park** (日比谷公園)
■ **Tsukiji Central Wholesale Market** (築地卸売市場)

The Hibiya, Yurakucho and Ginza districts of Tokyo are regarded as the heart of the city when it comes to entertainment and shopping. The Hibiya and Yurakucho districts adjoin the southeast corner of the Imperial Palace Grounds, and are in turn adjoined on the east side by the famous Ginza district, with Tsukiji a short distance further on.

In addition to famous hotels [the Imperial and the Peninsula], Hibiya and Yurakucho have several theaters, including the famous Takarazuka theater which features all-girl revues. The Ginza is the shopping and entertainment place in central Tokyo, with bars, clubs, restaurants, shops and department stores side-by-side. The famous Kabuki-Za theater is on the east side of the Ginza. And Tsukiji is most famous for its huge fish wholesale market.

In addition to two commuter train lines, this area is served by six subway lines that intersect, with all of the stations connected by underground corridors.

Map 3 SHIMBASHI, SHIODOME, HAMAMATSUCHO & SHIBA

■ **Shiodome Shio Sight (new business district)** (汐留シオサイト)
■ **Hamarikyu Garden** (浜離宮恩賜庭園)
■ **Zojo-ji** (増上寺)
■ **Tokyo Tower** (東京タワー)

Most of these communities in the north, south and western hilly portions of Edo/Tokyo grew up around the estates of fief lords who were required to have residences in Edo, keep their families there at all times and themselves spend every other year in their Edo mansions and serve in the shogun's court—a shogunate policy that began in the 1630s and lasted for over 240 years.

These districts are among the oldest in Tokyo, and played extraordinary roles in the history of the city. The following attractions are just three of their highlights: **Hamarikyu Gardens** is a public park in Tokyo's Chuo Ward, located at the mouth of the Sumida River. It is a landscaped garden surrounding a pond and a seawater moat, and was the site of a villa of the Shogun Tokugawa family in the 17th century. The garden is a short walk from Shiodome Station on the Toei Oedo Line, and a stroll from Shimbashi Station on the Ginza and Toei Asakusa subway lines.

Zojo Ji [Zojo Temple] is the chief temple of the Jodo-Buddist sect. Founded in 1393, it was the main temple of the Tokugawa shoguns. One of the trees on the grounds was planted by U.S. president Ulysses S. Grant in 1879. It remains popular with ordinary people and dignitaries.

Statues of Jizo Bosatsu—considered the protector of the souls of stillborn children,

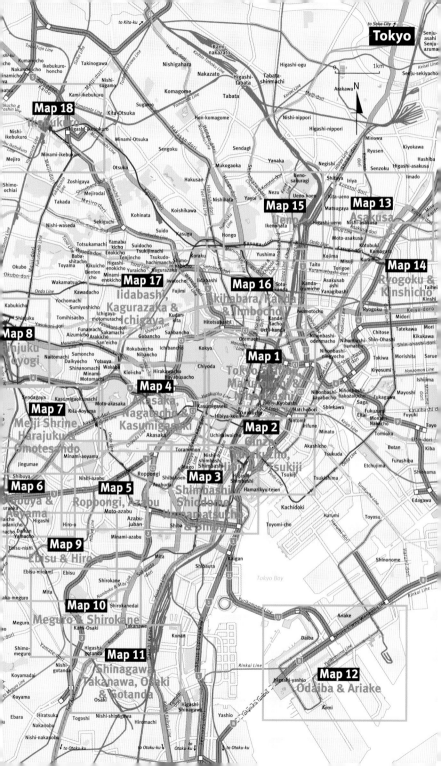

and are the Buddhist equivalent of angels—line the grounds in rows. There is also a gorgeous golden altar on the grounds where priests chant prayers that visitors may view.

Tokyo Tower attracts hundreds of thousands of people annually to enjoy a grand view of the city from its observation deck. It was built in 1958 and was modeled after the Eiffel Tower in Paris. It is 333 m (1,092 feet) high, 9 m (30 feet) higher than the Eiffel Tower in Paris. On a clear day you can see the towering pinnacle of Mt. Fuji and Mt. Tsukuba from the Observation Deck.

The tower is a short walk from the Shiba Park Prince Hotel, and a five-minute walk from Kamiyacho Station on the Hibiya Subway Line. Other subway stations within walking distance: Akabaneshi on the Toei Oedo Line, Onarimon on the Toei Mita Line, and Daimon on the Toei Asakusa Line. There are a variety of gift and other shops on the first four floors, access to which is free to visitors. Shiodome, next to Shimbashi Station, also has several prestige hotels.

Map 4 AKASAKA, NAGATACHO & KASUMIGASEKI

■ **National Diet Building (Kokkai Gijido)** (国会議事堂)
■ **New Otani Art Museum** (ニューオータニ美術館)

Nagatacho and Kasumigaseki together make up Japan's government center, with the Diet Building, the offices of the Upper and Lower House members, and all of the offices of agencies and departments that comprise the national government. Akasaka, which adjoins these two districts on the southwest side, is a hotel, office and restaurant center and the site of a number of geisha inns that cater to politicians, bureaucrats and their high-level business contacts.

Map 5 ROPPONGI & AZABU

■ **Roppongi Hills** (六本木ヒルズ)
■ **Tokyo Midtown** (東京ミッドタウン)
■ **The National Art Center** (国立新美術館)
■ **Azabujuban Shopping Town** (麻布十番商店街)

This bar and night club center is popular with both Japanese and foreign movie and TV stars and their fans, and is further noted for the restaurant and shop-filled Roppongi Hills and Tokyo Midtown high-rise complexes. The Roppongi Hills observation floor offers a 360-degree bird's eye view of the city. The entertainment areas and both of these complexes are within a short walk of Roppongi Intersection/Subway Station, served by the Hibiya Line and Toei No. 12 Line.

Other attractions: the Mori Art Center; 21-21 Design Sight, the Suntory Museum of Arts, and the nearby National Art Center. Azabu, one of Tokyo's most elite residential

Ginza—the ultimate shopping paradise for designer goods

areas, is also known for its large number of foreign embassies.

Map 6 SHIBUYA & AOYAMA

- ▓ **Hachiko Statue** (忠犬ハチ公像)
- ▓ **Shibuya 109 (ichi-maru-kyu) Shopping Building** (渋谷109)
- ▓ **Center-gai, Koen-dori Shopping District** (渋谷センター街、公園通り)
- ▓ **The Bunkamura Museum** (文化村ザ・ミュージアム)
- ▓ **Toguri Museum of Art** (戸栗美術館)

The Shibuya Station area, on the Yamanote Loop Line on the southwest side of Tokyo, is one of the city's most popular entertainment and shopping districts, with several department stores, theater complexes, fashion boutiques and specialty shops, and is especially popular with the younger set. The favorite meeting place: Hachiko, the statue of a faithful dog, in the center of the station plaza. Shibuya is a major transportation hub, with lines serving Yokohama and other satellite cities to the south and southwest.

The large upscale Aoyama district in the adjoining Minato Ward, which begins on the southwest corner of the Imperial Palace Grounds [near the Crown Prince's residence] is a major center of corporate headquarter office buildings, the south side entry way to the adjoining Meiji Park, fashion shops, jazz clubs [like The Blue Note], and the Nezu Museum.

Map 7 MEIJI SHRINE, HARAJUKU & OMOTESANDO

- ▓ **Meiji Jingu Shrine** (明治神宮)
- ▓ **Ota Museum of Ukiyo-e Prints** (太田記念美術館)
- ▓ **Watari-Um Museum (Contemporary Art)** (ワタリウム美術館)
- ▓ **Takeshitadori Shopping Street (for young people)** (竹下通り)
- ▓ **Omotesando Shopping Street (high-fashion street)** (表参道)

The Harajuku and Omotesando areas of Tokyo compete with the world-famous Ginza district for entertainment, dining, shopping and strolling. The centerpiece of all this activity is the broad tree-lined Omotesando Boulevard, which begins in front of Harajuku Station and runs eastward for about 1.5 kilometers [1 mile]. Virtually every high-end fashion designer and apparel outlet in the world has shops along the boulevard, with the large Omotesando Hills fashion shopping center adding to the attractions. On weekends and holidays hundreds of young men and women gather in the area to show off their latest far-out costumes, attracting thousands of viewers.

The main cultural/historical attraction in the Harajuku area is **Meiji Jingu Shrine**, about 15-minute walk from the Station. It honors Emperor Meiji and his empress Shoken, who reigned during Japan's transformation from a samurai-rule kingdom to a modern nation between 1870 until 1912. Several hundred thousand people visit the shrine on New Year's eve to greet the new year at midnight. Vendors on the shrine grounds sell a variety of refreshments and souvenirs. It is open from sunrise to sunset on regular days.

Other attractions in the area: **Ota Museum of Ukiyo-e Prints**, Japan's most famous ukiyo-e [uu-kee-yoh-eh] or woodblock print museum. It houses some 12,000 woodblock prints by traditional masters but displays only 80 to 100 at a time. Near the intersection of Omotesando Blvd. and Meiji Avenue behind La Foret, it is near the east entrance of Omotesando Station on the Chiyoda Line, and a three-minute walk from Harajuku Station on the Yamanote Train Line. Open from 10:30 am to 5:30 pm from Tuesday through Sunday, except from the 27th to the end of each month. There is an entrance fee.

Also: **Watari-Um Museum**, in the Jingumae section, a major museum featuring work by established artists as well as amateur youngsters. It is open from 11 am to 7 pm, and is near Gaienmae Station on the Ginza Subway Line on the eastern end of Omotesando Blvd. The museum building, designed by famed architect Mario Botta, is itself worth a visit.

Takeshita Dori Shopping Street is a short narrow street that starts at the west exit of Harajuku Station on the Yamanote Loop Line and goes down the slope to Meiji Avenue. The street and its narrow alleys are jam-packed with clothing shops, specialty shops, and fast food outlets. It is a haven for young people.

Map 8 SHINJUKU & YOYOGI

- ▓ **Tokyo Metropolitan Government Office Building** (東京都庁)
- ▓ **Nishi-Shinjuku Skyscrapers** (西新宿高層ビル群)
- ▓ **Shinjuku Gyoen Garden** (新宿御苑)
- ▓ **Kabuki-cho (night town)** (歌舞伎町)

Shinjuku on the west side of central Tokyo, is a huge city within itself, with a large number of international hotels, department stores, high-rise office buildings and the famous Kabukicho bar, cabaret, restaurant and theater district about 3 blocks northeast of Shinjuku Station. Shinjuku Ni-Chome, about three blocks from the station on Shinjuku Street, is a noted gay entertainment district. Shinjuku Station, the busiest transportation in the world, is also a major hub for subways and trains, and is the starting place for train service to the base of Mt. Fuji.

The south and southwest sides of Shinjuku Station include more than a dozen high-rise headquarter buildings of major Japanese corporations, and the 54-storey Tokyo Opera City. The west side has a large collection of major international hotels. The east side is noted for its department stores, restaurants, cafes and clubs. There is a spill-over of office buildings that continues on into the Yoyogi Station area on the southeast side.

The famous **Shinjuku Gyoen Garden** is about 2 kilometers east of Shinjuku Station on Shinjuku Street, the main east-west thorough-fare, near Gyoenmae Station on the Marunouchi Subway Line. This huge landscaped garden park, on the site of the estate of Shogunate-era Lord Naito, has one of the largest arrays of cherry trees and chrysanthemums in Japan, and is patronized by the Emperor and Empress. It is open daily except Mondays from 9 am to 4:30 pm, with longer hours during the flower blooming seasons. There is an admissions fee.

Map 9 EBISU & HIRO-O

■ **Yebisu Garden Place** (恵比寿ガーデンプレイス)
■ **Tokyo Metropolitian Museum of Photography** (東京都写真美術館)
■ **Yebisu Beer Museum** (ヱビスビール記念館)
■ **Yamatane Museum of Art** (山種美術館)
■ **Prince Arisugawa Memorial Park** (有栖川宮記念公園)

These two elite residential and entertainment areas in Southwest Tokyo on the Yamanote loop commuter train line have a number of unique attractions, including **Yebisu Garden Place**, a short ride on a covered moving sidewalk from the east side of Ebisu Station, which has been described as a city within a city. The centerpiece of the complex is a high-rise tower chocked full of shops and restaurants—the latter with fantastic night-time views of the city. It is surrounded by shops and other venues, and is one of Tokyo's most popular tourist attractions.

Also: **Tokyo Metro Museum of Photography** which has over 20,000 photographs in its collection but doesn't show all of them at once. Located in Yebisu Garden Place it is

open from 10 am to 6 pm Saturday to Wednesday and 10 am to 8 pm on Thursdays and Fridays. Take the Sky Walker from Ebisu Station to Yebisu Garden Place, proceed down the concourse to the top of Yebisu building. There is an entrance fee.

Yebisu Beer Garden on the original site of Japan Beer Brewing Company is now part of the famous Yebisu Garden Place. [See directions above.] Visitors can walk through the Yebisu Beer Museum and sample the product at the Sapporo Beer Station, which also serves food.

Yamatane Museum of Art, in adjoining Hiro-o, was founded in 1966 by Taneji Yamazaki and features exhibitions of outstanding Japanese artists. It is open from 10 am to 5 pm daily except Mondays and national holidays. It is a 10-minute walk from Exit 2 on the West side of Hiro-o Station.

Prince Arisugawa Memorial Park, described as an "enchanted park," is a heavily wooded area packed with ponds, rocks and trees which is in Hiro-o on the Hibiya Subway Line and surrounded by foreign embassies. Donated to Hiro-o by the family of Prince Arisugawa, it is dedicated to educating children about the richness of nature.

Map 10 MEGURO & SHIROKANE

■ **Tokyo Metro Teien Art Museum** (東京都庭園美術館)
■ **Institute for Nature Study** (国立科学博物館付属自然教育園)

Meguro, on the Yamanote Loop Line, is an elite residential area with the usual complex of businesses, cultural/historical attractions and restaurants in the vicinity of Meguro Station. The attractions include: **Tokyo Metro Teien Art Museum** at 5-chome, 21-9 Shirokane-dai, which caters to children and teens up to the age of 18. Its programs are free to teacher-led groups. Open from 10 am to 6 pm on most days. Call 3443-0201 for current days and exhibition schedule. It used to be the residence of Prince Asaka. **Institute for Nature Study**, next to the Teien Art Museum, contains over 8,000 trees and some marshy areas, and is a retreat for artists and bird spotters. No more than 300 people are allowed into the park at any time, making it a fairly quiet place to visit.

Map 11 SHINAGAWA, TAKANAWA, OSAKI & GOTANDA

■ **Epson Aqua Studium** (エプソン品川アクアスタジアム)
■ **Hara Museum of Contemporary Art** (原美術館)

Shinagawa Station on the Yamanote Loop Line

is a major transportation hub [where some "bullet trains" stop], and the gateway to several international hotels in the Shinagawa area and the adjoining Takanawa district. Its primary visitor attractions include the **Epson Aqua Stadium**, which is inside the Prince Hotel at 4-10-30 Takanawa. The site boasts more than 300 species and 20,000 water creatures. The dolphin show is very popular. Open Monday-Friday 12 noon to 10 pm; Saturday 10 am to 10 pm; Sunday & holidays 10 am to 9 pm.

The **Hara Museum of Contemporary Art** at 4-7-25 Kita-Shinagawa is a 15-minute walk from both Shinagawa and Takanawa Stations. It is Japan's oldest museum dedicated to contemporary art by both Japanese and foreign artists. Opening hours and days change. Call 3445-0651 for current days and house. There is an admissions fee.

The Osaki and Gotanda areas are further along from Shinagawa Station on the Loop Line. Osaki is a hub station for three other lines that serve areas south and southwest of Tokyo and beyond. The New Otani Hotel is in Osaki, which is described as an office district. Gotanda is also an office town, and is where the Tokyo Design Center is located, across from the Tokyu Stay Gotanda Hotel.

Map 12 ODAIBA & ARIAKE

- **Rainbow Bridge** (レインボーブリッジ)
- **Odaiba Marine Park** (お台場海浜公園)
- **Oedo Onsen Monogatari (spa)** (大江戸温泉物語)
- **Museum of Emerging Science and Innovation** (日本科学未来館)
- **Palette Town (Big Ferries Wheel, Mega Web amusement spot)** (パレットタウン)
- **Museum of Maritime Science** (船の科学館)
- **Tokyo Big Sight (exhibition hall)** (東京ビッグサイト)
- **Ariake Coliseum** (有明コロシアム)

Odaiba is a man-made island in the middle of Tokyo Bay, between the Shibaura waterfront area on the Tokyo side and Chiba Peninsula area on the east side. Constructed in 1851 as a fortress to protect the bay, it has since been developed into one of the most popular apartment, office, shopping and entertainment districts in Tokyo. It is connected to the Shibaura Dock area of central Tokyo by a spectacular suspension bridge known as **Rainbow Bridge**. Its primary attractions include the following:

Odaiba Marine Park—A popular tourist spot on the waterfront of Odaiba Island that is popular for strolling, picnicking and picture-taking. **Oedo Onsen Monogatari Spa**—A fabulous hot spring spa bathhouse/massage parlor done up in the style of the Shogunate period of Edo [Tokyo]. The ladies love it!

The Rainbow Bridge, Odaiba

Museum of Emerging Science & Innovation — A spectacular hall complex that is one of the most visited places on Odaiba Island.

Palette Town — A theme park/shopping center with a mega Ferris wheel and video game exhibits and pokemon trainers in the center of Odaiba Island. The name comes from a video character. **Tokyo Big Sight** — The nickname of the spectacular Tokyo International Business Center complex on Odaiba Island. It is BIG and includes public art places, exhibition halls and more. **Ariake Coliseum** — An indoor sports/entertainment arena that can hold 15,000 spectators. It has a retractable roof. The **Museum of Maritime Science** at 3-1 Higashi-Yashio, Shinagawa is an amazing museum housed in a 6-story tall ship with a higher still observation deck.

Map 13 ASAKUSA

- **Senso-ji** (浅草寺)
- **Nakamise Shopping Street** (仲見世通り)
- **Kappabashi-dori (area for purchases of kitchen tools)** (かっぱ橋道具街)

The Asakusa area became one of Edo's [Tokyo's] most famous and largest entertainment districts during the early decades of the Tokugawa Shogunate (1603–1868), and still today attracts over 30 million visitors a year. The biggest attraction in present-day Asakusa is the famed Senso-Ji (Senso Temple), which dates from the 7th century. The entrance to the large temple complex is marked by a huge Buddhist style gate, Kaminarimon, or "Thunder Gate."

The gate leads directly to Nakamise Dori,

Nakamise Shopping Street in Asakusa

or "Inside Shop Street," a third of a kilometer long open-air mall, with a retractable roof, that is lined with stalls selling accessories, apparel, crafts, food, gift items and Japanalia of all kinds. Asakusa was and still is famous for its annual festivals, including:

Sanja Matsuri with its massive fireworks displays over the Sumida River at the end of July; the **Brazilian Samba Festival** at the end of August; the **Golden Dragon Festival** on October 18 and again on March 18; and the **Tokyo Jidai Matsuri**, or Tokyo Period Festival, which depicts an outing by courtesans from Asakusa's Yoshiwara, Japan's largest and most famous redlight district, which flourished from the early decades of the Tokugawa or Edo period until 1956.

A large entertainment and shopping area adjoining the Senso-Ji grounds depicts the architecture and fashions of the Edo period.

Map 14 RYOGOKU & KINSHICHO

- **Tokyo Sky Tree** (東京スカイツリー)
- **Kokugikan Sumo Hall** (両国国技館)
- **Sumo Museum** (相撲博物館)
- **Edo Tokyo Museum** (江戸東京博物館)

The best-known landmarks and attractions in this area are the **Kokugikan Sumo Stadium**, where Japan's national sport is headquartered; the spectacular **Tokyo Sky Tree** highrise building, which at nearly 534 m (one-third of a mile) high dwarfs the famous Tokyo Tower; and the Edo Tokyo Museum, which brings the Edo [Tokyo]/Tokugawa Shogunate era alive. It is a must-see for devotees of Japan's samurai period, which lasted from 1192 until 1867. The spectacle of a sumo tournament is a once-in-a-lifetime experience, as is touring the Tokyo Sky Tree from bottom to top.

Map 15 UENO

- **Ueno Zoo** (上野動物園)
- **National Museum of Western Art** (国立西洋美術館)
- **National Science Museum** (国立科学博物館)
- **Tokyo National Museum** (国立博物館)
- **Kyu Iwasaki-tei House and Gardens** (旧岩崎邸庭園)
- **Yushima Tenjin Shrine** (湯島天神)
- **Ameyoko Shopping Street** (アメ横商店街)

The Ueno area was famous during the Tokyo's Yedo period as the estate grounds of a feudal lord, most of which has been converted into a park that now adjoins Ueno Station on the west side. The park boasts some of the most important cultural and historical attractions in the country, including: the **Ueno Zoo**, a world-class zoo, open from 9:30 am to 5 pm.

There is an admission fee except on special days; the **National Museum of Western Art**, a Japan's premiere museum of Western art. Open 9:30 am to 5:30 pm; closed on Mondays; the **National Science Museum**, a national treasure [there is a steam locomotive in front of the building]. It is closed on weekends and national holidays. The **Tokyo National Museum** is nearby. Also, the **Kyu Iwasaki-tei House & Gardens**, Ueno home and garden of the founder of the great Iwasaki industrial combine built in the Meiji Era [1867–1912]; the **Yushima Tenjin Shrine**, originally built in 458 A.D., and rebuilt in the 17th century. It is dedicated to scholars, and attracts thousands of students from nearby universities who pray for success in passing exams. It is a short walk from Ochanomizu Station and Yushima Station.

Ameyoko Shopping Street, a short walk south of Ueno Station along the train tracks, was a haven for black market goods after World War II. It is now a discount shopping mecca for clothing and other items that attracts bargain hunters, residents and visitors.

Map 16 AKIHABARA, KANDA & JIMBOCHO

■ Akihabara Electric City (秋葉原電気街)
■ Kanda Myojin Shrine (神田明神)
■ Holy Resurrection Cathedral (Nikolai-do) (ニコライ堂)
■ Tokyo Dome City (amusement spot) (東京ドームシティ)
■ Tokyo Dome (baseball studium) (東京ドーム)

Akihabara [Ah-kee-hah-bah-rah] **Electric City** on the Yamanote Loop Line is one place in Tokyo that is known by almost everyone who has ever been to Japan or contemplates going there. Adjoining Akihabara Station on the west side, it is Japan's most famous shopping mecca for all electric and electronic devices, from cameras, computers and e-dictionaries to refrigerators.

Other attractions in the area: **Kanda Myojin Shrine**, first built in 1270 in what is now Tokyo's Otemachi district, this landmark has been rebuilt many times, and is now located near Akihabara Station. It is the centerpiece of one of Japan's three most famous Shinto festivals held in May every other year; **Nikolai-Do** [Holy Resurrection Cathedral] in Surugadai, Kanda was first built in 1891 and rebuilt in 1929. It is the main orthodox Christian church in Japan, and is named after St. Nicholas, a Russian priest who came to Japan in 1860 and died there in 1911.

Jimbocho, near several universities, is known for its publishing houses and large number of book shops. Not far away is the **Tokyo Dome Amusement Center and Sports Stadium**, a huge complex that includes Tokyo's largest and most popular sports stadium, an amusement park shopping center and restaurant row. It also has a hot spring spa, a roller coaster, etc. and hotel. It is near Suidobashi Station on the Chuo Line.

Map 17 IIDABASHI, KAGURAZAKA & ICHIGAYA

■ Yasukuni Shrine (靖国神社)
■ Kagurazaka Shopping District (神楽坂)

These two districts have two noted attractions: **Yasukuni Shrine**, near Iidabashi Station where the Yurakucho and Tozai subway lines and the Chuo line intersect. Yasukuni dates from 1873, and is dedicated to the memory of the several million military men that have died in Japan's wars. On the west side of the Imperial Palace grounds, it is the site of numerous annul festivals. The entry way is marked by a huge torii gate.

Kagurazaka Shopping District on a slope just west of Ichigaya Station [on the west side of the Imperial Palace grounds], is a picturesque area that features Tokugawa Shogunate-style shops and restaurants that are popular attractions for both Japanese and visitors. The Chuo Line commuter train and the Yurakucho Subway Line intersect at both Iidabashi and Ichigaya Stations.

Map 18 IKEBUKURO

■ Sunshine 60 building (サンシャイン60ビル)
■ Sunshine Int'l Aquarium (サンシャイン国際水族館)
■ Otome Road (manga and anime street) (乙女ロード)
■ Tokyu Hands Department (東急ハンズ)

This northwest area of Tokyo used to be famous as a country-bumpkin town, but it has since morphed into a major shopping and entertainment district that is also known for its landmark 60-story **Sunshine 60 Building**, the **Sunshine International Aquarium**, and a street that is one of the anime and manga centers of Japan. The Yamanote Train Line and the Yurakucho Subway Line serve Ikebukuro and it is the hub for feeder train lines serving outlying areas. The 2nd and 3rd floors of Sunshine 60 Building are known as Namja Town that has unusual food shops and 14 other attractions. The Manten Planetarium is also located in the building and has ongoing programs. Other attractions include **The Metropolitan Art Space** on the west side of Ikebukuro Station [it has the world's longest escalator.]

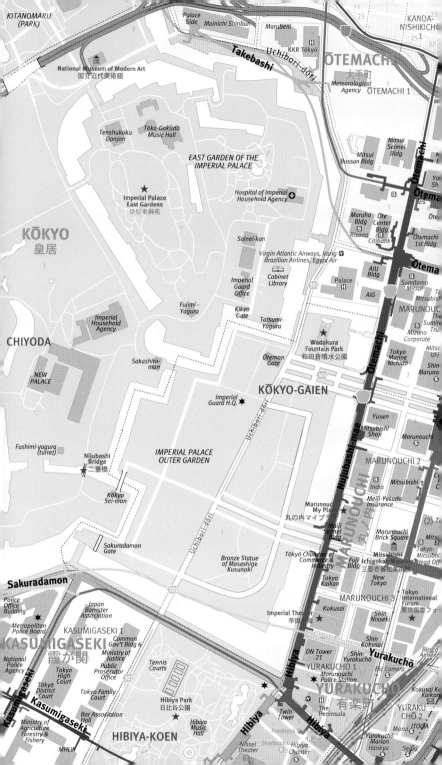

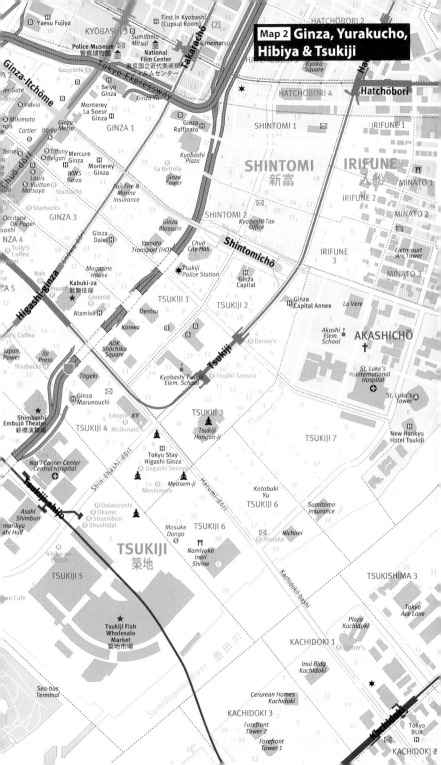

Map 2 Ginza, Yurakucho, Hibiya & Tsukiji

Yaesu Fujiya
First in Kyobashi (Cupsul Room) (2)
KYOBASHI 3
Police Museum
警察博物館
Sumitomo Mitsui
National Film Center
東京国立近代美術館
フィルムセンター
Kanematsu
HATCHŌBORI 2
Ginza-Itchōme
Tokyo Expressway
Takaracho
HATCHŌBORI 3
Kyoka Square
HATCHŌBORI 4
Hatchōbori
Gonpachi
ier Gate
Velvela
Mikimoto
Cartier
Itō-ya
Chanel
Tiffany
Bvlgari
Louis Vuitton
Matsuya
Occitane
Oji Paper
koshi
NZA 4
Tully's Coffee
ouvel
Nair
Promo
Higashi-ginza
A 5
ity's Coffee
Japan Power
Starbucks
Seiyō Ginza
Monterey La Soeur Ginza
Ginza Melso
GINZA 1
Mercure Ginza
Monterey Ginza
WINS Ginza
Starbucks
Starbucks
GINZA 3
Ginza Daiei
Shōwa-dōri
Chuō-dōri
Magazine House
Kabuki-za
歌舞伎座
Ginnotō
Atamisō
Konwa
Dentsu
Jiji Press
Tōgeki
Ginza Marunouchi
Shimbashi
Embujō Theater
新橋演舞場
TSUKIJI 4
Edogin
McDonald
KY
Nat'l Cancer Center Central Hospital
Asahi Shimbun
ahi Hall
Ichina-no
Shin-ōhashi-dōri
Tsukijishijō
TSUKIJI 5
an Cafe
Ginza Raffinato
Kyobashi Plaza
La Bettola
Ginza Tower
Fuji Fire & Marine Insurance
Ginza Blossom
Yamato Transport (HQ)
Chuō City Hall
Tsukiji Police Station
TSUKIJI 1
ADK Shōchiku Square
Kyobashi Tsukiji Elem. School
Tsukiji Tamura
Denny's
TSUKIJI 2
Tsukiji Hongan-ji
TSUKIJI 3
Tokyu Stay Higashi Ginza
Uogashi Senryō
Myōsem-ji
Meshimaru
Daiwazushi
Okame
Shushibun
Shushidai
Mosuke Dango
Namiyoke Inari Shrine
TSUKIJI 6
Harumi-dōri
Tsukiji Fish Wholesale Market
築地市場
Sea-bus Terminal
TSUKIJI
築地
SHINTOMI
新富
SHINTOMI 1
SHINTOMI 2
Kyobashi Tax Office
Shintomichō
Ginza Capital
Ginza Capital Annex
IRIFUNE
入船
IRIFUNE 1
IRIFUNE 2
MINATO 1
MINATO 2
IRIFUNE 3
MINATO 3
Lieocourt Arx Tower
La Vere
Akashi Elem. School
AKASHICHŌ
St. Luke's International Hospital
St. Luke's Tower
New Hankyu Hotel Tsukiji
TSUKIJI 7
Kotobuki Yu
TSUKIJI 6
Sumitomo Insurance
Nichirei
Tentake
TSUKISHIMA 3
Tokyo Ace Lane
Kachidoki-bashi
Plaza Kachidoki
KACHIDOKI 1
Inui Bldg Kachidoki
Cerurean Homes Kachidoki
KACHIDOKI 3
Forefront Tower 2
Forefront Tower 1
Tokyo BUK
KACHIDOKI 2
Sumidagawa River 墨田川

Map 3 **Shimbashi, Shiodome, Hamamatsucho & Shiba**

SHIMBASHI 1

NISHI-HIMBASHI
西新橋

-SHIMBASHI 2

SHI-BASHI 3

Univ. oital wa

Hibiya-dori

Da Vinci Oharimon

Yokohama Rubber Co.

SHIMBASHI 6

Tokyu Stay

Tokyo Art Club

Japan Red Cross Society

NBF Tower

Shiba Park Office

SHIBA-DAIMON
芝大門

SHIBA-DAIMON 2

Vince Shiba Park

arque

BA-EN 2

Tokyo Mitsubishi UFJ

A 2

Aviation

Dai-ichi

SHIMBASHI 1

Unizo Shimbashi

Malaysian Airline System

Hankyu Express International

SHIMBASHI
新橋

Torifuji

Matsuoka

China Airlines

SHIMBASHI 5

Shimbashi Sumitomo

SHIMBASHI 2

New Shimbashi Bldg

Torifuji

SHIMBASHI 3

SAKURADA PARK

Sunroute (4)

Rainbow

SHIBA-DAIMON 1

Mitsui Garden Shiodome

Tokyu Stay

HAMAMATSU CHŌ
浜松町

Daimon

Daimon

World Trade Center

HAMAMATSU CHŌ 2

Metr. Transportation Bureau

SHIBA 1

Mardi Gras

Kyubei

H&M Grocery Ginza

Ginza bu

Mitsui Garden

Shimbashi

Shimbashi

Ekimae Bldg No.4

Yakult (H.Q.)

Kyu-Shimbashi Teishajo 旧新橋停車場

Shiodome City Center

Nippon TV Tower

Shio Sight 汐サイト

Park Hotel Tokyo

Medi Tower

Toppan Forms

WINS Shiodome

HIGASHI-SHIMBASHI 2

Vita Italia イタリア街

Central Bldg

Acty Shiodome

Pokémon Center Tokyo

Shiba Comm. High School

KAIGAN 1

SHIBA RIKYU GARDEN

Tokyo Gas Bldg

Com Bldg

Panasonic

Caretta Shiodome

Royal Park Shiodome Tower

HIGASHI SHIMBASHI 1

Tokyo Shiodome Bldg

Sumitomo Bldg

Nittsu

Twin Parks

Shiki Theater (LUMI)

Tsukiji

Conrad

Starbucks

Excelsior

Villa Fontaine Shiodome

JR East Art Center, SHIKI Theater

Mitsui Garden

GINZA 8

Ginza Jr. H. School

Japan Post

TSUKIJI 5

Mitsui Engineering & Shipbuilding

HAMARIKYU-TEIEN

Hamarikyu Gardens
浜離宮恩賜庭園

CHUŌ-KU

MINATO-KU

Shiba Yayoi Kaikan

New Pier Takebashi North Tower

Aioi Takeshiba

Tokyo Trade Center

Tokyo Metr. Archives

Nittsu

New Pier Takeshiba South Tower

Takeshiba

Takeshiba Pier

Intercontinental Tokyo Bay

Tokyo Port Management Office

Tōshiba Bldg

Suzuya Hamamatsucho

0   250m

N

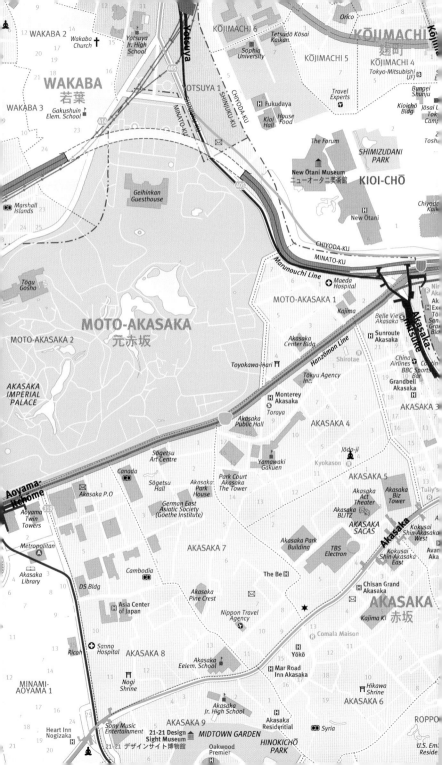

WAKABA 2
Wakaba Church
Yotsuya Jr. High School
WAKABA
若葉
WAKABA 3
Gakushuin Elem. School

KŌJIMACHI 6
Orico
Tetsudō Kōsai Kaikan
Sophia University
KŌJIMACHI 5
KŌJIMACHI 4
Tokyo-Mitsubishi UFJ
Travel Experts

KŌJIMACHI
麹町

Bungei Shunju
Kioichō Bldg
Jōsai U Tok Camp
Toshi

Yotsuya
KŌJIMACHI 1
CHIYODA-KU
SHINJUKU-KU
Fukudaya
Kioi Hall
House Food

Geihinkan Guesthouse

The Forum
New Ōtani Museum
ニューオータニ美術館
SHIMIZUDANI PARK
KIOI-CHŌ

Chiyoda Kaik
New Ōtani

Marshall Islands

CHIYODA-KU
MINATO-KU

Tōgu Gosho

Marunouchi Line
Maeda Hospital

Nir Aka
Ak
Exc Tō
San Gra Blo

MOTO-AKASAKA 1
Kajima
Belle Vie Akasaka
Sunroute Akasaka

MOTO-AKASAKA
元赤坂

MOTO-AKASAKA 2

Akasaka Center Bldg
Hanzōmon Line
Shirotae
China Airlines
BBC Sports Bar
Grandbell Akasaka

Toyokawa-Inari
Tokyu Agency Inc.

AKASAKA

AKASAKA IMPERIAL PALACE

Monterey Akasaka
Toraya

Akasaka Public Hall

AKASAKA 4

Sōgetsu Art Centre

Yamawaki Gakuen

Jōdo-ji
Kyokason
AKASAKA 5

Akasaka Biz Tower
Tully's

Canada
Sōgetsu Hall
Akasaka Park House
Park Court Akasaka The Tower

Akasaka Act Theater

Aoyama-itchome
Akasaka P.O
German East Asiatic Society (Goethe Institute)

Akasaka BLITZ
AKASAKA SACAS

Akasaka

Aoyama Twin Towers

AKASAKA 7

Akasaka Park Building
TBS Electron

Kokusai Shin-Akasaka West
Kokusai Shin-Akasaka East

Metropolitan
Cambodia

The Be
Avan

Akasaka Library
DS Bldg

Asia Center of Japan

Akasaka Pine Crest

Chisan Grand Akasaka

AKASAKA
赤坂

Nippon Travel Agency
Kajima KI

Ricoh
Sanno Hospital
AKASAKA 8

Comala Maison

MINAMI-AOYAMA 1

Akasaka Eelem. School

Yōkō

Nogi Shrine

Mar Road Inn Akasaka

Hikawa Shrine
AKASAKA 6

Heart Inn Nogizaka
Sony Music Entertainment
21-21 Design Sight Museum
21-21 デザインサイト博物館
AKASAKA 9
MIDTOWN GARDEN
Akasaka Jr. High School
Akasaka Residential
Syria

ROPPO

U.S. Em Reside

Oakwood Premier
HINOKICHŌ PARK

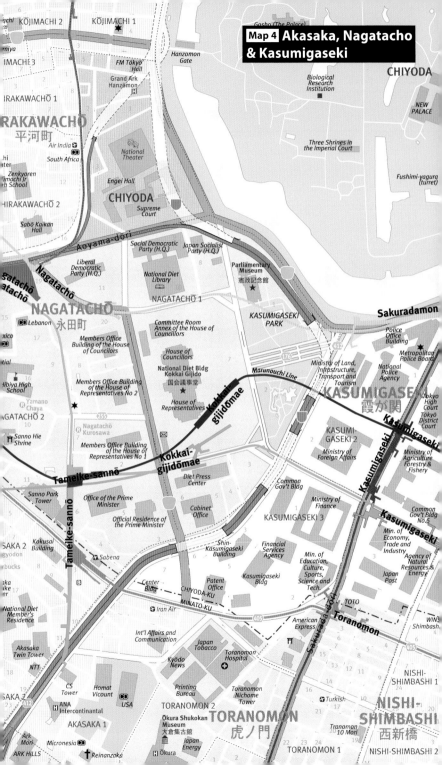

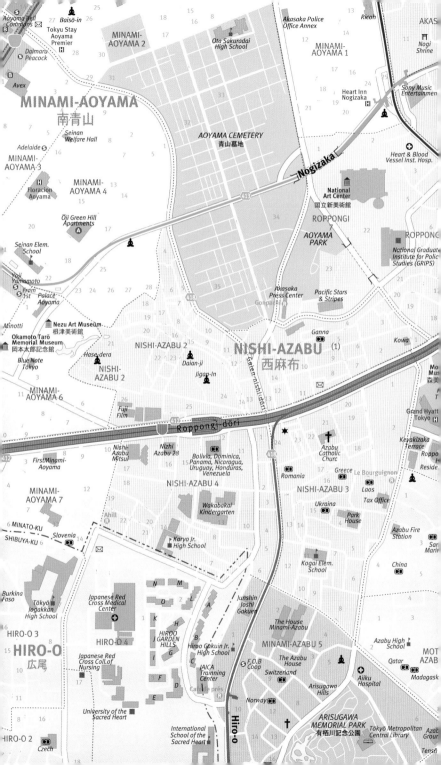

Map 5 Roppongi & Azabu

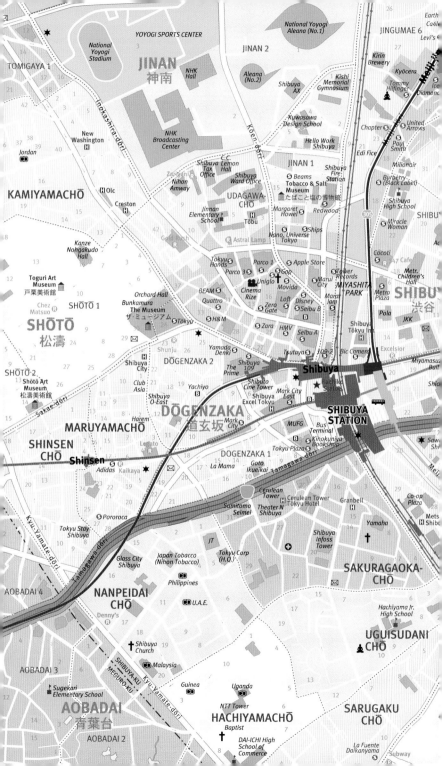

Map 7 **Meiji Shrine, Harajuku & Omotesando**

Shinanomachi

Tōkyō nasium

Kokuritsu-Kyogijo

Jingu Swimming Pool

Marshall

Prince Chichibu Memorial Sport Museum
秩父宮記念スポーツ博物館

National Athletic Field

Meiji Memorial Picture Museum
聖徳記念絵画館

Komeitō

MINATO-KU

Komei Hall

Meiji Kinenkan

Tōgu Gosho

KASUMIGAOKAMACHI

MOTO-AKASAKA

MEIJI PARK

Nippon Seinenkan Hall

Meiji Jingu Stadium 2 (Golf, Baseball ground)

MEIJI JINGU OUTER GARDEN

AKASAKA IMPERIAL PALACE

Metr. Kasumigaoka

Gaien House

SHINJUKU-KU

Kokugakuin High School

Meiji Jingu Stadium (Baseball ground)

SHINJUKU-KU

MINATO-KU

Met. Kita Aoyama Itchōme Apts

Aoyama Jr. High School

Aoyama-itchōme

Aoyama High School

TEPIA

KITA-AOYAMA 1

Metr. Kita-Aoyama

Aoyama

Aoyama-itchōme

SHIBUYA-KU

MINATO-KU

Kōtoku-in

Sompo Japan

Prince Chichibu Memorial Rugby Stadium

KITA-AOYAMA 2

Royal Garden Cafe

Idemitsu

Aoyama Twin Towers

Honda Motor

Metropolita

Akasaka Library

harajuku ots

Aoyama Plaza

Chōan-ji

Brazil

Aoyama OM Square

Tokyo Joshi-Idai Aoyama Hospital

Itōchu

Galemmae

Dai-Ichi Hoki Publishing

Gyokusō-ji

Akasaka Police

en-ji

tari Museum of ontemporary Art
タリウム美術館

GUMAE 3

KITA-AOYAMA 3

Aoyama Tower Bldg

Aoyama Elem. School

Akasaka Police Office Annex

MINAMI-AOYAMA 1

CSK Aoyama

Baisō-in

Aoyama Bell Commons

Tokyu Stay Aoyama Premier

MINAMI-AOYAMA 2

Ota Sakuradai High School

Tōkyu Store

Daimaru Peacock

MINAMI-AOYAMA

He No

Metr. Aoyama-Kitamachi Apts

Aoyama Intl Education of Japan

Avex

KITA-AOYAMA

北青山

MINAMI-AOYAMA
南青山

Zenkō-ji

Adelaide

Seinan Welfare Hall

AOYAMA CEMETERY
青山墓地

Nogizaka

Furula

MINAMI-AOYAMA 3

National Art Cente

OMOTESANDO
表参道

Floracion Aoyama

MINAMI-AOYAMA 4

Oji Green Hill Apartments

国立新美術

Aoyama-dori

Omotesando

ndersen

Issey Miyake

D&G

ROPPONG

Shimada Yōshō

Aveda

Prada

Sejinan Elem. School

AOYAMA PARK

Minami Aoyama Kaikan

Yokoi Moku

Yoji Yamamoto

From 1st

Palace Aoyama

Akasaka Press Center

Pacific Stars & Stripes

Ohara Kaikan

Gonpai

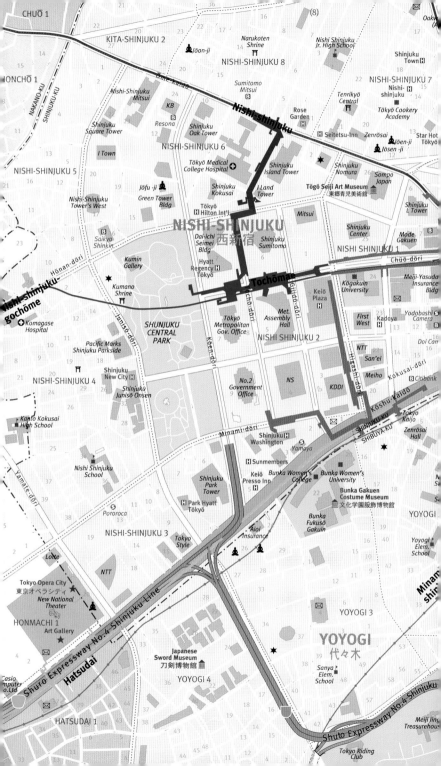

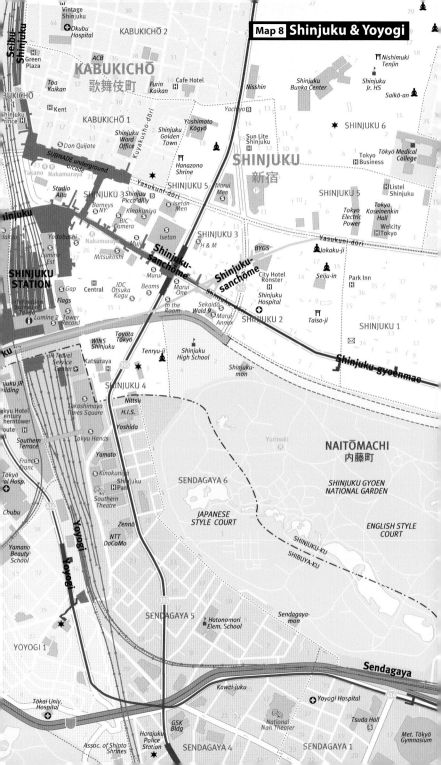

Map 8 **Shinjuku & Yoyogi**

Vintage Shinjuku
Okubo Hospital
KABUKICHŌ 2
Green Plaza
ACB
BUKICHŌ
KABUKICHŌ
歌舞伎町
Toa Kaikan
Furin Kaikan
Cafe Hotel
Nishimuki Tenjin
Shinjuku Bunka Center
Shinjuku Jr. HS
Saikō-an
hinjuku rince 1
Kent
KABUKICHŌ 1
Nisshin
Shinjuku Ward Office
Yachiyo
Shinjuku Golden Town
Yoshimoto Kōgyō
Sun Lite Shinjuku
SHINJUKU 6
Don Quijote
SUBNADE underground arcade
Tokyo Business
Tōkyō Medical College
Takano
Nakamuraya
Hanazono Shrine
SHINJUKU
新宿
SHINJUKU 5
Tokyo Electric Power
Listel Shinjuku
Studio Alta
SHINJUKU 3
Shinjuu Picca'dilly
Yasukuni-dōri
SHINJUKU 5
Marui Men
Tokyo Koseinenkin Hall
Welcity Tokyo
Barneys NY
Kinokuniya
Isetan Men
Yodobashi
BIC Camera
Lumine Est
Nakamuraya
Muji
Isetan
SHINJUKU 3
H & M
Yasukuni-dōri
Jokaku-ji
SHINJUKU
STATION
Mitsukoshi
BYGS
Seiju-in
Park Inn
Gap
Central
IDC Otsuka Kagu
Beams
Marui
Shinjuku-sanchōme
City Hotel Ronster
Shinjuku Hospital
Flags
Marui One
SHINJUKU 2
Tower Record
In the Room
Sekaidō Wald 9
Marui Annex
SHINJUKU 1
Lumine 2
WINS Shinjuku
Toyota Tokyo
Tenryu-ji
Taiso-ji
JR Travel Service Center
Katsuraya
Shinjuku High School
Shinjuku-mon
Shinjuku-gyoenmae
njuku JR ilding
SHINJUKU 4
Nittsu
Shinjuku-ku
kyu Hotel entury herntower oute
Takashimaya Times Square
H.I.S.
Yoshida
Yurinoki
NAITŌMACHI
内藤町
Southern Terrace
Tokyu Hands
Yamato
Franc Franc
Tōkyō al Hosp.
Kinokuniya
Shinjuku Park
SENDAGAYA 6
SHINJUKU GYOEN
NATIONAL GARDEN
Chubu
Southern Theatre
JAPANESE STYLE COURT
ENGLISH STYLE COURT
Yamano Beauty School
Zennō
NTT DoCoMo
SHINJUKU-KU
SHIBUYA-KU
YOYOGI 1
Yoyogi
SENDAGAYA 5
Hatonomori Elem. School
Sendagaya-mon
Sendagaya
Tōkai Univ. Hospital
Kawci-juku
Yoyogi Hospital
GSK Bldg
National Noh Theater
Tsuda Hall
Assoc. of Shinto Shrines
Harajuku Police Station
SENDAGAYA 4
SENDAGAYA 1
Met. Tōkyō Gymnasium

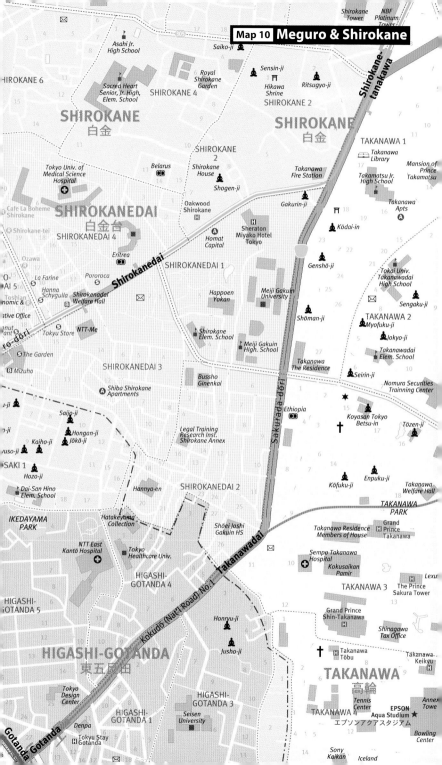

Map 10 Meguro & Shirokane

Shirokane Tower

NBF Platinum Tower

Saiko-ji

Asahi Jr. High School

Royal Shirokane Garden

Sensin-ji

Hikawa Shrine

Ritsugyo-ji

SHIROKANE 4

SHIROKANE 2

SHIROKANE
白金

SHIROKANE
白金

TAKANAWA 1

Sacred Heart Senior, Jr. High, Elem. School

SHIROKANE 6

Takanawa Library

Mansion of Prince Takamatsu

Takamatsu Jr. High School

SHIROKANE 2

Tokyo Univ. of Medical Science Hospital

Belarus

Shirokane House

Takanawa Fire Station

Takanawa Apts

Shogen-ji

SHIROKANEDAI
白金台

Cafe La Boheme Shirokane

Gakurin-ji

Shirokane-tei

Oakwood Shirokane

SHIROKANEDAI 4

Kōdai-in

Ozawa

Eritrea

Homat Capital

Sheraton Miyako Hotel Tokyo

Genshō-ji

La Farine

Pororoca

SHIROKANEDAI 1

Tokai Univ. Takanawadai High School

Hanna Schygulla

Shirokanedai Welfare Hall

Happoen Yokan

Meiji Gakuin University

Shōman-ji

Sengaku-ji

Toshiban nomic &

Tokyu Store

NTT-Me

TAKANAWA 2

Myofuku-ji

ative Office

Shōman-ji

Jokyo-ji

The Garden

Shirokane Elem. School

Meiji Gakuin High. School

Takanawadai Elem. School

Mizuho

SHIROKANEDAI 3

Takanawa The Residence

Seirin-ji

Shiba Shirokane Apartments

Bussho Ginenkai

Nomura Securities Training Center

-ji

Saijo-ji

Ethiopia

Koyasan Tokyo Betsu-in

Tōzen-ji

-ji

Hongan-ji

Jōkō-ji

Legal Training Research Insf. Shirokane Annex

Kaiho-ji

yuso-ji

SAKI 1

Hozo-ji

Hannya-en

SHIROKANEDAI 2

Kōfuku-ji

Enpuku-ji

Takanawa Welfare Hall

Dai-San Hino Elem. School

IKEDAYAMA PARK

Shoei Joshi Gakuin HS

TAKANAWA PARK

Hatakeyama Collection

NTT East Kantō Hospital

Tokyo Healthcare Univ.

Takanawa Residence Members of House

Grand Prince Takanawa

HIGASHI- GOTANDA 4

Sempo Takanawa Hospital

Kokusaikan Pamir

TAKANAWA 3

The Prince Sakura Tower

Lexu

HIGASHI- GOTANDA 5

Grand Prince Shin-Takanawa

Shinagawa Tax Office

Hanryu-ji

Takanawa Tōbu

Takanawa- Keikyu

Jusho-ji

Takanawa Annex Towe

HIGASHI-GOTANDA
東五反田

TAKANAWA
高輪

Tokyo Design Center

HIGASHI- GOTANDA 3

Tennis Center

TAKANAWA 4

EPSON Aqua Studium
エプソンアクアスタジアム

Denpa

Seisen University

Sony Kaikan

Iceland

Bowling Center

Tokyu Stay Gotanda

Gotanda Gotanda

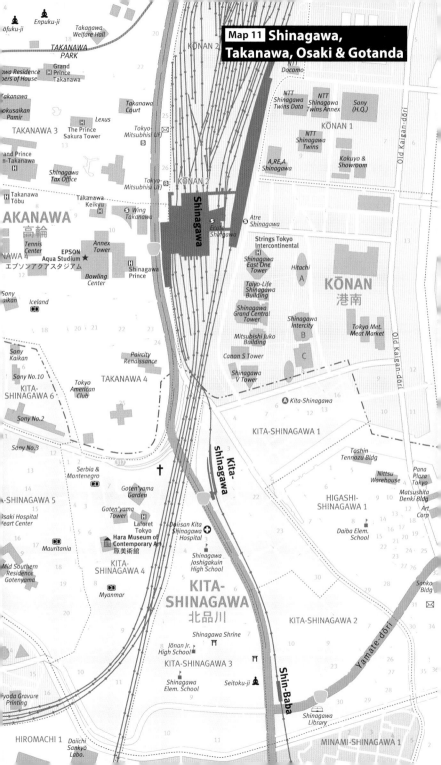

Map 11 Shinagawa, Takanawa, Osaki & Gotanda

ōfuku-ji
Enpuku-ji
Takanawa Welfare Hall

TAKANAWA PARK

KŌNAN 2

NTT Docomo

wa Residence
ers of House
Grand Prince Takanawa

NTT Shinagawa Twins Data
NTT Shinagawa Twins Annex
Sony (H.Q.)

Takanawa
okusaikan Pamir
Lexus
The Prince Sakura Tower

KŌNAN 1

TAKANAWA 3

Takanawa Court

Tokyo-Mitsubishi UFJ

NTT Shinagawa Twins

and Prince n-Takanawa

Shinagawa Tax Office

Tokyo-Mitsubishi UFJ

KŌNAN 2

A,RE,A Shinagawa

Kokuyo & Showroom

Takanawa Tōbu
Takanawa-Keikyu

Takanawa-Keikyu

Wing Takanawa

Shinagawa

Atre Shinagawa

Ecute Shinagawa

AKANAWA
高輪

Tennis Center

Annex Tower

EPSON
Aqua Studium ★
エプソンアクアスタジアム

Bowling Center

Shinagawa Prince

Strings Tokyo Intercontinental

Shinagawa East One Tower

Hitachi
A

KŌNAN
港南

NAWA 4

Sony
aikan
Iceland

Taiyo-Life Shinagawa Building

Shinagawa Grand Central Tower

Shinagawa Intercity
B

Tokyo Met. Meat Market

Sony Kaikan

Paircity Renaissance

Mitsubishi Juko Building

Sony No.10

KITA-SHINAGAWA 6

TAKANAWA 4

Tokyo American Club

Canon S Tower

C

Sony No.2

Shinagawa V Tower

Kita-Shinagawa

KITA-SHINAGAWA 1

Sony No.3

Serbia & Montenegro

Goten'yama Garden

Kita-shinagawa

Toshin Tennozu Bldg

Pana Plaza Tokyo

-SHINAGAWA 5

Goten'yama Tower

Nittsu Warehouse

Matsushita Denki Bldg

Osaki Hospital
eart Center

Laforet Tokyo

Doiisan Kita Shinagawa Hospital

HIGASHI-SHINAGAWA 1

Art Corp

Mauritania

Hara Museum of Contemporary Art
原美術館

Shinagawa Joshigakuin High School

Daiba Elem. School

Mid Southern Residence Gotenyama

KITA-SHINAGAWA 4

Myanmar

KITA-SHINAGAWA
北品川

Sanko Bldg

Shinagawa Shrine

KITA-SHINAGAWA 2

Yamate-dōri

Jōnan Jr. High School

KITA-SHINAGAWA 3

Shinagawa Elem. School

Seitoku-ji

Shin-Baba

Shinagawa Library

tyoda Gravure Printing

HIROMACHI 1

Daiichi Sankyo Labo.

MINAMI-SHINAGAWA 1

Old Kaigan-dōri

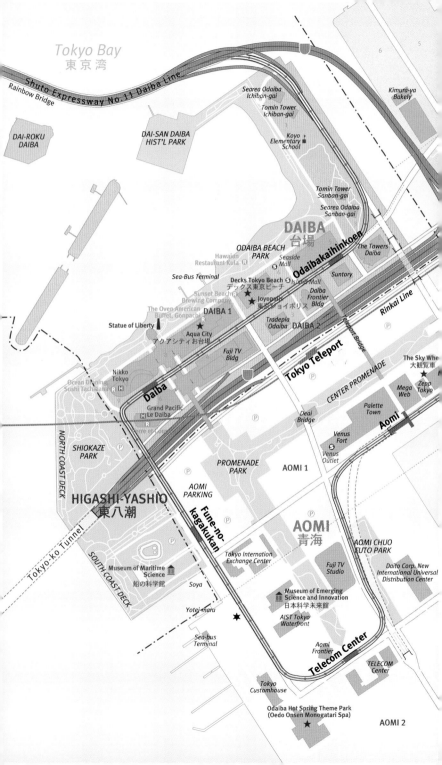

Map 12 **Odaiba & Ariake**

AKE 1

★ Ariake
Coliseum
有明コロシアム

ARIAKE 2

Shuto Expressway Wangan Line

Ariake

Kokusai-tenjijo

★ Ariake Tennis-no-mori Park
有明テニスの森公園

Cancer Institute
Hospital ✚   6

Panasonic
Center   2

TOC Ariake

Ariake
Park
Bldg

ᾶ Risupia

Tokyo Bay Ariake
Washington Ⓗ

2

ARIAKE
有明

ⓗ Sunroute
Ariake

Wanza Ariake ★

Ariake
Frontier

East Exhibition
Hall   13

Tokyo
Fashion
Town

IDC Otsuka-
kagu

Ⓡ Subway
McDonald's
Front

★
Tokyo International
Exhibition Hall
(Tokyo Big Sight)
東京国際展示場
（東京ビックサイト）

ᾶ Water Science
Museum
の科学館

Kokusai-tenjijo seimon

Conference
Tower

Nippon Steel

Partire
Tokyo Bay Wedding
Village

Sea-bus
Terminal

West Exhibition
Hall

o-ohashi
Tokyo
Bayside
Bridge)

Trusty
Tokyo
Bayside Ⓗ

15

shinkotsu Line

**Yurikamome
Train Base**

ARIAKE 3

Tokyo Waterfront
New Transit
Yurikamome
HQ

1

3

Nippon
Paper

16

17

Daio Paper's
Warehouse

22

Mitsubishi
Soko

Sumitomo Steel

**FERRY FUTO
PARK**

8

10

14

ARIAKE 4

11

15

18

Tokyo Ferry
Terminal

20

16

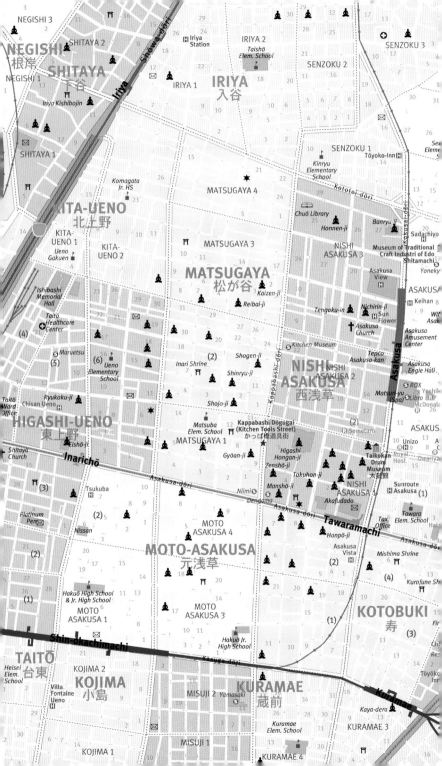

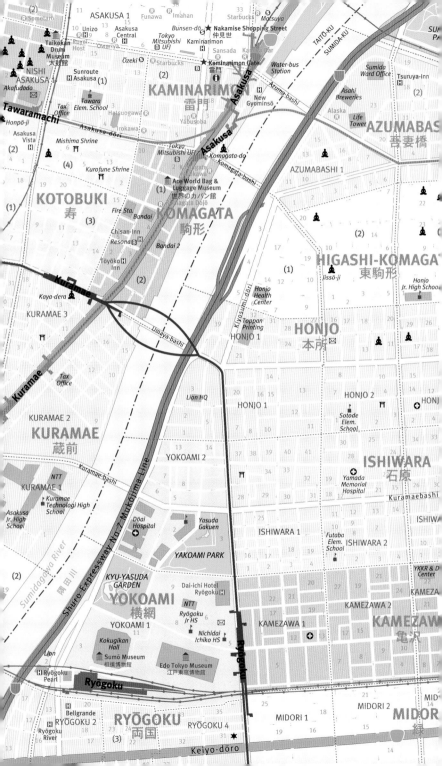

Map 14 Ryogoku & Kinshicho

OSHIAGE 2

OSHIAGE 1

Oshiage

OSHIAGE
押上

(3)

KŌJIMA 1

Kototoi-dōri

MUKŌJIMA
向島

Narihirabashi

Tokyo Sky Tree
東京スカイツリー ★

Postal
Museum
Japan

Kenseidō
Hospital

Oshiagekimae
Post Office

ZUMABASHI 3

Asakusa-dōri

Jo-
mabashi

Tax
Office

NARIHIRA 1

Yokokawa
Elem. School

(4)

NARIHIRA 2

NIRIHIRA
業平

NARIHIRA 3

NARIHIRA 4

Toba Store

NARIHIRA 5

Narihira
Elementary
School

Japan
Tobacco

YOKOKAWA 1

YOKOKAWA 5

Kasuga-dōri

YOKOKAWA
横川

YOKOKAWA 4

HONJO 4

YOKOKAWA 2

YOKOKAWA 3

Honjo
Fire Station

Yanagishima
Elementary
School

Honjo
Post Office

NTT

Kinshi Jr.
High School

TAIHEI 4

OLINAS MALL

Toho Cinemas

Olinas
Tower

Tower Records
Disney Store

OLINAS CORE

Brilla
Tower
Tokyo

Babiesrus
Simachu
Comme
Ça Store

TAIHEI
太平

TAIHEI 1

TAIHEI 2

TAIHEI 3

ISHIWARA 4

(3)

KINSHI PARK

Sumida
Ward Gym

(4)

KAMEZAWA 4

KINSHI 1

Kinshi
Elementary
School

KINSHI
錦糸

KINSHI 2

Ewatari

Kinshicho

Lotte
City

Charlotte
Chocolate Factory

Tatekawa
Jr. HS

Sumida
Triphony
Hall

Arca
West

ARCA TOWERS

Arca
Central

Tōbu Hotel
Levant Tokyo

Arca Kit

Arca
East

Kinshicho

Hello
Work
Sumida

Termina

Livin

to Kōtō-ku

Kinsia

Rakutenchi

(1)

(2)

KŌTOBASHI
江東橋

(4)

o-dōro

MIDORI 4

Ryogoku
High School

Kinshicho
Marui

(3)

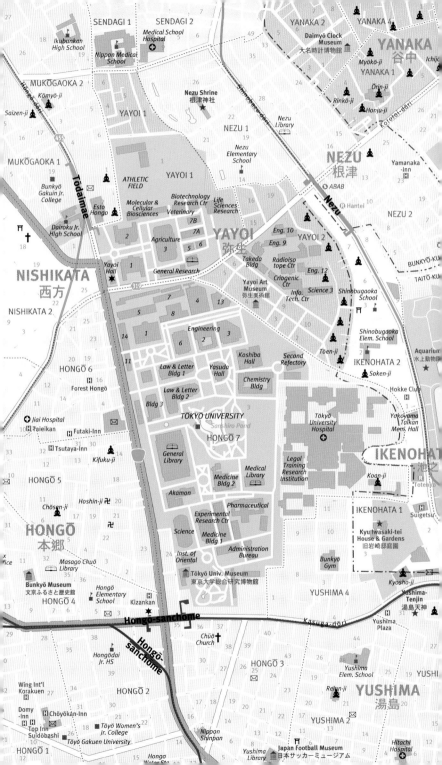

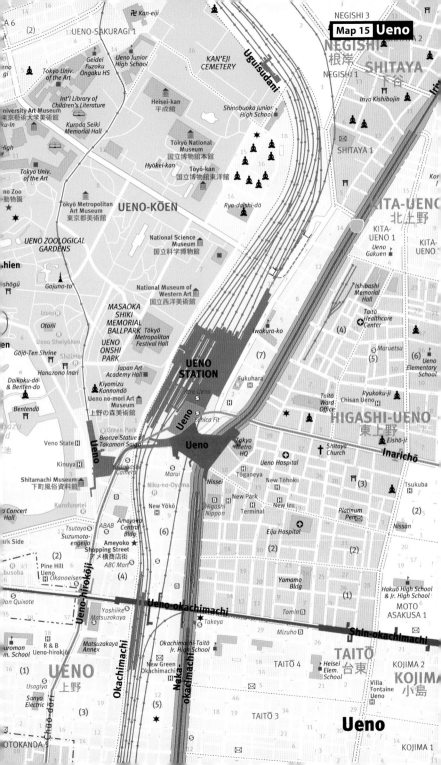

Map 15 Ueno

NEGISHI 3

NEGISHI
根岸

SHITAYA
下谷

NEGISHI 1

Iriya Kishibojin

Kan-eiji

UENO-SAKURAGI 1

Tōkyō Univ.
of the Art

Geidei
Fuzoku
Ongaku HS

Ueno Junior
High School

KAN'EJI
CEMETERY

Uguisudani

Int'l Library of
Children's Literature

Heisei-kan
平成館

Shinobuoka Junior
High School

SHITAYA 1

University Art Museum
東京藝術大学美術館

Kuroda Seiki
Memorial Hall

Tōkyō National
Museum
国立博物館本館

Hyōkei-kan

Tōyō-kan
国立博物館東洋館

KITA-UENO
北上野

KITA-
UENO 1

KITA-
UENO

Tokyo Univ.
of the Art

Tōkyō Metropolitan
Art Museum
東京都美術館

UENO-KŌEN

Ryo-daishi-dō

Ueno
Gakuen

Ueno Zoo
動物園

UENO ZOOLOGICAL
GARDENS

National Science
Museum
国立科学博物館

Ishibashi
Memorial
Hall

shōgū

Gojuno-to

National Museum of
Western Art
国立西洋美術館

Taitō
Healthcare
Center

Izuei

Otori

MASAOKA
SHIKI
MEMORIAL
BALLPARK

Iwakura-ko

(4)

Maruetsu

(5)

(6) Ueno
Elementary
School

Gojō-Ten Shrine

Shūntei

Hanazono Inari

UENO
ONSHI
PARK

Tōkyō
Metropolitan
Festival Hall

(7)

Daikoku-do
& Benten-do

Kiyomizu
Kannondō

Japan Art
Academy Hall

UENO
STATION

Fukuhara

Taitō
Ward
Office

Ryukoku-ji

Chisan Ueno

Bentendō

Ueno no-mori Art
Museum
上野の森美術館

Ueno

HIGASHI-UENO
東上野

pazu

Green Park

Eishō-ji

Veno State

Bronze Statue of
Takamori Saigō

Ueno

Ueno

Echica Fit

Tokyo
Metro
HQ

Shitaya
Church

Inarichō

Kinuya

Todobashi
Camera

Ueno Hospital

Shitamachi Museum
下町風俗資料館

Kurofunetei

Niku-no-Oyama

Marui

Nissei

Tōganeya

New Tōhoku

(3)

Tsukuba

Concert
Hall

Tsutaya

Suzumoto-
engeijo

New Yōkō

Higashi
Nippon

New Park
Terminal

New Izu

Platinum
Pen

Nissan

(2)

ark Side

ABAB

Ameyoko
Central
Bldg

(6)

Eiju Hospital

(2)

(2)

Ameyoko ★
Shopping Street
アメ横商店街

Pine Hill
Ueno

(2)

Okanoeisen

ABC Mart

(4)

Yamamo
Bldg

(1)

Hakuō High School
& Jr. High School

Don Quixote

Ueno-hirokōji

Ueno-okachimachi

Tomin

MOTO
ASAKUSA 1

Shin-okachimachi

Yoshiike
Matsuzakaya

Takeya

Mizuho

TAITŌ
台東

KOJIMA 2

uromon
m. School

R & B
Ueno-hirokōji

Matsuzakaya
Annex

Okachimachi

Naka-okachimachi

Okachimachi-Taitō
Jr. High School

Heisei
Elem.
School

KOJIMA
小島

(1)

UENO
上野

New Green
Okachimachi

TAITŌ 4

Villa
Fontaine
Ueno

Usagiya

Chuo-dori

(5)

Sanya
Electric

(3)

TAITŌ 3

Ueno

OTOKANDA

KOJIMA 1

Map 16 Akihabara, Kanda & Jimbocho

NGŌ 3

Kuromon Elem. School
Ueno-hirokoji
Matsuzakaya Annex
R & B
Okachimachi-Taitō Jr High School
Okachimachi

Yushima Elem. School
YUSHIMA 3
(1)
UE
上野
Okachimachi
Okachimachi-Taitō Jr High School

Reiun-ji
YUSHIMA
湯島
Usagiya
Sanya Electric
(3)
(5)

Japan Football Museum
日本サッカーミュージアム
Hitachi Hospital
SOTOKANDA 5

Ochanomizu St.
Hills
Tsumagoi Shrine
Tōkyō Garden Palace
Kanda Myōjin
神田明神
Moesham
Prama Rifle
Suehirochō
Dormy Inn
Kinki Nippon Tourist
TAITŌ-KU
CHIYODA-KU

Tōkyō Medical & Dental Univ.
Ochanomizu Inn
Kanda †
Cospatio G. Store
Don Quijote
Akiba
SOTOKANDA 4
Times Tower
KANDA IZUMICHŌ

YUSHIMA 1
Shohei Elem. School
SOTOKANDA 3
Kanda-ji
Comic Toranoana
Starbucks
AKIHABARA
秋葉原

anomizu
Yushima Seidō
Sofmap (Mac)
T Zone
Tokyo Anime Center
Akihabara UDX
Tower Records
Yurindo

Ochanomizu
SOTO-KANDA
外神田
Nippon Express
Sofmap
Yodobashi Camera

Maruzen
Ishimaru Audio
Yamagiwa
Flash Café Nagomi
Home Café
Akihabara DAI Bldg

dō
Ochanomizu Central
Ishimaru Denki
Sato Musen
(1)
Akihabara

hon Univ.
Hospital
Ochanomizu Juraku
Tsukumo Robot Kingdom
Laox
Akiba Gamers
Akihabara
Remm
KANDA

Nikorai-dō
Holly Resurrection Cathedral
Asobit City
Radio Kaikan
Yamada Labi
KANDA SAKUMACHŌ 1
(2)

Nihon Univ. (Sci & Engn)
Mitsui Sumitomo Annex
Volks Akiba, Kaiyō Dō
Remm

KANDA-AWAJICHŌ
My Stays Ochanomizu
Mansei

tsui Sumitomo Insurance
Tōkyō Green Hotel Awajichō
mAAch Ecute Kanda Manseibashi
KANDA SUDACHŌ
神田須田町
KANDA SUDACHŌ 2

Ryumeikan
The Be
KANDA SUDACHO 1

KANDA AWAMACHI
神田小川町
(1)
Ogawamachi
Awajichō
Iwamotochō
IWAMOTOCHŌ 3

uni-dori
(2)
KANDA-TACHŌ
New Central
KANDA KAJICHŌ 3
KANDA TOMIYAMACHŌ
IWAMOTOCHŌ 2

kyo Denki iversity
KANDA-TSUKASAMACHI
Tōkyō YMCA
Chiyoda Elem. School
Grand Central
Central
Olympic-Inn
KANDA KON'YACHŌ
KANDA HIGASHI KON'YACHŌ
IWAMOTO CHŌ

Kanda Mitoshirochō
KANDA KAJICHŌ
KANDA KAJICHŌ
神田鍛冶町
K. KITA-NORIMONOCHŌ
IWAMOTO CHŌ 1

KANDA-SHIKICHŌ 1
Niagai
UCHI-KANDA
内神田
Kanda Inst. of Foreign Language
Unizo Kanda
(3)
KANDA KAJICHŌ 1
KANDA KON'YACHŌ
K. NISHI-FUKUDACHŌ

UCHI-KANDA 1
Villa Fontaine Otemachi
UCHI-KANDA 2
KANDA KAJICHŌ 2
CHIYODA-KU
CHUŌ-KU
K. MIKURACHŌ
NIHONBASHI-HONCHŌ

CO-OP Bldg
Chiyoda Ward Gym
Kanda Station
Kazusaya
Shin-nihonbashi
Takarada Ebisu Shrine

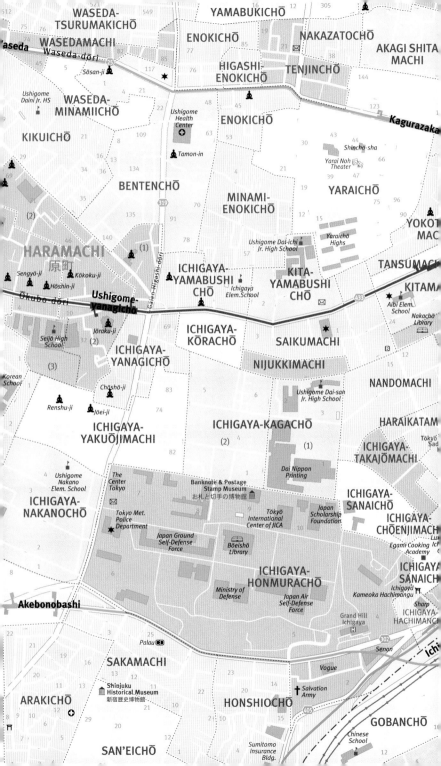

Map 17 Iidabashi, Kagurazaka & Ichigaya

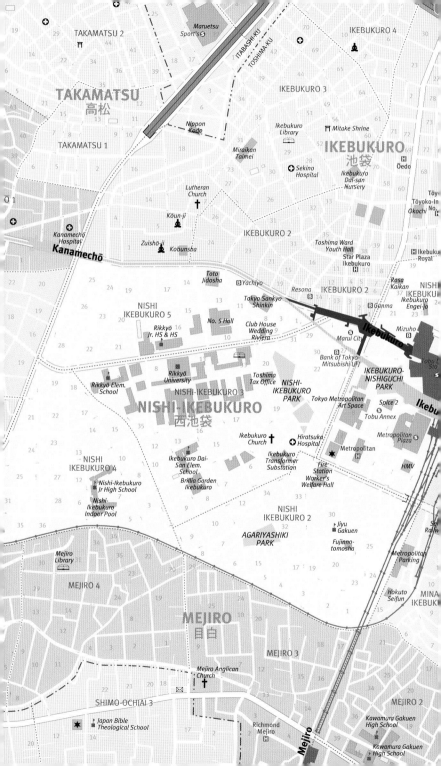

Map 18 **Ikebukuro**

0   250m

N

IKEBUKURO-HONCHŌ 1

Kawagoe Kaidō

KAMI-IKEBUKURO 3

KAMI-IKEBUKURO 2

KAMI-IKEBUKURO
上池袋

KAMI-IKEBUKURO 1

NISHI-SUGA

Kami-Ikebukuro Library

Toshima Central Hospital

Koyasu Inari Shrine

Sugamo Gakuen High School

Jpns. Foundation for Cancer Research Hospital

Peacock

IKEBUKURO 1

Nagashio Hospital

Toshima Garbage Incineration Plant

Kenko Plaza Toshima

Meiji Dōri

Hosei Elem. School

KITA-ŌTSUKA 3

Suitengu

Yachiyo

Meiji Yasuda Seimei

Teikyō Heisei University

HIGASHI IKEBUKURO 2

D-Box

The B

Meiji Dōri

Toshima City Office

Tokyo Electric Power Co.

City Tower Ikebukuro

Daiichi Inn

TG

Toshima Public Hall

Tokyo Electronics College

NTT ME

Tokyo Nissan

Sumitomo Trust

HIGASHI IKEBUKURO 1

Toshima Civic Center

Ark Tokyo

Daihatsu Tokyo

Bic Camera

Grand City

Ikebukuro Hospital

HIGASHI IKEBUKURO 3

Café Address

Yamada Denki

Urbannet Ikebukuro

HIGASHI-IKEBUKURO
東池袋

Mizuho

Tokyo Star

Otome Road
乙女ロード

Theatre Ikebukuro Cinema Sunshine

Toyota Amlux

Animate

Prince Hotel Sunshine City

Toshima Driver Training School

HIGASHI IKEBUKURO 4

Humax Pavilion

Tokyu Hands

Sunshine 60
サンシャイン60

World Import Mart

Hōyu Elem. School

Camera

JTB

Plantarium "Manten"
プラネタリウム「満天」

Sunshine Int'l Aquarium
サンシャイン国際水族館

Kinkadō

Times Spa Resta

ナンジャタウン

Namco Nanja Town

Ancient Orient Museum
古代オリエント博物館

Resona

Aozora

Ippia

Sunshine Theatre

Shoko Chukin

Toshimagaoka-joshi Gakuen

Kampo Health Plaza Tokyo

Seiyu

MINAMI-IKEBUKURO PARK

Minami-ikebukuro

Presso Inn Ikebukuro

Tokyo Mitsubishi UFJ

Mint Bureau Tokyo Branch

HIGASHI IKEBUKURO 5

Myoten-ji

Hōnryu-ji

MINAMI-IKEBUKURO 2

Air Rise Tower

Josai-ji

Sengyō-ji

Seita-ji

JTB Traveland

Higashi-ikebukuro

ŌTSUKA 6

MINAMI-IKEBUKURO
南池袋

Honkyo-ji

Kanju-in

Hōmyō-ji

Minami Ikebukuro Elem. School

Toden Zōshigaya

MINAMI-IKEBUKURO 3

Tokyo Music College

Zōshigaya Kishinojin

Honnō-ji

ZŌSHIGAYA 3

ZŌSHIGAYA CEMETERY

MINAMI-IKEBUKURO 4

TOSHIMAGA CEMETE

ZŌSHIGAYA 1

Green Ōdōri

Part 4: TOKYO'S JR RAILWAY LINES

Central Tokyo's JR Railway Lines

Tokyo is served by nine commuter railway lines and 13 subway lines that are integrated into one of the most comprehensive and efficient train-subway networks in the world. The railway lines include a number that are owned and operated by the huge JR Railway Group, along with several lines that are owned and operated by Metro Tokyo and smaller private companies

JR Railways is the major railway company in Japan, and accounts for approximately 70% of the country's network of trains. The JR Yamanote Line that encircles central Tokyo is a key in the city's transportation system. It links 29 stations that encircle central Tokyo in a 35 km loop, passing through such key stations as Tokyo Station, Ueno Station, Ikebukuro Station, Shinjuku Station, Shibuya Station, and Shinagawa Station and Yurakucho Station. All of these stations are hub stations for both train and subway lines. Commuters can therefore transfer to other train and subway lines along the loop, making it the primary link in Tokyo's transportation system. Morning trains come every 2.5 minutes and it takes about an hour to complete one loop. Morning and evening trains, especially on the Yamanote Line, can be so crowded that extra JR platform attendants are on hand to push the last passengers in so the doors will close. It is therefore best to avoid the morning [7 am–9 am] and evening [5 pm–7 pm] rush hours if possible.

All train and subway lines are color-coded according to the routes they cover, and station names and numbers are clearly posted in both Japanese and English, to help travelers choose the correct route to reach their desired destination. Be sure to familiarize yourself with where the sign posts are on the station platforms. Most are on the platform level but there are also some that are attached to the overhead ceiling.

In the larger hub stations there are signs on both the walls and ceilings of the corridors connecting the intersecting lines…and some of these corridors can be up to three or more blocks long. There can also be as many as three underground levels separating the intersecting lines so it is necessary to go up and down stairs and/or escalators.

Visitors going to Tokyo Station to board a Shinkansen "Bullet Train" should keep in mind that the Shinkansen boarding platforms are on the Yaesu Guchi [Yie-suu Guu-chee] east side of the large station. On the second basement level on the Marunouchi [west] side of the station there is a passageway that goes to the Yaesu east side. If you already have your ticket you can show it to an attendant on the ground level of the Marunouchi side and walk through the station to the Bullet Train entry wickets rather than use the basement-level passageway. [Signs noting the passageway hang down from the ceiling.]

On the second basement level on the Yaesu side of the station there is a quarter-of-a-mile long wide passageway that goes all the way to the Ginza-Kyobashi district, and is lined on both sides with shops and restaurants, including a McDonald's. The passageway is a great convenience when it is cold or raining.

Nine Major JR Lines in Central Tokyo

- ⦿ Yamanote Line
- ⦿ Keihin Tohoku Line (Omiya — Ofuna)
- ⦿ Ueno-Tokyo Line (Tokyo — Narita/Maebashi/Mito/Utsunomiya/Atami)
- ⦿ Chuo Line (Tokyo — Hachioji/Otsuki)
- ⦿ Sobu Line (Chiba — Mitaka)
- ⦿ Shonan-Shinjuku Line (Maebashi — Zushi)
- ⦿ Saikyo Line (Kawagoe — Osaki)
- ⦿ Keiyo Line (Tokyo — Soga)
- ⦿ Tokaido Line (Tokyo — Atami, see p. 147)
- ⦿ Yokosuka-Sobu Rapid Line (Narita Airport — Kurihama, see pp. 156, 181)

JR Yamanote Line 山手線

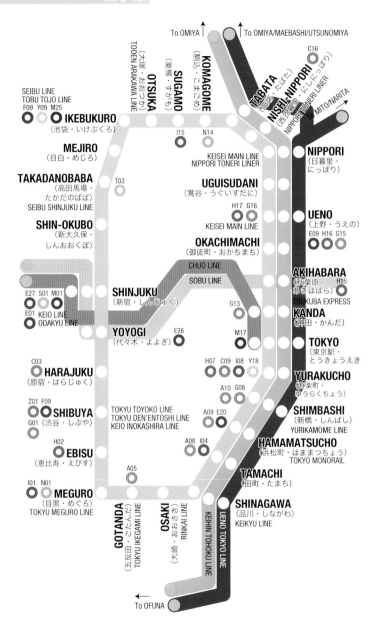

To OMIYA

To OMIYA/MAEBASHI/UTSUNOMIYA

C16

TABATA
（田端・たばた）

NISHI-NIPPORI
（西日暮里・にしにっぽり）

NIPPORI TONERI LINER

NISHI-NIPPORI

NIPPORI TONERI LINER

To MITO/NARITA

KOMAGOME
（駒込・こまごめ）

SUGAMO
（巣鴨・すがも）

OTSUKA
（大塚・おおつか）
TODEN ARAKAWA LINE

SEIBU LINE
TOBU TOJO LINE
F09 Y09 M25

IKEBUKURO
（池袋・いけぶくろ）

I15   N14

MEJIRO
（目白・めじろ）

KEISEI MAIN LINE
NIPPORI TONERI LINER

NIPPORI
（日暮里・
にっぽり）

TAKADANOBABA
（高田馬場・
たかだのばば）
SEIBU SHINJUKU LINE

T03

UGUISUDANI
（鶯谷・うぐいすだに）

H17 G16

UENO
（上野・うえの）
E09 H16 G15

SHIN-OKUBO
（新大久保・
しんおおくぼ）

KEISEI MAIN LINE

OKACHIMACHI
（御徒町・おかちまち）

CHUO LINE

SOBU LINE

AKIHABARA
（秋葉原・   H15
あきはばら）
TSUKUBA EXPRESS

E27 S01 M01

E01 KEIO LINE
ODAKYU LINE

SHINJUKU
（新宿・しんじゅく）

G13

KANDA
（神田・かんだ）

YOYOGI
（代々木・よよぎ）

E26

M17

TOKYO
（東京駅・
とうきょうえき

C03

HARAJUKU
（原宿・はらじゅく）

H07 C09 I08 Y18

YURAKUCHO
（有楽町・
ゆうらくちょう）

Z01 F09

SHIBUYA
G01 （渋谷・しぶや）

A10 G08

TOKYU TOYOKO LINE
TOKYU DEN'ENTOSHI LINE
KEIO INOKASHIRA LINE

A09 E20

SHIMBASHI
（新橋・しんばし）
YURIKAMOME LINE

H02

EBISU
（恵比寿・えびす）

A08 I04

HAMAMATSUCHO
（浜松町・はままつちょう）
TOKYO MONORAIL

A05

TAMACHI
（田町・たまち）

I01 N01

MEGURO
（目黒・めぐろ）
TOKYU MEGURO LINE

GOTANDA
（五反田・ごたんだ）
TOKYU IKEGAMI LINE

OSAKI
（大崎・おおさき）
RINKAI LINE

KEIHIN TOHOKU LINE

UENO TOKYO LINE

SHINAGAWA
（品川・しながわ）
KEIKYU LINE

To OFUNA

JR Keihin-Tohoku Line 京浜東北線

JR Chuo Line 中央線

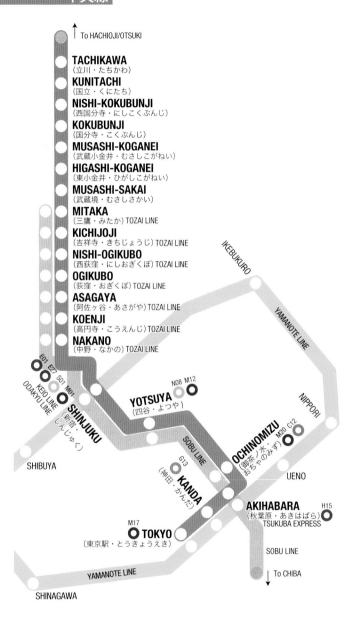

To HACHIOJI/OTSUKI

TACHIKAWA
（立川・たちかわ）

KUNITACHI
（国立・くにたち）

NISHI-KOKUBUNJI
（西国分寺・にしこくぶんじ）

KOKUBUNJI
（国分寺・こくぶんじ）

MUSASHI-KOGANEI
（武蔵小金井・むさしこがねい）

HIGASHI-KOGANEI
（東小金井・ひがしこがねい）

MUSASHI-SAKAI
（武蔵境・むさしさかい）

MITAKA
（三鷹・みたか）TOZAI LINE

KICHIJOJI
（吉祥寺・きちじょうじ）TOZAI LINE

NISHI-OGIKUBO
（西荻窪・にしおぎくぼ）TOZAI LINE

OGIKUBO
（荻窪・おぎくぼ）TOZAI LINE

ASAGAYA
（阿佐ヶ谷・あさがや）TOZAI LINE

KOENJI
（高円寺・こうえんじ）TOZAI LINE

NAKANO
（中野・なかの）TOZAI LINE

IKEBUKURO

YAMANOTE LINE

E01 E27 S01 M01
KEIO LINE
ODAKYU LINE

SHINJUKU
（新宿・しんじゅく）

N08 M12

YOTSUYA
（四谷・よつや）

NIPPORI

SHIBUYA

SOBU LINE

G13

M20 C12
OCHINOMIZU
（御茶ノ水・おちゃのみず）

UENO

KANDA
（神田・かんだ）

AKIHABARA
（秋葉原・あきはばら） H15
TSUKUBA EXPRESS

M17
TOKYO
（東京駅・とうきょうえき）

SOBU LINE

To CHIBA

YAMANOTE LINE

SHINAGAWA

JR Sobu Line 総武線

To HACHIOJI/
OTSUKI

MITAKA
(三鷹・みたか) TOZAI LINE

KICHIJOJI
(吉祥寺・きちじょうじ) TOZAI LINE

NISHI-OGIKUBO TOZAI LINE
(西荻窪・にしおぎくぼ)

OGIKUBO
(荻窪・おぎくぼ) TOZAI LINE

ASAGAYA
(阿佐ヶ谷・あさがや) TOZAI LINE

KOENJI
(高円寺・こうえんじ) TOZAI LINE

NAKANO(中野・なかの) TOZAI LINE

HIGASHI-NAKANO
(東中野・ひがしなかの)

OKUBO(大久保・おおくぼ)

IKEBUKURO

YAMANOTE LINE

To OMIYA

E26

YOYOGI (代々木・よよぎ)

SENDAGAYA (千駄ヶ谷・せんだがや)

E01 E27 S01 M01
KEIO LINE
ODAKYU LINE
SHINJUKU
(新宿・しんじゅく)

SHIBUYA

SHINANOMACHI (信濃町・しなのまち)

YOTSUYA
(四谷・よつや)
M12 N08

ICHIGAYA
(市ヶ谷・いちがや)
N09 Y14 S04

CHUO LINE

Y13 N10
T06
E06
IIDABASHI
(飯田橋・いいだばし)
I11
SUIDOBASHI
(水道橋・すいどうばし)
M20
C12
OCHINOMIZU
(御茶ノ水・おちゃのみず)

NIPPORI

UENO

H15
AKIHABARA
(秋葉原・あきはばら)
TSUKUBA EXPRESS

M17
TOKYO
(東京駅・とうきょうえき)

A16

E12
ASAKUSABASHI
(浅草橋・あさくさばし)

RYOGOKU
(両国・りょうごく)

Z13
KINSHICHO
(錦糸町・きんしちょう)

YAMANOTE LINE
KEIHIN-TOHOKU LINE
SHINAGAWA

To CHIBA

JR Shonan-Shinjuku Line 湘南新宿ライン線
JR Ueno-Tokyo Line 上野東京ライン線

To MAEBASHI

To KAWAGOE

To OMIYA/MAEBASHI/UTSUNOMIYA

AKABANE
(赤羽・あかばね)

UENO-TOKYO LINE

SEIBU LINE
TOBU TOJO LINE
F09 Y09 M25

IKEBUKURO
(池袋・いけぶくろ)

To MITO/
NARITA

NIPPORI

UENO

AKIHABARA

E01 E27 S01 M01
KEIO LINE
ODAKYU LINE

SHINJUKU
(新宿・しんじゅく)

TOKYU TOYOKO LINE
TOKYU DEN'ENTOSHI LINE
KEIO INOKASHIRA LINE

SHIBUYA
(渋谷・しぶや)

TOKYO

G01 Z01 F09

H02

EBISU
(恵比寿・えびす)

SAIKYO LINE

OSAKI
(大崎・おおさき)
RINKAI LINE

YAMANOTE LINE

KEIHIN-TOHOKU LINE

UENO-TOKYO LINE

TOKAIDO LINE

SHINAGAWA

KEIKYU LINE
TOKYU-TOYOKO LINE
MINATOMIRAI LINE
YOKOHAMA MUNICIPAL
SUBWAY LINE
SOTETSU LINE

To ZUSHI

YOKOHAMA
(横浜・よこはま)

SHIN-KAWASAKI
(新川崎・しんかわさき)

MUSASHI-KOSUGI
(武蔵小杉・むさしこすぎ)

To OFUNA

To ATAMI

JR Saikyo Line 埼京線

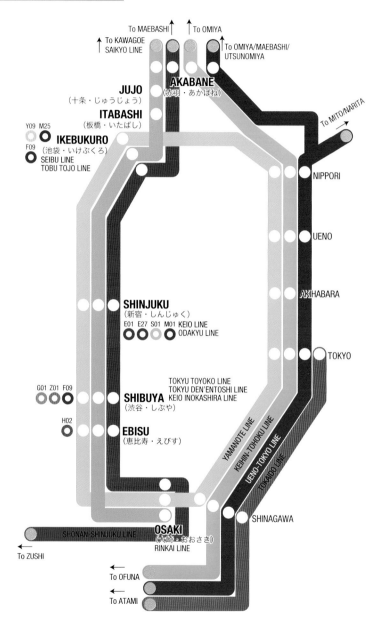

JR Keiyo Line 京葉線

UENO

AKIHABARA

M17
TOKYO
（東京駅・とうきょうえき）

YAMANOTE LINE

SHINAGAWA

HATCHOBORI
（八丁堀・はっちょうぼり）
H1

ETCHUJIMA
（越中島・えっちゅうじま）

SHIOMI
（潮見・しおみ）

Y24
SHIN-KIBA
（新木場・しんきば）
RINKAI LINE

KASAIRINKAIKOEN
（葛西臨海公園・
かさいりんかいこうえん）

MAIHAMA
（舞浜・まいはま）

SHIN-URAYASU
（新浦安・しんうらやす）

ICHIKAWA-SHIOHAMA
（市川塩浜・いちかわしおはま）

TO MINAMI-URAWA
MUSASHINO LINE

FUTAMATA-SHINMACHI
（二俣新町・ふたまたしんまち）

MINAMI-FUNABASHI
（南船橋・みなみふなばし）

SHIN-NARASHINO
（新習志野・しんならしの）

KAIHIN-MAKUHARI
（海浜幕張・かいひんまくはり）

KEMIGAWAHAMA
（検見川浜・けみがわはま）

INAGEKAIGAN
（稲毛海岸・いなげかいがん）

CHIBAMINATO
（千葉みなと・ちばみなと）

SOGA
（蘇我・そが）

Part 5: TOKYO'S MAIN SUBWAY LINES

Tokyo Metro and Toei Subway Lines

One of the world's largest subway systems lies in Tokyo where a total of 285 stations and 13 lines operate. The subway lines are operated by two separate companies: Tokyo Metro (9 lines) and by Toei (4 lines).

The 9 subway lines operated by Tokyo Metro are the following:

- ◯ **Ginza Line**
- ◯ **Marunouchi Line**
- ◯ **Hibiya Line**
- ◯ **Tozai Line**
- ◯ **Chiyoda Line**
- ◯ **Yurakucho Line**
- ◯ **Hanzomon Line**
- ◯ **Namboku Line**
- ◯ **Fukutoshin Line**

The 4 subway lines of the Toei network are:

- ◯ **Toei Asakusa Line**
- ◯ **Toei Oedo Line**
- ◯ **Toei Mita Line**
- ◯ **Toei Shinjuku Line**

Street Car
- ◯ **Toden Arakawa Line**

GINZA LINE: The Ginza Line, which starts on the southwest side of Tokyo in Shibuya and runs through the center of the city to Asakusa on the northeast side, was the first subway in Japan, beginning service in 1939. Its route through the city connects 20 districts that have been important since its inception. It intersects with other subway lines at nine of its stations, and with JR commuter trains at four of its stations.

MARUNOUCHI LINE: The Marunouchi Line begins in the far western outskirts of Tokyo in Ogikubo, enters central Tokyo at Shinjuku, goes through Japan's government center with a stop in front of the Diet Building, continues on eastward to the famous Ginza shopping and entertainment district, swings north to Tokyo Central Station and then curves to the northwest, ending up in Ikebukuro.

HIBIYA LINE: The Hibiya Line begins in Kikuna on the south side of Tokyo, connects with the Yamanote train loop line in Ebisu, stops at the famous Roppongi entertainment district, goes near Tokyo Tower, passes through the famous Hibiya and Ginza districts, stops near the great Tsukiji Fish Market and then swings northeast, ending up at Tobu-Dobutsu-Koen.

TOZAI LINE: The Tozai Line also begins on the far west side in the suburban city of Mitaka, goes by Waseda University, continues straight on to Nihonbashi [considered the starting point for all trips in Japan during the

A Ginza Line Train

Tokugawa era], then goes on in the direction of Chiba to Tsudanuma.

CHIYODA LINE: This line connects 18 districts from Hon-Atsugi in western Tokyo to Toride on the north side of the city, bisecting downtown Tokyo via Hibiya, Government Center and the Marunouchi and Otemachi business centers.

HANZOMON LINE: This line begins in Shibuya [where it connects with the private Shin Tamagawa Line that goes to distant Chuo Rinkan near Yokohama] and goes through the middle of central Tokyo, with a stop beneath the famous Mitsukoshi Department Store and the Tokyo Central Air Terminal], and on to Oshiage, where it connects with JR and private transportation to Narita Airport.

FUKUTOSHIN LINE: This line links Shibuya, Shinjuku and Ikebukuro with the huge outlying districts of Saitama on the north and Kanagawa on the south. The line has express trains that run from Shibuya to Ikebukuro in 11 minutes.

YURAKUCHO LINE: Beginning on the far northwest at Shinrin-Koen, this line cuts through Ikebukuro, Iidabashi, Nagatacho [Government Center] and Yurakucho and from there swings east to Shin-Kiba in the direction of Tokyo Bay and the Chiba Peninsula.

NAMBOKU LINE: The Namboku Line begins in Akabane on the north side of Tokyo, circles the Imperial Palace grounds on the west side, and ends up in Meguro on the south side of the city. It goes by Tokyo University, Sophia University [Jochi Daigaku], Government Center, and the upscale Azabu residential and embassy row areas.

TOEI ASAKUSA LINE: This line begins on the south side of Tokyo, bisects the center of the city at Shimbashi and Higashi Ginza, and goes on to Oshiage. Some of the coaches on this line continue on to Narita Airport, and have **Narita Kuko** signs on their front and on the sides. If you get on a train that makes its final stop at Oshiage, exit there and wait there for one that goes on to the airport, usually from the same platform. To make certain ask a platform attendant by saying "Narita dochira [Nah-ree-tah doh-chee-rah]?"

Toei Asakusa Line passes through the center of Tokyo, with stops and connections to other subway and train lines at Asakusa, Higashi-Nihonbashi, Nihonbashi, Higashi Ginza, Shimbashi and Mita, as well as at other subway and JR Railway stations.

TOEI OEDO LINE: The Oedo Line runs in a semi-loop around central Tokyo before branching out towards Nerima in the western suburbs, in the figure of a *6* lying on its side. It begins at Tocho-mae [front of the Tokyo Metro Government Building] and ends in Hikarigaoka. There are 38 stations; most in key areas of the city. [Read page 100 for more]

TOEI MITA LINE: The Toei Mita Line begins in Mita in south-central Tokyo, runs through the middle of the city [via the important districts of Shiba-Koen, Onarimon, and Hibiya] to Nishi-Takashimadaira on the northwest outskirts.

TOEI SHINJUKU LINE: This line begins in Shinjuku [the busiest rail terminal in the world!], connects to the Keio Line that goes to the southwestern outskirts of the city. Its more important stations in central Tokyo are Shinjuku Sanchome, Ichigaya and Jimbocho, the latter in Tokyo's university district and famous for its bookstores.

TOEI NO. 12 [KANJO SEN]: This line makes a long loop around Tokyo, beginning in Hikarigaoka, passes through Shinjuku and curves around through Iidabashi, Ryogoku, Tsukiji, Azabu Juban, Roppongi, Aoyama 1-chome, Yoyogi, and ends up back at Shinjuku Station.

TODEN ARAKAWA LINE: The Toden [Streetcar] Arakawa Line is the sole survivor of Tokyo's once-extensive streetcar system. It operates between Minowabashi Station and Waseda Station in the northern and eastern sections of the city. It runs along Meiji Street between Asukayama Station and Oji Eki-mae Station. Otherwise it operates on its own tracks. The streetcar stops at 30 stations, including eight stations that connect with different subway and train lines. The single driver-operated cars make the 12.2 km trip in 50 minutes.

The streetcar line operates in areas that tourists generally do not see; for that reason the quick trip is highly worthwhile. The Arakawa Line allows riders to have leisurely, street-level views of older sections of Tokyo that differ dramatically from the busy and increasingly high-rise neighborhoods like Shibuya, Shinjuku, and Ikebukuro.

Ginza Subway Line 銀座線

G19 **ASAKUSA**
（浅草・あさくさ）
A18

G18 **TAWARAMACHI**
（田原町・たわらまち）

G17 **INARICHO**
（稲荷町・いなりちょう）

G16 **UENO**
（上野・うえの）
H17 JR

G15 **UENO-HIROKOJI**
（上野広小路・うえのひろこうじ）
E09 H16

G14 **SUEHIROCHO**
（末広町・すえひろちょう）

G13 **KANDA**
（神田・かんだ）
JR

G12 **MITSUKOSHIMAE**
（三越前・みつこしまえ）
Z09 JR
SHIN-NIHOMBASHI Sta

G11 **NIHONBASHI**
（日本橋・にほんばし）
A13 T10

G10 **KYOBASHI**
（京橋・きょうばし）

H08 M16
G09 **GINZA**
（銀座・ぎんざ）

U01 A10
JR
G08 **SHIMBASHI**
（新橋・しんばし）

G07 **TORANOMON**
（虎ノ門・とらのもん）

C07 M13 N06
G06 **TAMEIKE-SANNO**
（溜池山王・ためいけさんのう）

Z04 Y16 N07 M13
G05 **AKASAKA-MITSUKE**
（赤坂見附・あかさかみつけ）

Z03 E24
G04 **AOYAMA-ITCHOME**
（青山一丁目・あおやまいっちょうめ）

G03 **GAIEMMAE**
（外苑前・がいえんまえ）

Z02 C04
G02 **OMOTE-SANDO**
（表参道・おもてさんどう）

Z01 F16
G01 **SHIBUYA** JR
（渋谷・しぶや）
TOKYU TOYOKO LINE
TOKYU DEN'ENTOSHI LINE
KEIO INOKASHIRA LINE

Marunouchi Subway Line 丸ノ内線

M01 OGIKUBO (JR)
（荻窪・おぎくぼ）

M02 MINAMI-ASAGAYA
（南阿佐ヶ谷・みなみあさがや）

M03 SHIN-KOENJI
（新高円寺・しんこうえんじ）

m01 HONANCHO
（方南町・ほうなんちょう）

m02 NAKANO-FUJIMICHO
（中野富士見町・なかのふじみちょう）

M04 HIGASHI-KOENJI
（東高円寺・ひがしこうえんじ）

Y09 F09 (JR)

TOBU TOJO LINE
SEIBU IKEBUKURO LINE

M25 IKEBUKURO
（池袋・いけぶくろ）

m03 NAKANO-SHIMBASHI
（中野新橋・なかのしんばし）

M05 SHIN-NAKANO
（新中野・しんなかの）

M06 NAKANO-SAKAUE
（中野坂上・なかのさかうえ）

E30

M24 SHIN-OTSUKA
（新大塚・しんおおつか）

M23 MYOGADANI
（茗荷谷・みょうがだに）

M07 NISHI-SHINJUKU
（西新宿・にししんじゅく）

E01 S01 (JR)

KEIO LINE
ODAKYU LINE

E07 I12 N11

M22 KORAKUEN
（後楽園・こうらくえん）

M08 SHINJUKU
（新宿・しんじゅく）

M09 SHINJUKU-SANCHOME
（新宿三丁目・しんじゅくさんちょうめ）

S02 F13

E08

M21 HONGO-SANCHOME
（本郷三丁目・ほんごうさんちょうめ）

M10 SHINJUKU-GYOEMMAE
（新宿御苑前・しんじゅくぎょえんまえ）

(JR)

M20 OCHANOMIZU
（御茶ノ水・おちゃのみず）

M11 YOTSUYA-SANCHOME
（四谷三丁目・よつやさんちょうめ）

C12 S07

M19 AWAJICHO
（淡路町・あわじちょう）

N08

(JR) **M12 YOTSUYA**
（四谷・よつや）

C11 Z08 I09 T09

M18 OTEMACHI
（大手町・おおてまち）

Z04 Y16 N07 G05 **M13 AKASAKA-MITSUKE**
（赤坂見附・あかさかみつけ）

M17 TOKYO (JR)
（東京・とうきょう）

G05 N06 C07 **M14 KOKKAI-GIJIDOMAE**
（国会議事堂前・こっかいぎじどうまえ）

G09 H08

M16 GINZA
（銀座・ぎんざ）

C08 H06 **M15 KASUMIGASEKI**
（霞ヶ関・かすみがせき）

Hibiya Subway Line 日比谷線

To ISESAKI

TOBU ISEZAKI LINE

C18

TOBU ISEZAKI LINE
TSUKUBA EXPRESS LINE (JR) **H21 KITA-SENJU**
（北千住・きたせんじゅ）

TSUKUBA EXPRESS LINE (JR) **H20 MINAMI-SENJU**
（南千住・みなみせんじゅ）

H19 MINOWA
（三ノ輪・みのわ）

H18 IRIYA
（入谷・いりや）

H17 UENO
（上野・うえの）

G16 (JR)

H16 NAKA-OKACHIMACHI
（仲御徒町・なかおかちまち）

G15 E09

H15 AKIHABARA
（秋葉原・あきはばら）

S08
TSUKUBA EXPRESS LINE

H14 KODEMMACHO
（小伝馬町・こでんまちょう）

A14

H13 NINGYOCHO
（人形町・にんぎょうちょう）

T11

H12 KAYABACHO
（茅場町・かやばちょう）

H11 HATCHOBORI (JR)
（八丁堀・はっちょうぼり）

H10 TSUKIJI
（築地・つきじ）

To YOKOHAMA
TOKYU TOYOKO LINE

H01 NAKA-MEGURO
（中目黒・なかめぐろ）

H02 EBISU (JR)
（恵比寿・えびす）

H03 HIRO-O
（広尾・ひろお）

H04 ROPPONGI
（六本木・ろっぽんぎ）

E23

H05 KAMIYACHO
（神谷町・かみやちょう）

H06 KASUMIGASEKI
（霞ヶ関・かすみがせき）

M15 C08

I08 Y18 C08
(JR)

H07 HIBIYA
（日比谷・ひびや）

M16 G09

H08 GINZA
（銀座・ぎんざ）

A11

H09 HIGASHI-GINZA
（東銀座・ひがしぎんざ）

Tozai Subway Line 東西線

Chiyoda Subway Line 千代田線

To TORIDE

H21
TOBU ISEZAKI LINE
TSUKUBA EXPRESS LINE
C18 KITA-SENJU（北千住・きたせんじゅ）

C20 KITA-AYASE
（北綾瀬・きたあやせ）

JR JOBAN LINE

KEISEI MAIN LINE
NIPPORI TONERI LINER
TODEN ARAKAWA LINE **C17 MACHIYA**（町屋・まちや）

C16 NISHI-NIPPORI（西日暮里・にしにっぽり）

C19 AYASE
（綾瀬・あやせ）

C15 SENDAGI
（千駄木・せんだぎ）

C14 NEZU
（根津・ねづ）

C13 YUSHIMA
（湯島・ゆしま）

M19 S07
OCHANOMIZU STATION
C12 SHIN-OCHANOMIZU
（新御茶ノ水・しんおちゃのみず）

M18 T09 I09 Z08
TOKYO STATION
C11 OTEMACHI
（大手町・おおてまち）

C10 NIJUBASHIMAE
（二重橋前・にじゅうばしまえ）

C07 KOKKAI-GIJIDOMAE（国会議事堂前・こっかいぎじどうまえ）

H07 Y18 I08
C09 HIBIYA
（日比谷・ひびや）

C06 AKASAKA（赤坂・あかさか）

H06 M15
C08 KASUMIGASEKI
（霞ヶ関・かすみがせき）

C05 NOGIZAKA（乃木坂・のぎざか）

G06
N06
M14

C04 OMOTE-SANDO（表参道・おもてさんどう）

C03 MEIJI-JINGUMAE（明治神宮前・めいじじんぐうまえ）

G02
Z02

C02 YOYOGI-KOEN（代々木公園・よよぎこうえん）

F15
JR HARAJUKU STATION

ODAKYU LINE

C01 YOYOGI-UEHARA
（代々木上原・よよぎうえはら）

To ODAWARA

Hanzomon Subway Line 半蔵門線

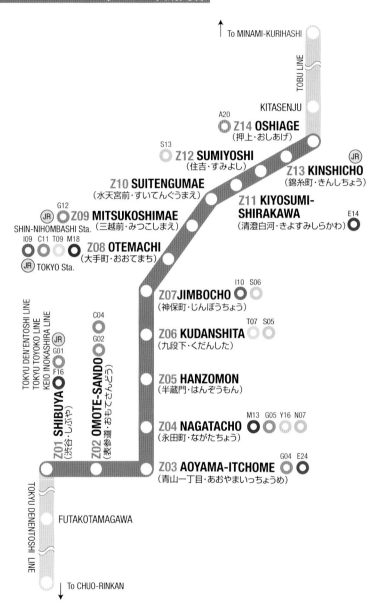

To MINAMI-KURIHASHI

TOBU LINE

KITASENJU

A20
Z14 **OSHIAGE**
（押上・おしあげ）

S13
Z12 **SUMIYOSHI**
（住吉・すみよし）

Z13 **KINSHICHO** (JR)
（錦糸町・きんしちょう）

Z10 **SUITENGUMAE**
（水天宮前・すいてんぐうまえ）

Z11 **KIYOSUMI-SHIRAKAWA**
（清澄白河・きよすみしらかわ） E14

G12
(JR) Z09 **MITSUKOSHIMAE**
SHIN-NIHOMBASHI Sta. （三越前・みつこしまえ）

I09 C11 T09 M18
Z08 **OTEMACHI**
（大手町・おおてまち）
(JR) TOKYO Sta.

Z07 **JIMBOCHO** I10 S06
（神保町・じんぼうちょう）

T07 S05
Z06 **KUDANSHITA**
（九段下・くだんした）

C04
Z05 **HANZOMON**
（半蔵門・はんぞうもん）

G02
Z04 **NAGATACHO** M13 G05 Y16 N07
（永田町・ながたちょう）

TOKYU DEN'ENTOSHI LINE
TOKYU TOYOKO LINE
KEIO INOKASHIRA LINE
(JR) G01
F16

G04 E24
Z03 **AOYAMA-ITCHOME**
（青山一丁目・あおやまいっちょうめ）

Z01 **SHIBUYA**
（渋谷・しぶや）

Z02 **OMOTE-SANDO**
（表参道・おもてさんどう）

TOKYU DENENTOSHI LINE

FUTAKOTAMAGAWA

To CHUO-RINKAN

Fukutoshin Subway Line 副都心線

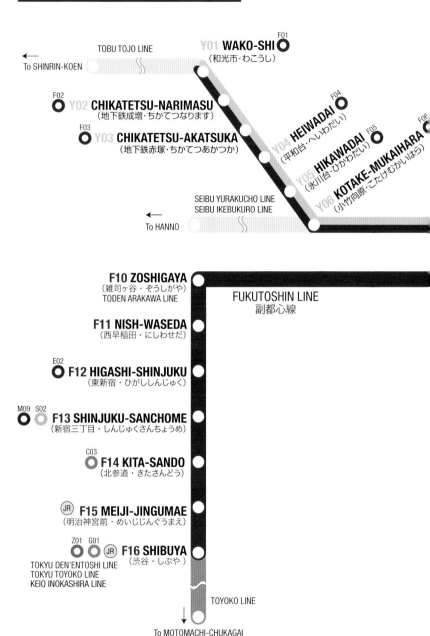

TOBU TOJO LINE

← To SHINRIN-KOEN

Y01 **WAKO-SHI** F01
（和光市・わこうし）

F02
Y02 **CHIKATETSU-NARIMASU**
（地下鉄成増・ちかてつなります）

F03
Y03 **CHIKATETSU-AKATSUKA**
（地下鉄赤塚・ちかてつあかつか）

F04
Y04 **HEIWADAI**
（平和台・へいわだい）

F05
Y05 **HIKAWADAI**
（氷川台・ひかわだい）

F06
Y06 **KOTAKE-MUKAIHARA**
（小竹向原・こたけむかいはら）

SEIBU YURAKUCHO LINE
SEIBU IKEBUKURO LINE

← To HANNO

F10 **ZOSHIGAYA**
（雑司ヶ谷・ぞうしがや）
TODEN ARAKAWA LINE

FUKUTOSHIN LINE
副都心線

F11 **NISH-WASEDA**
（西早稲田・にしわせだ）

E02
F12 **HIGASHI-SHINJUKU**
（東新宿・ひがししんじゅく）

M09 S02
F13 **SHINJUKU-SANCHOME**
（新宿三丁目・しんじゅくさんちょうめ）

C03
F14 **KITA-SANDO**
（北参道・きたさんどう）

JR F15 **MEIJI-JINGUMAE**
（明治神宮前・めいじじんぐうまえ）

Z01 G01
JR F16 **SHIBUYA**
（渋谷・しぶや）
TOKYU DEN'ENTOSHI LINE
TOKYU TOYOKO LINE
KEIO INOKASHIRA LINE

TOYOKO LINE

↓ To MOTOMACHI-CHUKAGAI

Yurakucho Subway Line 有楽町線

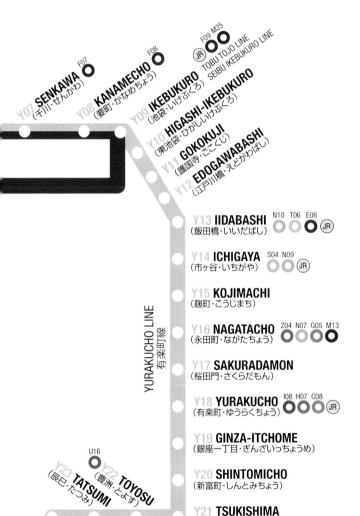

Y07 SENKAWA F07
（千川・せんかわ）

Y08 KANAMECHO F08
（要町・かなめちょう）

Y09 IKEBUKURO F09 M25 JR TOBU TOJO LINE SEIBU IKEBUKURO LINE
（池袋・いけぶくろ）

Y10 HIGASHI-IKEBUKURO
（東池袋・ひがしいけぶくろ）

Y11 GOKOKUJI
（護国寺・ごこくじ）

Y12 EDOGAWABASHI
（江戸川橋・えどがわばし）

Y13 IIDABASHI N10 T06 E06 JR
（飯田橋・いいだばし）

Y14 ICHIGAYA S04 N09 JR
（市ヶ谷・いちがや）

Y15 KOJIMACHI
（麹町・こうじまち）

Y16 NAGATACHO Z04 N07 G05 M13
（永田町・ながたちょう）

Y17 SAKURADAMON
（桜田門・さくらだもん）

Y18 YURAKUCHO I08 H07 C08 JR
（有楽町・ゆうらくちょう）

Y19 GINZA-ITCHOME
（銀座一丁目・ぎんざいっちょうめ）

Y20 SHINTOMICHO
（新富町・しんとみちょう）

Y21 TSUKISHIMA
（月島・つきしま）

YURAKUCHO LINE 有楽町線

U16

Y23 TATSUMI
（辰巳・たつみ）

Y22 TOYOSU
（豊洲・とよす）

Y24 SHIN-KIBA JR
（新木場・しんきば） RINKAI LINE

Namboku Subway Line 南北線
(Saitama Kosoku Railway 埼玉高速鉄道)

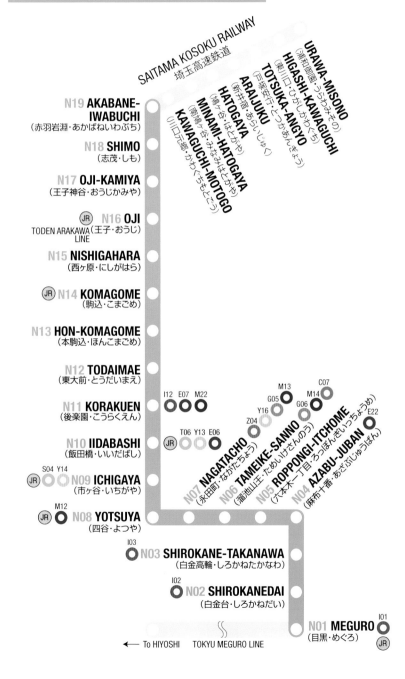

SAITAMA KOSOKU RAILWAY 埼玉高速鉄道

URAWA-MISONO（浦和美園・うらわみその）
HIGASHI-KAWAGUCHI（東川口・ひがしかわぐち）
TOTSUKA-ANGYO（戸塚安行・とつかあんぎょう）
ARAIJUKU（新井宿・あらいじゅく）
HATOGAYA（鳩ヶ谷・はとがや）
MINAMI-HATOGAYA（南鳩ヶ谷・みなみはとがや）
KAWAGUCHI-MOTOGO（川口元郷・かわぐちもとごう）

N19 **AKABANE-IWABUCHI**（赤羽岩淵・あかばねいわぶち）

N18 **SHIMO**（志茂・しも）

N17 **OJI-KAMIYA**（王子神谷・おうじかみや）

(JR) N16 **OJI**
TODEN ARAKAWA LINE（王子・おうじ）

N15 **NISHIGAHARA**（西ヶ原・にしがはら）

(JR) N14 **KOMAGOME**（駒込・こまごめ）

N13 **HON-KOMAGOME**（本駒込・ほんこまごめ）

N12 **TODAIMAE**（東大前・とうだいまえ）

N11 **KORAKUEN**（後楽園・こうらくえん）
I12 E07 M22

N10 **IIDABASHI**（飯田橋・いいだばし）
(JR) T06 Y13 E06

S04 Y14
(JR) N09 **ICHIGAYA**（市ヶ谷・いちがや）

M12
(JR) N08 **YOTSUYA**（四谷・よつや）

M13 C07
G05 M14
Y16 G06
Z04

N07 **NAGATACHO**（永田町・ながたちょう）
N06 **TAMEIKE-SANNO**（溜池山王・ためいけさんのう）
N05 **ROPPONGI-ITCHOME**（六本木一丁目・ろっぽんぎいっちょうめ）
E22
N04 **AZABU-JUBAN**（麻布十番・あざぶじゅうばん）

I03
N03 **SHIROKANE-TAKANAWA**（白金高輪・しろかねたかなわ）

I02
N02 **SHIROKANEDAI**（白金台・しろかねだい）

I01
N01 **MEGURO**（目黒・めぐろ）
(JR)

← To HIYOSHI   TOKYU MEGURO LINE

Toei Asakusa Subway Line 都営浅草線
(Hokuso Railway 北総鉄道)

INBA-NIHONIDAI
（印旛日本医大・いんばにほんいだい）

CHIBA-NEW TOWN-CHUO
（千葉ニュータウン中央・
ちばにゅーたうんちゅうおう）

JR LINE
SHIN-KEISEI LINE **SHIN-KAMAGAYA**
TOBU NODA LINE （新鎌ケ谷・しんかまがや）

HIGASHI-MATSUDO
（東松戸・ひがしまつど）

TAKASAGO
（高砂・たかさご）

NARITA SKY ACCESS

NARITA AIRPORT

HOKUSO RAILWAY 北総鉄道

KEISEI LINE

AOTO

A20 OSHIAGE Z14
（押上・おしあげ）

A19 HONJO-AZUMABASHI
（本所吾妻橋・ほんじょあづまばし）

E11
A17 KURAMAE
（蔵前・くらまえ）

A18 ASAKUSA G19
（浅草・あさくさ）

A16 ASAKUSABASHI (JR)
（浅草橋・あさくさばし）

S09
A15 HIGASHI-NIHONBASHI (JR)
（東日本橋・ひがしにほんばし）BAKUROCHO Sta.

H13
A14 NINGYOCHO
（人形町・にんぎょうちょう）

G11 T10
A13 NIHONBASHI
（日本橋・にほんばし）

A12 TAKARACHO
（宝町・たからちょう）

H09
A11 HIGASHI-GINZA
（東銀座・ひがしぎんざ）

U01 G08
A10 SHIMBASHI (JR)
（新橋・しんばし）

E20
A09 DAIMON (JR)
（大門・だいもん）HAMAMATSUCHO Sta.

A08 MITA (JR)
（三田・みた）I04 TAMACHI Sta.

A07 SENGAKUJI（泉岳寺・せんがくじ）

A06 TAKANAWADAI（高輪台・たかなわだい）

TOKYU OIMACHI LINE
(JR) **A05 GOTANDA**（五反田・ごたんだ）

A04 TOGOSHI（戸越・とごし）

A03 NAKANOBU（中延・なかのぶ）

A02 MAGOME（馬込・まごめ）

A01 NISHI-MAGOME（西馬込・にしまごめ）

KEIHIN-KYUKO LINE

KEIKYU-KAMATA

KEIKYU KUKO LINE

To MISAKIGUCHI   To HANEDAKUKO

Toei Oedo Subway Line 都営大江戸線

E38 **HIKARIGAOKA**
（光が丘・ひかりがおか）

E37 **NERIMA-KASUGACHO**
（練馬春日町・ねりまかすがちょう）

E36 **TOSHIMAEN**
（豊島園・としまえん）

E35 **NERIMA**
（練馬・ねりま）
SEIBU YURAKUCHO LINE
SEIBU IKEBUKURO LINE

E34 **SHIN-EGOTA**
（新江古田・しんえごた）

E33 **OCHIAI-MINAMI-NAGASAKI**
（落合南長崎・おちあいみなみながさき）

E32 **NAKAI**
（中井・なかい）

E31 **HIGASHI-NAKANO** (JR)
（東中野・ひがしなかの）

M06
E30 **NAKANO-SAKAUE**
（中野坂上・なかのさかうえ）

E29 **NISHI-SHINJUKU-GOCHOME**
（西新宿五丁目・
にししんじゅくごちょうめ）

E28 **TOCHOMAE**
（都庁前・とちょうまえ）

M08 S01
KEIO LINE (JR)
ODAKYU LINE
E27 **SHINJUKU**
（新宿・しんじゅく）

(JR) E26 **YOYOGI**
（代々木・よよぎ）

E25 **KOKURITU-KYOGIJO**
（国立競技場・こくりつきょうぎじょう）

G04 Z03 E24 **AOYAMA-ITCHOME**
（青山一丁目・あおやまいっちょうめ）

H04 E23 **ROPPONGI**
（六本木・ろっぽんぎ）

N04 E22 **AZABU-JUBAN**
（麻布十番・あざぶじゅうばん）

Y13 N10 T06
E06 **IIDABA**
（飯田橋・いいた

E05 **USHIGO**
（牛込神楽坂・うし

E04 **USHIGOME-YAN**
（牛込柳町・うしごめやなぎ

E03 **WAKAMATSU-KAWADA**
（若松河田・わかまつかわだ）

E02 **HIGASHI-SHINJUKU**
（東新宿・ひがししんじゅく）

E01 **SHINJUKU-NISHIGUCHI**
（新宿西口・しんじゅくにしぐち）
F12

M08
(JR)

Toei Oedo Line can also be called the "Sightseers' Subway Line." Refer to page 100 for more information.

G15 H16 JR OKACHIMACHI Sta.

M21

I12 N11 M22

E07 KASUGA
（春日・かすが）

E08 HONGO-SANCHOME
（本郷三丁目・ほんごうさんちょうめ）

E09 UENO-OKACHIMACHI
（上野御徒町・うえのおかちまち）

E10 SHIN-OKACHIMACHI
（新御徒町・しんおかちまち）

A17

E11 KURAMAE
（蔵前・くらまえ）

JR E12 RYOGOKU
（両国・りょうごく）

S11
E13 MORISHITA
（森下・もりした）

Z11
E14 KIYOSUMI-SHIRAKAWA
（清澄白河・きよすみしらかわ）

T12
E15 MONZEN-NAKACHO
（門前仲町・もんぜんなかちょう）

E16 TSUKISHIMA
（月島・つきしま）

E17 KACHIDOKI
（勝どき・かちどき）

Y21

SHIMBASHI STATION JR

U02

AMATSUCHO STATION JR

E18 TSUKIJISHIJO
（築地市場・つきじしじょう）

A09

E19 SHIODOME
（汐留・しおどめ）

AKABANEBASHI
橋・あかばねばし）

E20 DAIMON
（大門・だいもん）

TOEI OEDO—THE SIGHTSEERS' SUBWAY LINE

Tokyo's new upscale Toei No. 12 Loop Line, popularly known as the Oedo Line [which might be translated as *The Greater Tokyo Line*] could also be called *The Sightseers' Subway Line* because it connects areas that have more than a dozen of the most outstanding attractions in the city. [See pages 98-99 for the route.] Some of the more outstanding of these attractions, listed by the names of the Oedo Line subway stations that serve them, are:

Tochomae

Tochomae [Tohh-chohh-my] literally means "In Front of the Metropolitan Government Building". This spectacular building complex [where the governor hangs out] includes restaurants, shops, a visitor information center, a bookstore, a high-rise view floor that provides a grand view of the city—and the towering peak of Mt. Fuji on clear days. At first criticized because of its cost and elaborate architectural features, the building is now one of Tokyo's most popular tourist attractions.

Shinjuku Nishiguchi

Shinjuku Nishiguchi [Sheen-juu-kuu Nee-she-guu-chee], literally "Shinjuku West Exit/Entrance", is the west entrance to Japan's busiest train station, with over a million people passing through it daily. In addition to being a hub station for commuter and long-distance train lines, Shinjuku Station is the locus for a large complex of international hotels, department stores, restaurants and the famous Kabukicho [Kah-buu-kee-choh] entertainment district with its bars, cafés, pubs and restaurants on the northeast side of the station.

Ueno-Okachimachi

Ueno-Okachimachi [Way-no Oh-kah-chee-mah-chee] Station is the gateway to Ueno Park, originally the estate of a samurai feudal lord and now the location of some of Japan's most important cultural attractions, from museums and galleries to the top zoo. In addition to these popular attractions, the whole Ueno-Okachimachi area is known for its ethnic restaurants and the Okachimachi bargain shopping area.

Ryogoku

For those who are interested in or would like to know more about Japan's world of sumo,

Ryogoku [Rio-go-kuu] is the place. In addition to the spectacular sumo stadium where the bouts are staged, Ryogoku is replete with sumo training stables that are open to the public, *chanko nabe* [chahn-koh nah-bay] restaurants that serve the famous stew eaten by sumo wrestlers, a sumo museum and shops that offer a variety of sumo paraphernalia for sumo fans. Ryogoku has been the center of the sumo world for over 300 years.

Tsukijishijo

Tsukijishijo [T-sue-kee-jee-she-johh] is one of the gateways to Tokyo's internationally famous wholesale fish market and its complex of sushi restaurants. Hordes of visitors and local residents converge on the Tsukiji Fish Market in the early morning hours to see the sight of tons of freshly caught fish being off-loaded and auctioned off to buyers for restaurants and restaurant chains… and often to dine on the fresh fish.

Shiodome

In addition to its complex of international hotels and high-rise office buildings Shiodome [She-oh-doh-may], which adjoins Shimbashi Station at the south end of the famous Ginza shopping district, is a short walk from the famous Hamarikyu Garden, once the estate of a feudal lord, and is the starting point of the elevated Yurikamome train line that goes to Odaiba Island Tokyo Bay—the latter one of Tokyo's newest and most popular entertainment and shopping districts.

Roppongi

Roppongi [Rope-pon-ghee] has been noted since the 1960s as a night-time entertainment center that caters to foreign residents and visitors and the Japanese movie and model crowd who like the international atmosphere. It is now also the gateway to the huge Roppongi Hills and Tokyo Midtown office complexes that include hotels, upscale restaurants and shops by the dozens. Like most of Tokyo's new high-rise buildings the Roppongi Hills complex includes a "sightseeing floor" that provides a 360-degree view of Tokyo.

Maps of the Oedo Subway Line are available at some tourist information shops, including the one in the Metro Tokyo Government Building, accessible via an underground corridor from Tochomae Station.

Toei Mita Subway Line 都営三田線

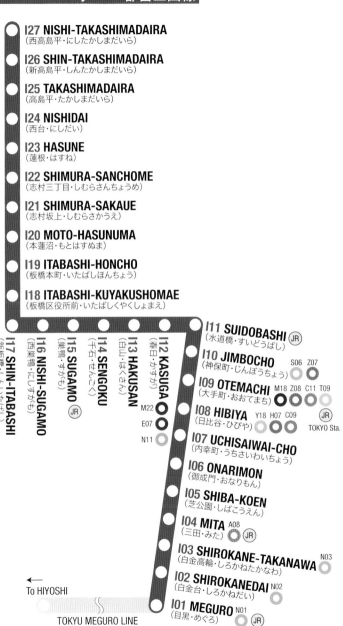

I27 **NISHI-TAKASHIMADAIRA**
(西高島平・にしたかしまだいら)

I26 **SHIN-TAKASHIMADAIRA**
(新高島平・しんたかしまだいら)

I25 **TAKASHIMADAIRA**
(高島平・たかしまだいら)

I24 **NISHIDAI**
(西台・にしだい)

I23 **HASUNE**
(蓮根・はすね)

I22 **SHIMURA-SANCHOME**
(志村三丁目・しむらさんちょうめ)

I21 **SHIMURA-SAKAUE**
(志村坂上・しむらさかうえ)

I20 **MOTO-HASUNUMA**
(本蓮沼・もとはすぬま)

I19 **ITABASHI-HONCHO**
(板橋本町・いたばしほんちょう)

I18 **ITABASHI-KUYAKUSHOMAE**
(板橋区役所前・いたばしくやくしょまえ)

I17 **SHIN-ITABASHI**
(新板橋・しんいたばし)

I16 **NISHI-SUGAMO**
(西巣鴨・にしすがも)

I15 **SUGAMO** (JR)
(巣鴨・すがも)

I14 **SENGOKU**
(千石・せんごく)

I13 **HAKUSAN**
(白山・はくさん)

I12 **KASUGA** M22 E07 N11
(春日・かすが)

I11 **SUIDOBASHI** (JR)
(水道橋・すいどうばし)

I10 **JIMBOCHO** S06 Z07
(神保町・じんぼうちょう)

I09 **OTEMACHI** M18 Z08 C11 T09
(大手町・おおてまち)

I08 **HIBIYA** Y18 H07 C09 (JR)
(日比谷・ひびや) TOKYO Sta.

I07 **UCHISAIWAI-CHO**
(内幸町・うちさいわいちょう)

I06 **ONARIMON**
(御成門・おなりもん)

I05 **SHIBA-KOEN**
(芝公園・しばこうえん)

I04 **MITA** A08 (JR)
(三田・みた)

I03 **SHIROKANE-TAKANAWA** N03
(白金高輪・しろかねたかなわ)

I02 **SHIROKANEDAI** N02
(白金台・しろかねだい)

I01 **MEGURO** N01 (JR)
(目黒・めぐろ)

← To HIYOSHI

TOKYU MEGURO LINE

Toei Shinjuku Subway Line 都営新宿線

To HASHIMOTO
KEIO LINE

M08 E01 JR
KEIO LINE
ODAKYU LINE
M09 F13

S01 SHINJUKU
（新宿・しんじゅく）

S02 SHINJUKU-SANCHOME
（新宿三丁目・しんじゅくさんちょうめ）

S03 AKEBONOBASHI
（曙橋・あけぼのばし）

Y14 N09 JR

S04 ICHIGAYA
（市ケ谷・いちがや）

Z06 T07

S05 KUDANSHITA
（九段下・くだんした）

Z07 I10

S06 JIMBOCHO
（神保町・じんぼうちょう）

M19 C12

S07 OGAWAMACHI
（小川町・おがわまち）

TSUKUBA
EXPRESS LINE   JR H08

S08 IWAMOTOCHO
（岩本町・いわもとちょう）

JR A15
BAKUROCHO ST.

S09 BAKUROYOKOYAMA
（馬喰横山・ばくろよこやま）

S10 HAMACHO
（浜町・はまちょう）

E13
S11 MORISHITA
（森下・もりした）

S12 KIKUKAWA
（菊川・きくかわ）

S13 SUMIYOSHI
（住吉・すみよし）   Z12

S14 NISHI-OJIMA
（西大島・にしおおじま）

S15 OJIMA
（大島・おおじま）

S16 HIGASHI-OJIMA
（東大島・ひがしおおじま）

S17 FUNABORI
（船堀・ふなぼり）

S21 MOTOYAWATA   JR
（本八幡・もとやわた）

S20 SHINOZAKI
（篠崎・しのざき）

S19 MIZUE
（瑞江・みずえ）

S18 ICHINOE
（一之江・いちのえ）

Toden Arakawa Subway Line 都電荒川線

MACHIYA-EKIMAE KEISEI LINE C17
(町屋駅前・まちやえきまえ)

MACHIYA NICHOME
(町屋二丁目・まちやにちょうめ)

ARAKAWA NANACHOME
(荒川七丁目・あらかわななちょうめ)

HIGASHIOGU SANCHOME
(東尾久三丁目・ひがしおぐさんちょうめ)

ARAKAWA NICHOME
(荒川二丁目・あらかわにちょうめ)

KUMANOMAE
(熊野前・くまのまえ)

ARAKAWAKUYAKUSHOMAE
(荒川区役所前・あらかわくやくしょまえ)

MIYANOMAE
(宮ノ前・みやのまえ)

ARAKAWA ITCHUMAE
(荒川一中前・あらかわいっちゅうまえ)

ODAI
(小台・おだい)

MINOWABASHI H19
(三ノ輪橋・みのわばし)

ARAKAWA YUENCHIMAE
(荒川遊園地前・あらかわゆうえんまえ)

ARAKAWA-SHAKOMAE (荒川車庫前・あらかわしゃこまえ)

KAJIWARA (梶原・かじわら)

SAKAECHO (栄町・さかえちょう)

OJI-EKIMAE JR N16
(王子駅前・おうじえきまえ)

ASUKAYAMA
(飛鳥山・あすかやま)

TAKINOGAWA ITCHOME
(滝野川一丁目・たきのがわいっちょうめ)

NISHIGAHARA YONCHOME
(西ヶ原四丁目・にしがはらよんちょうめ)

SHIN-KOSHINZUKA I08 NISHI-SUGAMO Sta.
(新庚申塚・しんこうしんづか)

KOSHINZUKA
(庚申塚・こうしんづか)

SUGAMOSHINDEN
(巣鴨新田・すがもしんでん)

OTSUKA-EKIMAE JR
(大塚駅前・おおつか駅前)

MUKOHARA
(向原・むこうはら)

HIGASHI-IKEBUKURO Y10
YONCHOME (東池袋4丁目・
ひがしいけぶくろよんちょうめ)

WASEDA
(早稲田・わせだ)

OMOKAGEBASHI
(面影橋・おもかげばし)

GAKUSHUINSHITA
(学習院下・がくしゅういんした)

TODEN ZOSHIGAYA
(都電雑司ヶ谷・とでんぞうしがや)

KISHIBOJINMAE F10
(鬼子母神前・きしぼじんまえ)

Tokyo's Private Commuter Rail Lines

Metropolitan Tokyo consists of 23 central wards that are surrounded by 27 suburban cities and 8 towns that encompass most of three prefectures—Chiba, Kanagawa and Saitama. Approximately 36 million people live in this area, making it the most densely populated place on Earth.

This huge area is served by one of the world's most extensive urban rail networks; of which the following are the major private rail lines:

○ **Keio Electric Railway (to Shinjuku)**

○ **Odakyu Electric Railway (to Hakone) (page 184)**

○ **Tokyu Electric Railway**

○ **Seibu Railway (to Chichibu and Kawagoe)**

○ **Tobu Railway (to Nikko and Kinugawa Onsen (spa))**

○ **Yurikamome Line (to Odaiba)**

○ **Rinkai Line (to Odaiba)**

○ **Tsukuba Express Line (to Akihabara)**

○ **Tokyo Monorail (to Haneda Airport)**

○ **Keihin-Kyuko (Keikyu)(to Haneda Airport, Yokohama, Zushi, Kanazawa Hakkei) (pages 33, 138, 170)**

○ **Keisei Electric Railway (to Narita Airport, Ueno) (page 20)**

This network consists of 79 public and private train and subway lines that are used on weekdays by an estimated 20 million people—workers, students, shoppers and visitors…the latter including thousands of people from around the country who are in Tokyo on business and personal visits.

Approximately 15 million people commute from outlying wards, cities and towns to central Tokyo each weekday, most of them passing through the following eight hub stations: Shinjuku, Ikebukuro, Shibuya, Yokohama, Tokyo, Shinagawa, Takadanobaba and Shimbashi. Shinjuku Station on the western side of central Tokyo is rated by the *Guinness Book of World Records* as the busiest commuter railway station in the world, with some 3.7 million passengers using it daily.

Eleven major private commuter lines, shown on the adjoining map, provide transportation from the outlying cities and towns to hub stations in central Tokyo. All of these lines include connections in central Tokyo to the three lines that serve Narita Airport and the two lines that serve Haneda Airport. Tokyo's extensive public bus lines primarily serve as feeder lines from residential districts to the nearest train and subway hub stations.

The morning rush-hours on the private suburban lines going to central Tokyo hub stations begin as early as 6 am and last until around 9 am. During the first two hours most of these trains are so crowded that railway platform staff serve as "pushers" to jam passengers into coaches so the doors can close. The evening rush-hour when people are leaving central Tokyo is a bit less hectic because it is spread over a longer period of time— from about 5:30 pm to 9:30 pm.

Both public and private train and subway lines that serve central Tokyo destinations from the major hub stations are generally more crowded during rush-hours than the private suburban lines that feed into them from outlying cities and towns.

When possible, visitors from overseas who plan on using these suburban feeder lines should keep in mind that trains going out of central Tokyo in the early morning rush hours and during the day are usually not crowded, while those leaving central Tokyo during rush hours can be very crowded.

Tokyo's Private Commuter Railways

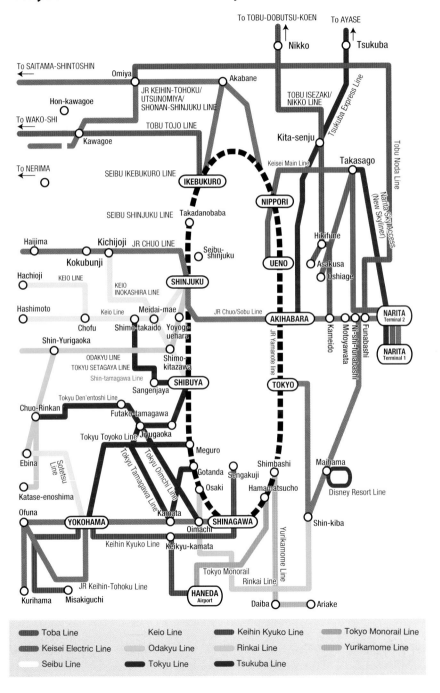

To TOBU-DOBUTSU-KOEN
To AYASE
Nikko
Tsukuba
To SAITAMA-SHINTOSHIN
Omiya
Akabane
JR KEIHIN-TOHOKU/
UTSUNOMIYA/
SHONAN-SHINJUKU LINE
TOBU ISEZAKI/
NIKKO LINE
Hon-kawagoe
Tsukuba Express Line
To WAKO-SHI
TOBU TOJO LINE
Kita-senju
Takasago
Kawagoe
Keisei Main Line
Tobu Noda Line
To NERIMA
SEIBU IKEBUKURO LINE
IKEBUKURO
Narita SkyAccess (New Skyliner)
SEIBU SHINJUKU LINE
Takadanobaba
NIPPORI
Hikifune
Haijima
Kichijoji
JR CHUO LINE
Seibu-shinjuku
UENO
Asakusa
Kokubunji
Oshiage
Hachioji
KEIO LINE
SHINJUKU
Hashimoto
KEIO INOKASHIRA LINE
Keio Line
Meidai-mae
JR Chuo/Sobu Line
AKIHABARA
NARITA Terminal 2
Chofu
Shimo-takaido
Yoyogi-uehara
Kameido
Nishi-funabashi
Motoyawata
Funabashi
Shin-Yurigaoka
ODAKYU LINE
TOKYU SETAGAYA LINE
Shimo-kitazawa
NARITA Terminal 1
Shin-tamagawa Line
SHIBUYA
JR Yamanote line
Sangenjaya
TOKYO
Chuo-Rinkan
Tokyu Den'entoshi Line
Futako-tamagawa
Tokyu Toyoko Line
Jiyugaoka
Meguro
Maihama
Ebina
Sotetsu Line
Tokyu Tamagawa Line
Tokyu Oimachi Line
Gotanda
Sengakuji
Shimbashi
Disney Resort Line
Katase-enoshima
Osaki
Hamamatsucho
Ofuna
YOKOHAMA
Kamata
Oimachi
SHINAGAWA
Shin-kiba
Keihin Kyuko Line
Keikyu-kamata
Yurikamome Line
Tokyo Monorail
Kurihama
Misakiguchi
JR Keihin-Tohoku Line
HANEDA Airport
Rinkai Line
Daiba
Ariake

Toba Line	Keio Line	Keihin Kyuko Line	Tokyo Monorail Line
Keisei Electric Line	Odakyu Line	Rinkai Line	Yurikamome Line
Seibu Line	Tokyu Line	Tsukuba Line	

KEIO ELECTRIC RAILWAY: The Keio Electric Line and its seven branch lines connect Tokyo's main west side Shinjuku hub station with more than a dozen key satellite cities as well as several hub stations in central Tokyo. Among the primary satellite cities going westward from Shinjuku that are served by the Keio line and its branch lines are Shimo-Kitazawa, Eifukucho, Kichijoji, Chofu, Fuchu and Keio-Hachioji. The branch Inokashira Line also serves Shibuya, one of the primary shopping and entertainment districts on the southwest side of central Tokyo. Fuchu, on the main Keio Line, was formerly an air station for the U.S. Forces Japan, but the facility was moved to Yokota City in 2005.

SEIBU SHINJUKU LINE: The Seibu Shinjuku Line begins at Seibu Shinjuku Station, a short distance northwest of the huge Shinjuku Station and goes all the way to Hon-Kawagoe Station in Kawagoe, Saitama Prefecture. The line operates six types of trains: Local, Semi-Express, Express, Commuter Express Rapid Express Kawagoe and Limited Express Koedo. Stops on the Seibu Shinjuku Line include the important Tokyo districts of Takadanobaba and Shimo-Ochiai and the satellite towns of Saginomiya, Kodaira, Tokorozawa, Shin-Tokorozawa and Hon-Kawagoe.

SEIBU IKEBUKURO LINE: This line begins at Tokyo's Yamanote Loop Line Ikebukuro Station on the northwestern side of the city and serves the important city of Tokorozawa in Saitama Prefecture. The Ikebukuro Line has three branch lines: the Toshima Line, the Seibu Yurakucho Line and the Seibu Sayama Line. Yurakucho is a major district in Central Tokyo, adjoining the famous Ginza, Hibiya and Marunouchi shopping, entertainment and business districts.

TOBU-NIKKO LINE: This line is popular because it provides the fastest and most convenient service from Tokyo to the historically famous mountain town of Nikko in Tochigi Prefecture north of Tokyo, where the mausoleum of Ieyasu Tokugawa, the founder of the Tokugawa Shogunate in 1603, is located…the gateway to the mausoleum is so impressive many visitors think it is the mausoleum. Tokugawa chose the site before dying in 1616 because it had been famous for more than 1,000 years as the site of a Buddhist temple in a scenic setting of indescribable beauty.

Hundreds of thousands of visitors board the Tobu-Nikko Line for Nikko at Asakusa Station, a primary hub station on the northeast side of central Tokyo. There is a famous saying in Japanese that you should never say "Magnificent" until you have seen Nikko. There is a non-stop daily service from Asakusa Station to Nikko Station, allowing passengers to go up in the morning and come back in the evening. Nikko is also famous for its Kegon Waterfalls and a huge lake (Lake Chizenji) further up the mountain from Nikko.

TOBU-ISEZAKI LINE: This line, the longest private railway line in Japan, connects Asakusa Station in Tokyo with Isezaki Station in Gunma Prefecture…114.5 kilometers. Some of the trains on the line connect with Tokyo's Metro Hibiya and Hanzomon lines, which serve many of the most important districts in Central Tokyo, including the Hibiya and Ginza shopping and entertainment districts and Shibuya on the southwest side of the city and the Tokyo City Air Terminal [TCAT] on the east side of Central Tokyo.

RINKAI LINE: This line starts in Tokyo's Shin-Kiba district and runs mostly underground beneath the Port of Tokyo to the man-made islands of Aomi and Odaiba in Tokyo Bay. It serves eight stations along the Tokyo waterfront.

YURIKAMONE LINE: This elevated train line soars on a high bridge from Shimbashi just south of the famed Ginza district to Odaiba Island in Tokyo Bay, a famed shopping, sightseeing and business district. The trains have rubber wheels and are fully automated—no drivers! It is a spectacular ride. The Yurikamone station is a few dozen yards from Shimbashi Station, a hub station for several subway lines and commuter train lines.

TSUKUBA EXPRESS LINE: This connects Akihabara Station [famed electronic appliance and device town] in Chiyoda Ward with Tsukuba Station in Tsukuba, Ibaraki Prefecture. Tsukuba is known as Japan's "Science City," and is home to many major research facilities. These facilities attract many Japanese as well as foreign researchers and visiting scientists. The city is also noted for its historic shrines and temples. High-speed trains make the trip from Tokyo to Tsukuba in about an hour and forty minutes.

Keio Electric Railway 京王電鉄

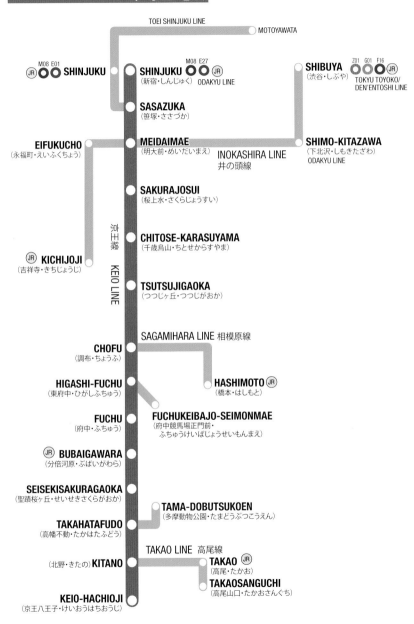

TOEI SHINJUKU LINE

MOTOYAWATA

M08 E01
(JR) ⚪⚪ SHINJUKU

M08 E27
SHINJUKU ⚪⚪ (JR)
(新宿・しんじゅく) ODAKYU LINE

SHIBUYA
(渋谷・しぶや)

Z01 G01 F16
⚪⚪⚪ (JR)
TOKYU TOYOKO/
DEN'ENTOSHI LINE

SASAZUKA
(笹塚・ささづか)

EIFUKUCHO
(永福町・えいふくちょう)

MEIDAIMAE
(明大前・めいだいまえ)

INOKASHIRA LINE
井の頭線

SHIMO-KITAZAWA
(下北沢・しもきたざわ)
ODAKYU LINE

SAKURAJOSUI
(桜上水・さくらじょうすい)

京王線

CHITOSE-KARASUYAMA
(千歳烏山・ちとせからすやま)

(JR) KICHIJOJI
(吉祥寺・きちじょうじ)

KEIO LINE

TSUTSUJIGAOKA
(つつじヶ丘・つつじがおか)

SAGAMIHARA LINE 相模原線

CHOFU
(調布・ちょうふ)

HIGASHI-FUCHU
(東府中・ひがしふちゅう)

HASHIMOTO (JR)
(橋本・はしもと)

FUCHU
(府中・ふちゅう)

FUCHUKEIBAJO-SEIMONMAE
(府中競馬場正門前・
ふちゅうけいばじょうせいもんまえ)

(JR) BUBAIGAWARA
(分倍河原・ぶばいがわら)

SEISEKISAKURAGAOKA
(聖蹟桜ヶ丘・せいせきさくらがおか)

TAMA-DOBUTSUKOEN
(多摩動物公園・たまどうぶつこうえん)

TAKAHATAFUDO
(高幡不動・たかはたふどう)

TAKAO LINE 高尾線

(北野・きたの) KITANO

TAKAO (JR)
(高尾・たかお)

TAKAOSANGUCHI
(高尾山口・たかおさんぐち)

KEIO-HACHIOJI
(京王八王子・けいおうはちおうじ)

Seibu Shinjuku Line 西武新宿線
Seibu Ikebukuro Line 西武池袋線

NAGATORO
（長瀞・ながとろ）

CHICHIBU RAILWAY
秩父鉄道

SEIBU-CHICHIBU
（西武秩父・せいぶちちぶ）

HIGASHI-HANNO JR
（東飯能・ひがしはんのう）

HANNO
（飯能・はんのう）

IRUMA
（入間・いるま）

MUSASHI-FUJISAWA

SAYAMAGAOKA

KOTESASHI

SHIN-TOKOROZAWA
（新所沢・しんところざわ）

NISHI-TOKOROZAWA
（西所沢・にしところざわ）

OHANABATAKE
（御花畑・おはなばたけ）

SEIBU CHICHIBU LINE
西武秩父線

SAYAMA LINE　狭山線

TOKOROZAWA
（所沢・ところざわ）

HIGASHI-MURAYAMA
（東村山・ひがしむらやま）

SEIBU KYUJOMAE
（西武球場前・
せいぶきゅうじょうまえ）

YAMAGUCHI LINE
山口線

MITSUMINEGUCHI
（三峰口・みつみねぐち）

SEIBUEN LINE
西武園線

SEIBUEN
（西武園・せいぶえん）

YUENCHI-NISHI
（遊園地西・ゆうえんちにし）

KUMEGAWA
（久米川・くめがわ）

OGIYAMA
（荻山・おぎやま）

SEIBU YUENCHI
（西武遊園地・せいぶゆうえんち）

HAIJIMA LINE　拝島線

OGAWA
（小川・おがわ）

KODAIRA
（小平・こだいら）

HANAKOGANEI

HAIJIMA JR
（拝島・はいじま）

TAMAGAWAJOSUI
（玉川上水・たまがわじょうすい）

KOKUBUNJI LINE
国分寺線

TAMAKO LINE
多摩湖線

OUMEKAIDO
（青梅街道・
おうめかいどう）

**HITOTSUBASHI
GAKUEN**
（一橋学園・
ひとつばしがくえん）

JR CHUO LINE

KOKUBUNJI JR
（国分寺・こくぶんじ）

KOREMASA
（是政・これまさ）

HON-KAWAGOE
（本川越・ほんかわごえ）

To WAKO-SHI

TOSHIMA LINE 豊島線
TOSHIMAEN
（豊島園・としまえん）

SEIBU YURAKUCHO LINE 西武有楽町線

KOTAKE-MUKAIHARA

F09　M25　Y09
JR ○ ○
TOBU TOJO LINE

IKEBUKURO
（池袋・いけぶくろ）

BUKURO LINE 池袋線

AKITSU
（秋津・あきつ）JR

OOIZUMIGAKUEN
（大泉学園・おおいずみがくえん）

SHAKUJII-KOEN
（石神井公園・しゃくじいこうえん）

NERIMA
（練馬・ねりま）E35

EKODA
（江古田・えこだ）

To SHIN-KIBA
YURAKUCHO LINE

T03
JR

SHINJUKU LINE 新宿線

TAKADANOBABA
（高田馬場・たかだのばば）

SHI-SEKI

KAMI-SHAKUJII

NOGATA

ARAIYAKUSHI-MAE

NAKAI E32
（中井・なかい）

SHIMO-OCHIAI

SEIBU SHINJUKU
（西武新宿・せいぶしんじゅく）

SASHI-SAKAI JR
（武蔵境・むさしさかい）

TAMAGAWA LINE
多摩川線

Tobu-Nikko Line 東武日光線 | Tobu-Isezaki Line 東武伊勢崎線

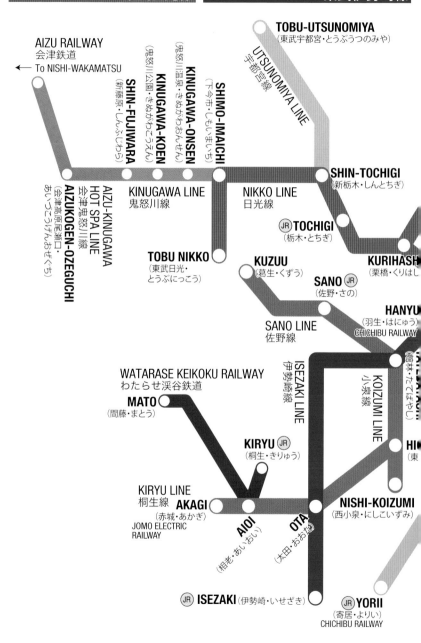

TOBU-UTSUNOMIYA
（東武宇都宮・とうぶうつのみや）

UTSUNOMIYA LINE
宇都宮線

AIZU RAILWAY
会津鉄道
← To NISHI-WAKAMATSU

SHIN-FUJIWARA
（新藤原・しんふじわら）

KINUGAWA-KOEN
（鬼怒川公園・きぬがわこうえん）

KINUGAWA-ONSEN
（鬼怒川温泉・きぬがわおんせん）

SHIMO-IMAICHI
（下今市・しもいまいち）

SHIN-TOCHIGI
（新栃木・しんとちぎ）

AIZUKOGEN-OZEGUCHI
（会津高原尾瀬口・あいづこうげんおぜぐち）

AIZU-KINUGAWA HOT SPA LINE
会津鬼怒川線

KINUGAWA LINE
鬼怒川線

NIKKO LINE
日光線

TOCHIGI
（栃木・とちぎ）

TOBU NIKKO
（東武日光・とうぶにっこう）

KUZUU
（葛生・くずう）

SANO
（佐野・さの）

KURIHASH
（栗橋・くりはし

HANYU
（羽生・はにゅう）
CHICHIBU RAILWAY

SANO LINE
佐野線

WATARASE KEIKOKU RAILWAY
わたらせ渓谷鉄道

MATO
（間藤・まとう）

ISEZAKI LINE
伊勢崎線

KOIZUMI LINE
小泉線

（館林・たてばやし）

KIRYU
（桐生・きりゅう）

HIG
（東

KIRYU LINE
桐生線

AKAGI
（赤城・あかぎ）
JOMO ELECTRIC
RAILWAY

AIOI
（相老・あいおい）

OTA
（太田・おおた）

NISHI-KOIZUMI
（西小泉・にしこいずみ）

ISEZAKI（伊勢崎・いせざき）

YORII
（寄居・よりい）
CHICHIBU RAILWAY

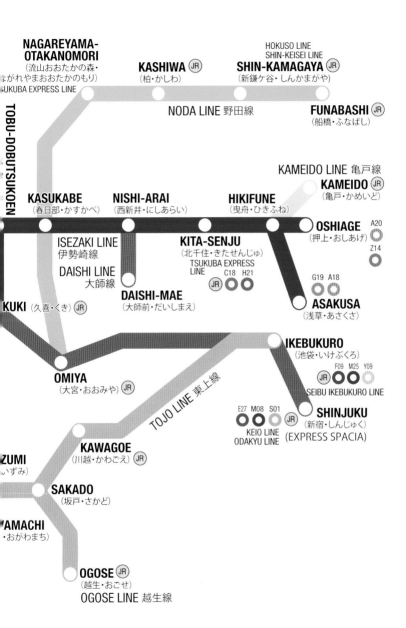

NAGAREYAMA-OTAKANOMORI
（流山おおたかの森・
ながれやまおおたかのもり）
TSUKUBA EXPRESS LINE

KASHIWA (JR)
（柏・かしわ）

HOKUSO LINE
SHIN-KEISEI LINE
SHIN-KAMAGAYA (JR)
（新鎌ケ谷・しんかまがや）

NODA LINE 野田線

FUNABASHI (JR)
（船橋・ふなばし）

TOBU-DOBUTSUKOEN

KAMEIDO LINE 亀戸線
KAMEIDO (JR)
（亀戸・かめいど）

KASUKABE
（春日部・かすかべ）

NISHI-ARAI
（西新井・にしあらい）

HIKIFUNE
（曳舟・ひきふね）

OSHIAGE   A20
（押上・おしあげ）
Z14

ISEZAKI LINE
伊勢崎線

KITA-SENJU
（北千住・きたせんじゅ）
TSUKUBA EXPRESS
LINE   C18 H21
(JR)

DAISHI LINE
大師線

G19 A18

KUKI （久喜・くき）(JR)

DAISHI-MAE
（大師前・だいしまえ）

ASAKUSA
（浅草・あさくさ）

IKEBUKURO
（池袋・いけぶくろ）
F09 M25 Y09
(JR)
SEIBU IKEBUKURO LINE

OMIYA
（大宮・おおみや）(JR)

TOJO LINE 東上線

E27 M08 S01
SHINJUKU
（新宿・しんじゅく）
KEIO LINE   (JR)   (EXPRESS SPACIA)
ODAKYU LINE

ZUMI
（いずみ）

KAWAGOE
（川越・かわごえ）(JR)

SAKADO
（坂戸・さかど）

AMACHI
（おがわまち）

OGOSE (JR)
（越生・おごせ）
OGOSE LINE 越生線

Rinkai Line りんかい線   Yurikamome Line ゆりかもめ線

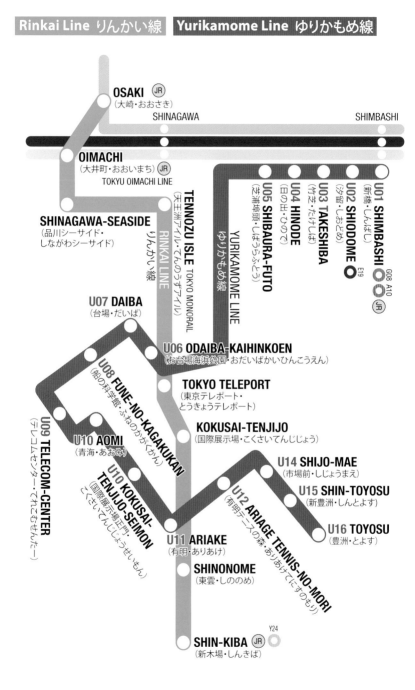

OSAKI (JR)
(大崎・おおさき)

SHINAGAWA

SHIMBASHI

OIMACHI
(大井町・おおいまち) (JR)
TOKYU OIMACHI LINE

SHINAGAWA-SEASIDE
(品川シーサイド・
しながわシーサイド)

りんかい線 RINKAI LINE

TENNOZU ISLE TOKYO MONORAIL
天王洲アイル・てんのうずアイル

ゆりかもめ線 YURIKAMOME LINE

U05 **SHIBAURA-FUTO**
(芝浦埠頭・しばうらふとう)

U04 **HINODE**
(日の出・ひので)

U03 **TAKESHIBA**
(竹芝・たけしば)

U02 **SHIODOME**
(汐留・しおどめ)

U01 **SHIMBASHI**
(新橋・しんばし)
G08 A10
(JR)
E19

U07 **DAIBA**
(台場・だいば)

U06 **ODAIBA-KAIHINKOEN**
(お台場海浜公園・おだいばかいひんこうえん)

TOKYO TELEPORT
(東京テレポート・
とうきょうテレポート)

U08 **FUNE-NO-KAGAKUKAN**
(船の科学館・ふねのかがくかん)

KOKUSAI-TENJIJO
(国際展示場・こくさいてんじじょう)

U09 **TELECOM-CENTER**
(テレコムセンター・てれこむせんたー)

U10 **AOMI**
(青海・あおみ)

U10 **KOKUSAI-TENJIJO-SEIMON**
(国際展示場正門・こくさいてんじじょうせいもん)

U14 **SHIJO-MAE**
(市場前・しじょうまえ)

U15 **SHIN-TOYOSU**
(新豊洲・しんとよす)

U12 **ARIAGE TENNIS-NO-MORI**
(有明テニスの森・ありあけてにすのもり)

U16 **TOYOSU**
(豊洲・とよす)

U11 **ARIAKE**
(有明・ありあけ)

SHINONOME
(東雲・しののめ)

SHIN-KIBA (JR)
(新木場・しんきば)
Y24

Tsukuba Express Line つくばエクスプレス線

TSUKUBA
（つくば）

KENKYUGAKUEN
（研究学園・けんきゅうがくえん）

BAMPAKU-KINENKOEN
（万博記念公園・ばんぱくきねんこうえん）

MIDORINO
（みどりの）

MIRAIDAIRA
（みらい平・みらいだいら）

MORIYA JOSO LINE
（守谷・もりや）

KASHIWA-TANAKA
（柏たなか・かしわたなか）

KASHIWANOHA-CAMPUS
（柏の葉キャンパス・かしわのはキャンパス）

NAGAREYAMA-ŌTAKANOMORI TOBU NODA LINE
（流山おおたかの森・ながれやまおおたかのもり）

NAGAREYAMA-CENTRALPARK
（流山セントラルパーク・ながれやまセントラルパーク）

MINAMI-NAGAREYAMA JR
（南流山・みなみながれやま）

MISATO-CHUO
（三郷中央・みさとちゅうおう）

YASHIO
（八潮・やしお）

ROKUCHO
（六町・ろくちょう）

AOI
（青井・あおい）

H21 C18
KITA-SENJU JR ○ ○ TOBU ISEZAKI LINE
（北千住・きたせんじゅ）

H20
MINAMI-SENJU JR ○
（南千住・みなみせんじゅ）

ASAKUSA
（浅草・あさくさ）

E10
SHIN-OKACHIMACHI ○
（新御徒町・しんおかちまち）

H15
AKIHABARA JR ○
（秋葉原・あきはばら）

Part 7: TOKYO'S BUS ROUTES

Tokyo's Convenient Public Bus Services

Tokyo's Metropolitan government (abbreviated to Toei) operates a large public bus network in the city's 23 wards. There are also a number of private companies as well as adjoining cities that operate bus services to and from Tokyo. All of these bus lines generally cover residential areas not served by subways and trains.

There are over 160 bus routes within Tokyo, most of them departing from terminals at JR stations, and the remainder from terminals in centralized areas of the city. Some of the buses depart at approximately 10-minute intervals and others at 20-minute intervals, depending on the routes. They start operations as early as 6:30 am and the last bus is before 12 midnight. There are special midnight services for a few routes.

Passengers can buy a variety of bus passes that eliminate the need for having to carry cash and figure out the fares. These bus passes include:

TOEI ONE-DAY ECONOMY BUS PASS:
This pass entitles passengers to an unlimited number of rides on Toei buses, trains and streetcars and is valid on any day within a six-month period. Another type of one-day pass is good only on the day of purchase. Cost is ¥500 (adult) and ¥250 (child). The One-Day Economy Pass can be purchased from any of the Arakawa Line or Toei subway stations, and from sales offices of Toei buses at various places in Tokyo.

TOEI ONE-DAY BUS PASS: This pass is good only on Toei buses in Tokyo's 23 wards, and can be purchased at Toei bus depots, at Toei bus information centers, and on buses. It is valid on any day during a six-month period. Cost is ¥500 (adult) and ¥250 (child).

Long-time visitors and residents can buy commuter passes that are valid for one to three months.

A private company, PASMO Co. Ltd., also sells a special bus and train pass that is used by passing it over an electronic reader that automatically deducts the fare from the amount stored in the card. It is valid in all of the city's 23 wards. The company also sells a card that is good on Toei subway lines. Such PASMO cards can be bought with prepaid amounts from ¥1,000 to ¥20,000 — plus a ¥500 deposit.

However, using city buses is generally not recommended for short-time visitors to Tokyo for a number of reasons. For one, all of the signs are in Japanese, either ideograms or Roman letters. Drivers generally speak only Japanese and typically cannot answer questions by foreign passengers about such things as fares and stops. Most buses are not equipped to accommodate disabled persons. [Getting luggage on and off the buses is a special hassle.]

Visitors who need or choose to use buses are advised to have their destinations written out in Japanese, along with the correct bus-line name and/or number and the number of the Stand from which it leaves the bus terminal. [There are, for example, over two dozen Departure Stands at the two open-air Shibuya Bus Terminals adjoining the JR Shibuya Station (one on the east side and one of the west side).]

Some bus lines charge set fares; others charge by the distance. Stops are often as far apart as 1.6 km or more. If you do choose or need to ride a city bus, pick up a copy of the **TOEI Bus Route Map**, published by the city's Bureau of Transportation, at a Tourist Information Center desk in Narita Airport and at other key locations in Tokyo, including bus information centers and larger train and subway station offices.

Toei One-Day Bus Pass

Public Bus

Most of the local public bus routes in Tokyo's 23 Wards are run by Toei Bus Company, while a couple of smaller bus companies run bus routes to and from Tokyo. These bus routes usually cover routes not served by the train or subway lines. There are also other special tour buses that enable the passenger to travel beyond Tokyo. (Please refer to pages 158–159, 169, 189–191, 194).

Most of the city-operated bus lines in Tokyo charge a flat fare regardless of the distance traveled. Board at the front of the bus, 1) drop your fare into the fare slot and the driver will give you change if there are any. 2) Tap a PASMO or Suica card (IC card) against the IC reader. When your stop is announced, press the Disembark button nearest to you, and leave by the rear door.

Slot Ticket Machine

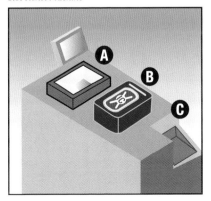

For local buses, the fare is fixed at ¥210 (adult) and ¥110 (child; 6 to 11 years). The regular fare for a shuttle bus is ¥190 (adult) and ¥100 (child), while that for Access Line bus is ¥100 (adult) and ¥50 (child). Up to two children below the age of 5 (this includes a 6-year child, who has not started elementary schooling) can ride free-of-charge if accompanied by an adult or a child passenger. Infants also ride free-of-charge.

GET ON BOARD FROM THE FRONT DOOR.

Pay the Fare
THE FARE IS 200 YEN PER RIDE.
1. Insert coins in (A). Insert a 1,000-yen bill in (C).
2. If you have a PASMO or Suica card, tap it against (B).
* If you require a Toei Bus One-Day Pass, please purchase it from the driver.

PRESS THE DISEMBARK BUTTON
When your stop is announced, press the Disembark button on the nearest window pillar.

Tokyo's Skybus Tours

Skybus Tokyo, Japan's first open-top double-decker sightseeing bus, tours the central districts of the city, giving riders a good view of the outer grounds of the Imperial Palace, the Otemachi financial district, the Diet Building, the government center, the famous Ginza shopping district and the Nihonbashi business district. The trip takes about 45 minutes and features a recorded audio guide in Japanese and English. The bus leaves from the front of Tokyo Station daily from 10 am to 6 pm. Tickets are available from the Skybus Ticket Office in the lobby of the Mitsubishi Building across from the Marunouchi [west side] South Entrance of Tokyo Station. The colorful bus seats 45. Modest fees, vary with the season.

RESERVATIONS ARE REQUIRED FOR THE TOURS

Reservations are accepted one month in advance. To make a reservation, call 03-3215-0008 (9:30 to 18:00). Reservations can be made at the ticket counter (9:00 to 18:00) on the first floor of Mitsubishi Building, at the Marunouchi South Entrance of Tokyo Station. For information: http://skybus.jp/explains/index/00033.

If seats are available, you may board the bus without reservations.

Route 1:

Kokyo (Imperial Palace), Ginza, Marunouchi
Daily*, from 10 am to 6 pm (Mar 1 to Nov 30); 10 am to 5 pm (Dec 1 to Feb 28). Buses arrive and depart every 60 minutes for the 50-minute tour. Tickets are ¥1,600 for adults and ¥700 for children. Pre-recorded audio information about the sights on the tour is available in Chinese, English and Korean.

Route 2:

Tokyo Tower, Rainbow Bridge
Daily*, from 10:40 am to 5:40 pm (Mar 1 to Sep 30); 10:40 am to 4:40 pm (Oct 1 to Nov 30). Buses arrive and depart every 60 minutes for the 1-hour tour. Tickets are ¥1,800 for adults and ¥900 for children. Pre-recorded audio information about the sights is available in Japanese.

Route 3:

Odaiba night view
Daily*, from 6:30 pm. Buses arrive and depart every 60 minutes for the 2-hour tour. Tickets are ¥2,100 for adults and ¥1,000 for children. Pre-recorded audio information about the sights is available in Japanese..

Route 4:

Tokyo Sky Tree, Asakusa, Akihabara
Daily*, from 10:20 am to 5:20 pm (Aug 7 to Sep 30); 10:20 am to 3:20 pm (Oct 1 to Mar 18). Buses arrive and depart every 60 minutes for the 80-minute tour. Tickets are ¥2,500/¥3,500** for adults and ¥1,200/¥1,700** for children. Pre-recorded audio information about the sights is available in Japanese.
*Except for Jan 1, Feb 28. **one-day ticket/two-days ticket

ROUTE 1	IMPERIAL PALACE, GINZA, MARUNOUCHI
●	**TOKYO STATION (MITSUBISHI BLDG.)** (東京駅：三菱ビル前)
●	**IMPERIAL PALACE** (皇居)
●	**NATIONAL MUSEUM OF MODERN ART** (国立近代美術館)
●	**BRITISH EMBASSY** (イギリス大使館)
●	**NATIONAL THEATER** (国立劇場)
●	**SUPREME COURT** (最高裁判所)
●	**DIET BUILDING** (国会議事堂)
●	**KASUMIGASEKI (GAVERNMENT MINISTRIES)** (霞ヶ関)
●	**GINZA** (銀座)
●	**TOKYO STATION (MITSUBISHI BLDG.)** (東京駅：三菱ビル前)

ROUTE 2	**TOKYO TOWER, RAINBOW BRIDGE**	
	ROUTE 3	**ODAIBA NIGHT VIEW**
●	●	**TOKYO STATION (MITSUBISHI BLDG.)** (東京駅：三菱ビル前)
●	●	**IMPERIAL PALACE** (皇居)
●	●	**TOKYO TOWER** (東京タワー)
●	●	**RAINBOW BRIDGE** (レインボーブリッジ)
	●	**ODAIBA** (お台場) (A break at 60 min. interval at AQUA CITY)
	●	**RAINBOW BRIDGE** (レインボーブリッジ)
●	●	**TOYOSU** (豊洲)
●	●	**TSUKIJI** (築地)
●	●	**GINZA** (銀座)
●	●	**HIBIYA** (日比谷)
●	●	**MARUNOUCHI** (丸の内)
●	●	**TOKYO STATION (MITSUBISHI BLDG.)** (東京駅：三菱ビル前)

ROUTE 4	**TOKYO SKY TREE, ASAKUSA, AKIHABARA**
●	**TOKYO STATION (MITSUBISHI BLDG.)** (東京駅：三菱ビル前)
●	**UENO STATION** (上野駅)
●	**TOKYO SKY TREE** (東京スカイツリー)
●	**ASAKUSA HANAKAWADO** (浅草花川戸(浅草寺東参道))
●	**UENO MATSUZAKAYA** (上野松坂屋)
●	**AKIHABARA** (秋葉原)
●	**SHIN-NIHONBASHI** (新日本橋駅(三井タワー／三越))
●	**TOKYO STATION (MITSUBISHI BLDG.)** (東京駅：三菱ビル前)

Tokyo Station — Ginza — Tsukiji 東京駅 — 銀座 — 築地

ROUTE NUMBER	START	VIA	TERMINUS
都 04	TOKYO STATION MARUNOUCHI SOUTH EXIT	KACHIDOKI STATION/GINZA YONCHOME	TOYOMI SUISAN PIER

都 04

Toei Bus Route 04

TOKYO STATION MARUNOUCHI SOUTH EXIT （東京駅丸の内南口） (JR) ○ M17

TOKYO INTERNATIONAL FORUM （東京国際フォーラム） (JR) ○ Y18

YURAKUCHO STATION （有楽町駅） (JR) ○ Y18

SUKIYABASHI （数寄屋橋） ○ H08 ○ M08

GINZA-YONCHOME (MITSUKOSHI DEPT STORE) （銀座四丁目（三越前）） ○ G09

TSUKIJI FISH MARKET （築地） ○ H10

TSUKIJI SANCHOME （築地三丁目）

TSUKIJI ROKUCHOME (CHUO-SHIJO) （築地六丁目（中央市場前）） ○ E18

KACHIDOKIBASHI SOUTH END （勝どき橋南詰）

KACHIDOKI STATION （勝どき駅） ○ E17

KACHIDOKI SANCHOME （勝どき三丁目）

NIIJIMABASHI （新島橋）

TSUKISHIMA POLICE POST （月島警察署）

TOYOMI SUISAN PIER （豊海水産埠頭）

Tokyo Station — Yurakucho — Ginza — Tsukiji
東京駅 — 有楽 — 銀座 — 築地

ROUTE NUMBER	START	VIA	TERMINUS
都 05	TOKYO STATION MARUNOUCHI SOUTH EXIT	GINZA YONCHOME/ YURAKUCHO STATION	HARUMI PIER

都 05

Toei Bus Route 05

TOKYO STATION MARUNOUCHI SOUTH EXIT （東京駅丸の内南口） JR ● M17

TOKYO INTERNATIONAL FORUM （東京国際フォーラム） JR ● Y18

YURAKUCHO STATION （有楽町駅） JR ● Y18

SUKIYABASHI （数寄屋橋） ● H08 ● M08

GINZA YONCHOME (MITSUKOSHI DEPT STORE) （銀座四丁目（三越前）） ● G09

TSUKIJI FISH MARKET （築地） ● H10

TSUKIJI SANCHOME （築地三丁目）

TSUKIJI ROKUCHOME (CHUO-SHIJO) （築地六丁目（中央市場前）） ● E18

KACHIDOKIBASHI SOUTH END （勝どき橋南詰）

KACHIDOKI STATION （勝どき駅） ● E17

HARUMI TORITON SQUARE （晴海トリトンスクエア）

HARUMI-SANCHOME （晴海三丁目）

HOTEL MARINERS' COURT TOKYO （ホテルマリナーズコート東京）

HOTTO PURAZA HARUMI EXIT （ほっとプラザはるみ入り口）

HARUMI PIER （晴海埠頭）

TOKYO TOURIST BUS: Tokyo Station — Ueno — Asakusa — Tokyo SkyTree — Kinshicho
東京→夢の下町バス: 上野 — 浅草 — 東京スカイツリー —錦糸町

ROUTE NUMBER	START	VIA	TERMINUS	REMARKS
	UENO MATSUZAKAYA	ASAKUSA / TOKYO SKYTREE	JR KINSHICHO STATION	The bus runs every day, every 30 minutes. No reservations required.
	JR KINSHICHO STATION	TOKYO SKYTREE / ASAKUSA	UENO MATSUZAKAYA	

CATEGORY	REGULAR FARES	Toei One-Day Economy Bus Pass
ADULT	¥210	¥500
CHILD	¥110	¥250

Toei Bus Route S1

BUS STOP	Famous sights around each bus stop
TOKYO STATION **MARUNOUCHI NORTH EXIT** (JR) M17 (Saturday, Sunday and Holiday) (東京駅丸の内北口)	Imperial Palace Outer Gardens 皇居外苑 Nijubashi Bridge 二重橋 Wadakura Fountain Park 和田倉噴水公園 Marunouchi Naka-dori Shopping Street 丸の内仲通り
NIHONBASHI MITSUKOSHI G12 Z09 (Saturday, Sunday and Holiday) (日本橋三越)	Bank of Japan 日本銀行 Mitsui Memorial Museum 三井記念美術館 Mitsukoshi Department Store 三越デパート Nihonbashi Bridge 日本橋
SUDACHO (AKIHABARA ELECTRONICS CITY) (Saturday, Sunday and Holiday) (JR) (須田町(秋葉原電気街入口))	Akihabara Electronics City 秋葉原電気街 Tsukumo Robot Kingdom ツクモロボット王国 Tokyo Anime Center 東京アニメセンター
UENO MATSUZAKAYA MAE (UENO OKACHI-MACHI STATION) (上野松坂屋前(上野御徒町駅前))	Ameyoko Shopping Street アメ横商店街 Matsuzakaya Department Store 上野松坂屋
UENO PARK-YAMASHITA G16 H17 (上野公園山下) (JR) KEISEI LINE	Ameyoko Shopping Street アメ横商店街 Tokyo National Museum 東京国立博物館 Ueno Zoo 上野動物公園
KIKUYA-BASHI G18 **(KAPPABASHI-DOUGUGAI)** (菊屋橋(かっぱ橋道具街))	Kappabashi Dougugai (Kitchenware Town) Shopping Street かっぱ橋道具街
ASAKUSA-KAMINARIMON G19 A18 (浅草雷門) TOBU LINE	Kaminarimon Gate 雷門 Nakamise-dori Street 仲見世通り Senso-ji Temple 浅草寺
TOKYO SKYTREE STATION (東京スカイツリー駅入口(業平橋)) TOBU LINE	Tokyo Skytree 東京スカイツリー Tokyo Sora Machi (shopping mall) 東京ソラマチ Sumida Aquarium すみだ水族館
OSHIAGE STATION Z14 A20 (押上駅)	
KINSHICHO STATION (錦糸町駅) (JR) Z13	

Free Shuttle Bus : Tokyo Station — Otemachi — Hibiya — Yurakucho 丸の内シャトル

GENERAL ROUTE	10:00 ~ 20:00 (daily, except Jan 1)	This free tourist bus service covers Maru-nouchi, the premiere business district in central Tokyo. Buses leave every 15 to 20 minutes, and the tour lasts about 45 minutes. No reservations required. It is first come, first served.
OTEMACHI ROUTE	8:00 ~ 10:00 (weekdays only)	
FARE	**FREE**	

GENERAL ROUTE	OTEMACHI ROUTE	STOPS	LINKED STATIONS
		MITSUBISHI BLDG. (三菱ビル)	TOKYO STATION (JR LINE, MARUNOUCHI LINE)
		SHIN-MARUNOUCHI BLDG. (新丸ビル)	TOKYO STATION (JR LINE, MARUNOUCHI LINE)
		OTEMACHI TOWER (大手町タワー)	OTEMACHI STATION
		TOKYO SANKEI BLDG. (東京サンケイビル)	
		NIKKEI BLDG. (日経ビル)	
		KEIDANREN KAIKAN & JA BLDG. (経団連会館、JAビル)	
		YOMIURI SHIMBUN (読売新聞)	OTEMACHI STATION (TOZAI LINE, CHIYODA LINE, MITA LINE, HANZOMON LINE, MARUNOUCHI LINE)
		YUSEN BLDG. (郵船ビル)	TOKYO STATION (JR LINE, MARUNOUCHI LINE)
		MARUNOUCHI MY PLAZA (丸の内マイプラザ)	NIJUBASHI-MAE STATION (CHIYODA LINE)
		DAIICHI LIFE (第一生命)	NIJUBASHI-MAE STATION (CHIYODA LINE)
		HIBIYA (日比谷)	HIBIYA STATION (HIBIYA LINE, MITA LINE, CHIYODA LINE)
		SHIN-KOKUSAI BLDG. (BIC CAMERA) (新国際ビル(ビックカメラ))	YURAKUCHO STATION (JR LINE, YURAKUCHO LINE)
		MITSUBISHI BLDG. (三菱ビル)	TOKYO STATION (JR LINE, MARUNOUCHI LINE)

Free Shuttle Bus: Tokyo Station — Ginza — Nihonbashi
メトロリンク日本橋

TIMES	10:00 ~ 20:00	This free daily bus tour takes you around the Nihonbashi [Japan Bridge] district—the main district during the famed Edo Shogunate period. Buses leave about every 10 minutes, and reservations are not required.
FARE	**FREE**	

GENERAL ROUTE	STOPS	LINKED STATIONS / NEAREST SITES
	TOKYO STATION YAESU EXIT (東京駅八重洲口)	JR LINE
	GOFUKUBASHI (呉服橋)	
	NIHONBASHI STATION (地下鉄日本橋駅)	TOZAI LINE, GINZA LINE, ASAKUSA LINE NEAREST SITE: COREDO Nihonbashi, TAKASHIMAYA DEPARTMENT STORE
	MITSUKOSHI-MAE STATION (地下鉄三越前駅)	GINZA LINE, HANZOMON LINE NEAREST SITE: MITSUKOSHI NIHOBASHI DEPARTMENT STORE
	MITSUI MEMORIAL MUSEUM (三井記念美術館)	MITSUKOSHI-MAE STATION (GINZA LINE), SHIN-NIHONBASHI STATION (JR LINE) NEAREST SITE: MITSUI MEMORIAL MUSEUM
	JR SHIN-NIHONBASHI STATION (JR新日本橋駅)	JR LINE
	NIHONBASHI-MUROMACHI-ITCHOME (日本橋室町一丁目)	MITSUKOSHI-MAE STATION (GINZA LINE, HANZOMON LINE)
	NIHONBASHI SOUTH (日本橋南詰)	NEAREST SITE: COREDO NIHONBASHI
	NIHONBASHI-NICHOME (日本橋二丁目)	MITSUKOSHI-MAE STATION (GINZA LINE) NEAREST SITE: TAKASHIMAYA DEPARTMENT STORE
	NIHONBASHI-SANCHOME (日本橋三丁目)	MITSUKOSHI-MAE STATION (GINZA LINE)
	KYOBASHI STATION, MUROMACHI STATION (京橋駅、室町駅)	KYOBASHI STATION (GINZA LINE), MUROMACHI STATION (ASAKUSA LINE) NEAREST SITE: NATIONAL FILM CENTER
	KYOBASHI-NICHOME (京橋二丁目)	NEAREST SITE: BRIDGESTONE MUSEUM
	KYOBASHI-ITCHOME (京橋一丁目)	NEAREST SITE: YAESU SHOPPING MALL

Tokyo Station — Ginza — Harumi — Tokyo Bigsight
東京駅 — 銀座 — 築地 — 晴海 — 東京ビッグサイト

ROUTE NUMBER	START	VIA	TERMINUS
都 05	TOKYO STATION MARUNOUCHI SOUTH EXIT	ARIAKE TENNIS-NO-MORI/GINZA YONCHOME	TOKYO BIG SIGHT

Toei Bus Route 5

TOKYO STATION MARUNOUCHI SOUTH EXIT　（東京駅丸の内南口）　(JR) M17

TOKYO KOKUSAI FORUM　（東京国際フォーラム）(JR) Y18

YURAKUCHO STATION　（有楽町駅）(JR) Y18

SUKIYABASHI　（数寄屋橋）H08 M08

GINZA-YONCHOME (MITSUKOSHI-MAE)　（銀座四丁目（三越前））G09

TSUKIJI　（築地）H10

TSUKIJI-SANCHOME　（築地三丁目）

TSUKIJI-ROKUCHOME (CENTRAL MARKET)　（築地六丁目（中央市場前））E18

KACHIDOKIBASHI SOUTH END　（勝どき橋南詰）

KACHIDOKI STATION　（勝どき駅）E17

HARUMI TORITON SQUARE　（晴海トリトンスクエア）

HARUMI-FUTO (HARUMI PASSENGER TURMINAL)
（晴海埠頭（晴海客船ターミナル））

SHIN-TOYOSU STATION　（新豊洲駅前）U15

ARIAKE-NICHOME　（有明二丁目）

ARIAKE COLOSSEUM　（有明コロシアム）

ARIAKE TENNIS-NO-MORI　（有明テニスの森）

ARIAKE-ITCHOME　（有明一丁目）

TOKYO BIG SIGHT　（東京ビッグサイト）

The following shuttle bus tours of the famed Asakusa and Ueno districts cover the most important, historical and present-day attractions.

MEGURIN BUS	START & TERMINUS	FARE	7:30 (holiday 8:30) ~ 19:45 Runs daily, every 15 minutes
	ASAKUSA Station UENO Station	¥100 ¥300 (One-day ticket)	

Asakusa Senso Ji Temple Shuttle 浅草—浅草寺シャトルバス

NORTH ROUTE	BUS STOPS	LINKED STATIONS / NEAREST SITES
	ASAKUSA STATION (浅草駅)	TOBU LINE, GINZA LINE, ASAKUSA LINE
	SUMIDA PARK (隅田公園)	
	RIVERSIDE SPORTS CENTER (リバーサイド・スポーツセンター前)	
	IMADO-NICHOME (今戸二丁目)	
	MINOWA STATION (三ノ輪駅)	HIBIYA LINE, TODEN ARAKAWA LINE
	ICHIYO MEMORIAL EXIT (一葉記念館入口)	
	UGUISUDANI STATION (鴬谷駅)	JR LINE
	IRIYA STATION ENTRANCE (入谷駅入口)	HIBIYA LINE
	SENZOKU-NICHOME (千束二丁目)	
	ASAKUSA-GOCHOME (浅草五丁目)	
	ASAKUSA POLICE POST (浅草警察署前)	SENSO-JI
	SENSO-JI TEMPLE NORTH (浅草寺北)	
	NITENMON (二天門)	SENSO-JI
	ASAKUSA STATION (浅草駅)	TOBU LINE, GINZA LINE, ASAKUSA LINE

Ueno-Asakusa Shuttle 上野—浅草シャトルバス

SOUTH ROUTE	BUS STOPS	LINKED STATIONS / NEAREST SITES
	UENO STATION (上野駅)	JR LINE, GINZA LINE, HIBIYA LINE
	OKACHIMACHI (御徒町)	
	SHIN-OKACHIMACHI STATION (新御徒町駅)	OEDO LINE
	MITSUIKINEN HOSPITAL (三井記念病院前)	
	ASAKUSABASHI STATION NORTH (浅草橋駅北)	
	TORIGOE JINJA (鳥越神社前)	
	OEDO-SEN KURAMAE STATION (大江戸線蔵前駅)	OEDO LINE
	TAWARAMACHI STATION (田原町駅)	GINZA LINE
	KAPPABASHI (かっぱ橋)	OEDO LINE
	TAITO KUYAKUSHO WARD OFFICE (台東区役所)	
	UENO STATION (上野駅)	JR LINE, GINZA LINE, HIBIYA LINE

Shinagawa—Telecom Center 品川駅ー東京テレポート

ROUTE NUMBER	START	TERMINUS
波 01	SHINAGAWA STATION	TOKYO TELEPORT STATION

Toei Bus: Odaiba Route 01

SHINAGAWA STATION (KONAN EXIT) （品川駅港南口）(JR)

HAMAJI-BASHI （浜路橋）

KONAN-SANCHOME （港南三丁目）

GOSHIKI-BASHI （五色橋）

KAIGAN-DORI （海岸通）

(Cross THE RAINBOW BRIDGE)

ODAIBA KAIHIN PARK STATON （お台場海浜公園駅） U06

DAIBA-NICHOME （台場二丁目）

FUJI TELEVISION （フジテレビ）

DAIBA STATION （台場駅） U07

FUNENOKAGAKU-KAN STATION （船の科学館駅） U08

NIHON KAGAKU MIRAIKAN （日本科学未来館）
(National Museum of Emerging Science & Innovation)

TOKYO KOWAN GODO CHOSHA （東京港湾合同庁舎）

TELECOM CENTER STATION （テレコムセンター駅） U09

TOKYO TELEPORT STATION （東京テレポート駅）

Odaiba Bay Shuttle Bus (Loop Line) 東京ベイシャトル

GENERAL ROUTE	11:00 ~ 20:00	This daily shuttle bus service loops around Odaiba Island in Tokyo Bay, departing every 15-20 minutes and dropping you off wherever you wish to shop or sight-see. There are eight scheduled stops at key locations.
FARE	**FREE**	

GENERAL ROUTE	BUS STOPS	LINKED STATIONS / NEAREST SITES
●	**MIRAIKAN** (日本科学未来館)	FUNENOKAGAKUKAN STATION (YURIKAMOME LINE)
●	**FUJI TV WANGAN STUDIO** (フジテレビ湾岸スタジオ)	
●	**VENUS FORT** (ヴィーナスフォート)	AOMI STATION (YURIKAMOME LINE) NEAREST SITE: PALETTE TOWN
●	**TOKYO TELEPORT** (東京テレポート駅)	TOKYO TELEPORT STATION (RINKAI LINE)
●	**DIVER CITY TOKYO** (ダイバーシティ東京)	DAIBA STATION (YURIKAMOME LINE)
●	**AQUA CITY ODAIBA** (アクアシティお台場)	DAIBA STATION (YURIKAMOME LINE)
●	**FUJI TELEVISION** (フジテレビ)	DAIBA STATION (YURIKAMOME LINE)
●	**HOTEL GRAND PACIFIC LE DAIBA** (ホテルグランパシフィック LE DAIBA)	DAIBA STATION (YURIKAMOME LINE)
●	**AOMI PARKING LOT** (青海臨時駐車場)	FUNENOKAGAKUKAN STATION (YURIKAMOME LINE)

Meguro — Shirokane — Ebisu — Azabu — Tokyo Tower
目黒 — 白金 — 恵比寿 — 麻布 — 東京タワー

ROUTE NUMBER	START	VIA	TERMINUS
橋86折返	MEGURO STATION	AZABU-JUBAN STATION	TOKYO TOWER

Toei Bus Route 94

MEGURO STATION （目黒駅）(JR) A05

KAMI-OSAKI （上大崎）

SHIROKANEDAI-GOCHOME （白金台五丁目）

TODAI IKAKEN HOSPITAL WEST GATE （東大医科研病院西門）

SHIROKANE-ROKUCHOME （白金六丁目）

EBISU-SANCHOME （恵比寿三丁目）

TENGENJIBASHI （天現寺橋）

HIROBASHI （広尾橋）

AIIKU HOSPITAL （愛育病院）

MOTO AZAZU-NICHOME （元麻布二丁目）

SENDAIZAKA-UE （仙台坂上）

SENDAIZAKA-SHITA （仙台坂下）

NINOHASHI （二ノ橋）

AZABU-JUBAN STATION （麻布十番駅（一ノ橋）) E22 N04

NAKANOHASHI （中ノ橋）

AKABANEBASHI STATION （赤羽橋駅） E21

HIGASHI AZABU-ITCHOME （東麻布一丁目）

TORANOMON-GOCHOME （虎ノ門五丁目）

KAMIYACHO STATION （神谷町駅） H05

ONARIMON （御成門） A09

TOKYO TOWER （東京タワー）

Shibuya — Roppongi — Shimbashi 渋谷駅 — 六本木 — 新橋

ROUTE NUMBER	START	VIA	TERMINUS
都01	SHIBUYA STATION	ROPPONGI STATION, TAMEIKE	SHIMBASHI STATION
都01 折返	SHIBUYA STATION	NISHI-AZABU	ROPPONGI HILLS
RH01	SHIBUYA STATION	(DIRECT)	ROPPONGI HILLS

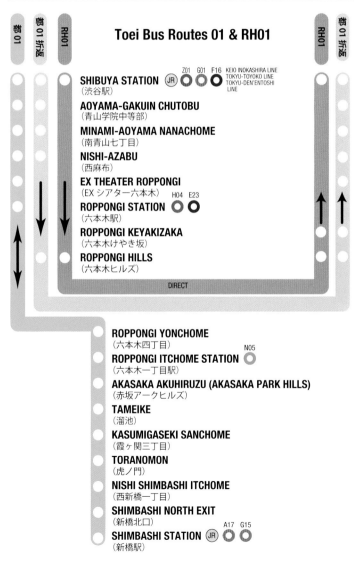

Toei Bus Routes 01 & RH01

都01　都01折返　RH01

SHIBUYA STATION (JR) ○ ○ ○
Z01　G01　F16　KEIO INOKASHIRA LINE
TOKYU-TOYOKO LINE
TOKYU-DEN'ENTOSHI LINE
(渋谷駅)

AOYAMA-GAKUIN CHUTOBU
(青山学院中等部)

MINAMI-AOYAMA NANACHOME
(南青山七丁目)

NISHI-AZABU
(西麻布)

EX THEATER ROPPONGI
(EX シアター六本木)

ROPPONGI STATION ○ ○
H04　E23
(六本木駅)

ROPPONGI KEYAKIZAKA
(六本木けやき坂)

ROPPONGI HILLS
(六本木ヒルズ)

DIRECT

ROPPONGI YONCHOME
(六本木四丁目)

ROPPONGI ITCHOME STATION ○
N05
(六本木一丁目駅)

AKASAKA AKUHIRUZU (AKASAKA PARK HILLS)
(赤坂アークヒルズ)

TAMEIKE
(溜池)

KASUMIGASEKI SANCHOME
(霞ヶ関三丁目)

TORANOMON
(虎ノ門)

NISHI SHIMBASHI ITCHOME
(西新橋一丁目)

SHIMBASHI NORTH EXIT
(新橋北口)

SHIMBASHI STATION (JR) ○ ○
A17　G15
(新橋駅)

Roppongi-Azabu-Asakusa Shuttle ちいばす [赤坂・田町ルート]

CHII BUS	START & TERMINUS		FARE	7:30 ~ 19:45 Runs daily, every 15 minutes
	ROUTE 1: TAMACHI STATION — ROPPONGI HILLS ROUTE 2: ROPPONGI HILLS — ROPPONGI STATION		¥100	

ROUTE 1	ROUTE 2	BUS STOPS	CONNECTING TO
●		**TAMACHI STATION EAST EXIT** (田町駅東口)	JR LINE
●		**TAMACHI STATION** (田町駅)	JR LINE
●		**MITA STATION** (三田線三田駅)	MITA LINE
●		**AKABANEBASHI STATION** (赤羽橋駅)	OEDO LINE
●		**AZABU-JUBAN STATION** (麻布十番駅)	OEDO LINE, NAMBOKU LINE
●		**ROPPONGI KEYAKIZAKA** (六本木けやき坂)	
●	○	**ROPPONGI HILLS** (六本木ヒルズ)	
●	○	**ROPPONGI KEYAKIZAKA** (六本木けやき坂)	
●	○	**ROPPONGI STATION** (六本木駅)	HIBIYA LINE, OEDO LINE
	○	**AKASAKA STATION** (赤坂駅)	CHOYODA LINE
	○	**AKASAKA-MITSUKE STATION** (赤坂見附駅)	GINZA LINE, MARUNOUCHI LINE
	○	**AOYAMA-ITCHOME STATION** (青山一丁目駅)	GINZA LINE, HANZOMON LINE, OEDO LINE
	○	**ROPPONGI STATION** (六本木駅)	HIBIYA LINE, OEDO LINE
	○	**ROPPONGI HILLS** (六本木ヒルズ)	
●		**TAMACHI STATION EAST EXIT** (田町駅東口)	JR LINE

Shibuya—Harajuku—Omotesando Shuttle
ハチ公バス [神宮の杜、夕焼けこやけルート]

HACHIKO BUS	START & TERMINUS		FARE	8:00 ~ 20:00 Runs daily, every 15 minutes
	ROUTE 1: SHIBUYA STATION — HARAJUKU, OMOTESANDO ROUTE 2: SHIBUYA WARD OFFICE — DAIKANYAMA		¥100	

ROUTE 1	ROUTE 2	BUS STOPS	CONNECTING TO
●		**SHIBUYA STATION HACHIKO EXIT** (渋谷駅ハチ公口)	JR, GINZA, HANZOMON, FUKUTOSHIN, TOKYU, INOKASHIRA LINE
●		**DENRYOKU KAN** (電力館)	
●	●	**SHIBUYA WARD GOVT OFFICES** (渋谷区役所)	
●	●	**KOKURITSU-YOYOGI STADIUM** (国立代々木競技場)	OEDO LINE
●	●	**HARAJUKU STATION EXIT** (原宿駅入口)	JR, CHIYODA LINE
●	●	**MEIJI-JINGU SHRINE (HARAJUKU STATION)** (明治神宮(原宿駅))	JR, CHIYODA LINE
●	●	**MEIJI-JINGU SHRINE-MAE STATION** (明治神宮前駅)	CHIYODA LINE, FUKUTOSHIN LINE
●	●	**OMOTESANDO HILLS** (表参道ヒルズ)	JR LINE
●	●	**OMOTESANDO STATION** (表参道駅)	GINZA LINE, CHIYODA LINE, HANZOMON LINE
●	●	**KOKURITSU NOHGAKUDO** (国立能楽堂)	
●	●	**YOYOGI STATION** (代々木駅)	JR, OEDO LINE
●	●	**SHIBUYA STATION HACHIKO EXIT** (渋谷駅ハチ公口)	JR, KEIO INOKASHIRA LINE, GINZA, FUKUTOSHIN, HANZOMON LINE
	●	**SHIBUYA STATION EAST EXIT** (渋谷駅東口)	JR, KEIO INOKASHIRA LINE, GINZA, FUKUTOSHIN, HANZOMON LINE
	●	**EBISU STATION EAST EXIT** (恵比寿駅東口)	JR, HIBIYA LINE
	●	**YEBISU GARDEN PLACE** (恵比寿ガーデンプレイス)	
	●	**EBISU STATION EXIT** (恵比寿駅入口)	JR, HIBIYA LINE
	●	**DAIKANYAMA STATION** (代官山駅)	TOKYU DEN'EN TOSHI LINE
	●	**SHIBUYA STATION WEST EXIT** (渋谷駅西口)	JR, KEIO INOKASHIRA LINE, GINZA, FUKUTOSHIN, HANZOMON LINE
	●	**DENRYOKUKAN** (電力館)	
	●	**KOKURITSU-YOYOGI STADIUM** (国立代々木競技場)	OEDO LINE
	●	**SHUBUYA WARD GOVT. OFFICES** (渋谷区役所)	

Roppongi — Azabu-juban — Shinagawa — Gotanda
六本木 — 麻布十番 — 品川 — 五反田

ROUTE NUMBER	START	VIA	TERMINUS
反 96	GOTANDA STATION	ROPPONGI HILLS/ROPPONGI STATION	GOTANDA STATION

Toei Bus Route 96

ROPPONGI HILLS （六本木ヒルズ）

ROPPONGI STATION （六本木駅） ○ ○ E23 H04

ROPPONGI GOCHOME （六本木五丁目）

ROPPONGI KEYAKIZAKA （六本木けやき坂）

IIKURA KATAMACHI （飯倉片町）

AZABU-JUBAN STATION (ICHI-NO-HASHI) （麻布十番駅（一ノ橋）） ○ ○ E22 N04

NINOHASHI （二ノ橋）

SANNOHASHI （三ノ橋）

FURUKAWA-BASHI （古川橋）

GYORANZAKA-SHITA （魚藍坂下）

TAKANAWA-ITCHOME （高輪一丁目）

SENGAKUJI （泉岳寺） ○ A07

TAKANAWA-KITAMACHI （高輪北町）

SHINAGAWA STATION （品川駅） JR KEIKYU LINE

YATSUYAMA-BASHI （八ツ山橋）

GOTENYAMA （御殿山）

HIGASHI-GOTANDA-SANCHOME （東五反田三丁目）

HIGASHI-GOTANDA-ITCHOME （東五反田一丁目）

GOTANDA STATION （五反田駅） JR ○ A05

LOOPLINE

Factory Outlet Malls

Most Tokyo suburbs now have large outlet malls where you can buy branded goods at discount prices. Here are some of the best ones.

Gotemba Outlet Malls 御殿場 プレミアム アウトレット

Approximately 95 minutes by train from Tokyo, these malls offer a wide range of international brands (Gucci, Armani, D&G, etc) for fashion wear, and sportswear (Adidas, etc), kidswear and accessories (watches, belts, shoes). It is open daily from 10 am to 7 pm. http:// www.premiumoutlets. co.jp/en/gotemba/

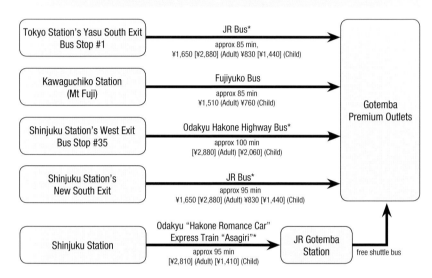

Tokyo Station's Yasu South Exit Bus Stop #1	JR Bus* approx 85 min, ¥1,650 [¥2,880] (Adult) ¥830 [¥1,440] (Child)
Kawaguchiko Station (Mt Fuji)	Fujiyuko Bus approx 85 min ¥1,510 (Adult) ¥760 (Child)
Shinjuku Station's West Exit Bus Stop #35	Odakyu Hakone Highway Bus* approx 100 min [¥2,880] (Adult) [¥2,060] (Child)
Shinjuku Station's New South Exit	JR Bus* approx 95 min ¥1,650 [¥2,880] (Adult) ¥830 [¥1,440] (Child)

Gotemba Premium Outlets

Shinjuku Station → Odakyu "Hakone Romance Car" Express Train "Asagiri"* approx 95 min [¥2,810] (Adult) [¥1,410] (Child) → JR Gotemba Station → free shuttle bus → Gotemba Premium Outlets

Grandberry Malls Machida 三井アウトレットパーク多摩南大沢

The largest commercial complex in Japan, it is reached approximately 36 minutes by train from Tokyo. It offers international brands of fashion wear and accessories (like Coach, Gap), FrancFranc furniture, etc. It is also a favorite place for dog lovers—items for dogs are available here. It is open daily from 10 am to 8 pm. http://www.grandberry.com

Shibuya Station → Toku Den-en-toshi Line* approx 36 min, ¥290 (Adult) ¥150 (Child) → Minami-Machida Station → direct access → Grandberry Mall Machida

*Reservation is required.
Fares in brackets denote round-trip fares.
All trains and buses above operate daily.

Mitsui Outlet Park Makuhari 三井アウトレットパーク幕張

This outlet can be reached by a 30-minute train ride from Tokyo. Kids', men's and women's clothes and sportswear are available, with Japanese brand goods being offered at 30–80% off the regular prices. It opens daily from 10 am to 8 pm. http://www.31op.com/makuhari/foreign/index_en.html

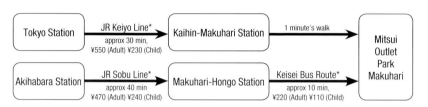

Venus Outlet ヴィーナスアウトレット

Another easily-accessible mall from Tokyo (approximately 25 minutes by train), this mall offers well-known brands of fashion wear (Hunting, Marni, Levi etc), and made-in-Japan cosmetics and electronic goods. Opening hours are 11 am to 9 pm daily. http://www.venusfort.co.jp/multi/en/floormap/3f_list.html

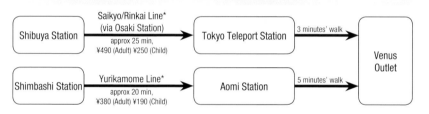

Karuizawa Prince Shopping Plaza 軽井沢プリンスショッピングプラザ

This huge shopping paradise in Nagano can be reached by an-hour Shinkansen ride from Tokyo. Famous brands of fashion (e.g. Gucci, Harrods) and sportswear (Adidas, Oakley) are available here. Its opening hours are 10 am to 7 pm daily. The mall is surrounded by hotels and other facilities. http://www.karuizawa-psp.jp/en/index.html

*Reservation is required.

Part 8: TOKYO DISNEY RESORT

Visiting Tokyo Disney Resort

Tokyo Disney Resort, in Urayasu City, a short distance east of Tokyo, consists of two theme parks, Tokyo Disneyland and Tokyo DisneySea. Tokyo Disneyland, a "Magic Kingdom" park, just like all the others, was the first Disney theme park to be built on non-U.S. territory. Tokyo Disneyland's sister park, Tokyo DisneySea is an oceanic-themed park exclusive to Japan. Tokyo Disney Resort also includes the Ikspiari shopping and entertainment complex.

With over 14 million annual visitors, Tokyo Disneyland is the third most visited theme park in the world behind Walt Disney World's Magic Kingdom and the original Disneyland; DisneySea follows in fifth place, behind fourth-place Disneyland Paris.

The hours of the resort change according to the season. It generally opens between 8 and 9 am and closes between 9 and 10 pm.

Train Service to Disney Resort

For most visitors the most practical way to get to Tokyo Disney Resort is via the JR Keiyo Line from Tokyo Central Station, getting off at Maihama, the 6th stop, which is adjacent to the resort entrance. The trip takes 15 minutes by Express Train and costs ¥210. The Tokyo Disney Resort Welcome Center, where you buy tickets to enter the resort, is immediately to your right after you exit Maihama Station.

Your best ticket bet is the 1-Day Passport, which gives you entry into either Tokyo Disneyland or DisneySea, but not both. Here

Subway and Railway Lines to Tokyo Disney Resort

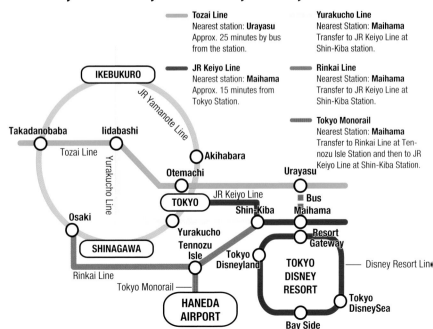

Tozai Line
Nearest station: **Urayasu**
Approx. 25 minutes by bus from the station.

JR Keiyo Line
Nearest station: **Maihama**
Approx. 15 minutes from Tokyo Station.

Yurakucho Line
Nearest Station: **Maihama**
Transfer to JR Keiyo Line at Shin-Kiba station.

Rinkai Line
Nearest Station: **Maihama**
Transfer to JR Keiyo Line at Shin-Kiba Station.

Tokyo Monorail
Nearest Station: **Maihama**
Transfer to Rinkai Line at Tennozu Isle Station and then to JR Keiyo Line at Shin-Kiba Station.

are the Passport charges as of this writing: Adult (18+) ¥5,800, Junior (12–17) ¥5,000, Child (4–11) ¥3,900, Senior (60+) ¥5,100. Tickets can also be purchased from travel agents in Japan.

Bus Service to Disney Resort

A direct bus service to Disneyland and DisneySea is available daily from and to the JR Highway Bus Terminal Tokyo at JR Shinjuku Station's New South Exit. Travel time to Tokyo DisneySea is about 40 minutes; to Disneyland about 50 minutes. Adult fare is ¥800 and children's fare is ¥400, one-way.

It is generally best for visitors staying in Shinjuku hotels as well as other areas of Tokyo to go to Tokyo Central Station via the Marunouchi Subway Line, the Chuo Line or the Yamanote Line, and there transfer to the JR Keiyo Line, which goes to Maihama, the Disneyland station.

There is a limousine bus service from Narita Airport that goes directly to and from Disney Resort. Buy your ticket at one of the limousine bus counters in the Arrival Lobby. The one-way fare is ¥2,400. Travel time is about 60 minutes.

Subway Service to Disney Resort

The Tozai Line goes to Urayasu, requiring a short bus ride to Maihama, the Disneyland station.

The Yurakucho Line goes to Shin-Kiba Station, requiring a transfer to the Keiyo train line to continue on to Maihama. Again, it may be more practical for visitors who have easy access to the Yamanote JR line that encircles central Tokyo to go to Tokyo Central Station and catch a Keiyo train directly to Maihama.

Disney Hotels

Disney Ambassador Hotel (adjacent to Ikspiari): This hotel is themed to the Art Deco era of the 1930's. ¥28,000–¥300,000.

Tokyo Disneyland Hotel (outside the Tokyo Disneyland entrance): An opulent Victorian-style hotel with the best view of Tokyo Disneyland on the side. ¥33,000–¥500,000.

Tokyo DisneySea Hotel MiraCosta (within the Mediterranean Harbor area of Tokyo DisneySea): An Italian-style hotel complete with rooms overlooking Mediterranean Harbor. ¥33,000–¥500,000.

"Official Hotels"

The following hotels are served by the free Disney Resort Cruiser bus service from Bayside Station on the Disney Resort Line monorail:

Hilton Tokyo Bay, 1-8 Maihama Urayasu-shi, 81-047-355-5000

Hotel Okura Tokyo Bay, 1-8 Maihama Urayasu-shi, 81-047-355-3333

Sheraton Grande Tokyo Bay Hotel, 1-9 Maihama Urayasu-shi, 81-047-355-5555

Sunroute Plaza Tokyo, 1-6 Maihama Urayasu-shi, 81-047-355-1111

Tokyo Bay Hotel Tokyu, 1-7 Maihama Urayasu-shi, 81-047-355-2411

Tokyo Bay Maihama Hotel, 1-34 Maihama Urayasu-shi, 81-047-355-1222

Bus Routes to Tokyo Disney Resort

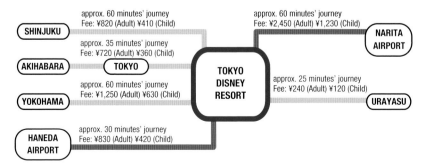

Buses to Tokyo Disney Resort

DEPARTURE POINT	DEPARTURE TIME	FARE		REMARKS
		ADULT	CHILD	
SHINJUKU STATION (NEW SOUTH EXIT, HIGHWAY BUS TERMINAL) 新宿駅新南口、高速バスターミナル	6:40 ~ 9:50	¥820	¥410	To Tokyo DisneySea: 40 mins. To Tokyo Disneyland: 50 mins. Runs daily, every 30–40 mins. No reservations required.
AKIHABARA STATION (CHUO EXIT, BUS TERMINAL) 秋葉原駅中央口バスのりば	WEEKDAY 8:30 ~ 9:40 SAT, SUN & HOLIDAY 10:05 ~ 13:40	¥720	¥360	To Tokyo DisneySea: 35 mins. To Tokyo Disneyland: 40 mins. Runs daily, every 30–55 mins. No reservations required.
TOKYO STATION (YAESU CHUO EXIT; TERMINAL NO. 1) 東京駅八重洲中央口1番バスのりば	WEEKDAY 8:45 ~ 9:25 SAT, SUN & HOLIDAY 10:20 ~ 13:55	¥720	¥360	To Tokyo DisneySea: 35 mins. To Tokyo Disneyland: 40 mins. Runs daily, every 30–60 mins. No reservations required.
KOIWA STATION (SOUTH EXIT; TERMINAL NUMBER 0; ROUTE NO. 07) 小岩駅南口0番バスのりば; 環 07	6:26 ~ 21:10	¥410	¥210	To Tokyo DisneySea: 45 mins. To Tokyo Disneyland: 50 mins. Runs daily, every 30–60 mins. No reservations required.
TOKYO METRO TOZAI LINE URAYASU STATION (SOUTH EXIT; ROUTE NOS. 4, 8, 12) 東京メトロ東西線浦安駅南口 4番、8番、12番バスのりば	WEEKDAY 7:23 ~ 21:09 SAT, SUN & HOLIDAY 7:47 ~ 17:45	¥240	¥120	To Tokyo DisneySea: 25 mins. To Tokyo Disneyland: 25 mins. Runs daily, every 60 mins. No reservations required.
YOKOHAMA STATION (EAST EXIT: TERMINAL NO. 17) 横浜駅東口17番バスのりば	6:15 ~ 18:20	¥1,250	¥630	To Tokyo DisneySea: 50 mins. To Tokyo Disneyland: 60 mins. Runs daily, every 10–30 mins. No reservations required.
KAWASAKI STATION (EAST EXIT; TERMINAL NO. 18) 川崎駅東口18番バスのりば	6:15 ~ 9:35	¥1,230	¥610	To Tokyo DisneySea: 65 mins. To Tokyo Disneyland: 75 mins. Runs daily, every 60–80 mins. No reservations required.
KAMATA STATION (EAST EXIT; TERMINAL NO. 6) 蒲田駅東口6番バスのりば	6:35 ~ 9:55	¥1,130	¥570	To Tokyo DisneySea: 50 mins. To Tokyo Disneyland: 60 mins. Runs daily. No reservations required.
HANEDA AIRPORT (ARRIVAL FLOOR; BUS TERMINAL NO. 6) 羽田空港到着フロア6番バスのりば	7:35 ~ 19:00	¥830	¥420	To Tokyo DisneySea: 50 mins. To Tokyo Disneyland: 60 mins. Runs daily, every 10–20 mins. No reservations required.
NARITA AIRPORT (DAIICHI TERMINAL NO. 7/DAINI TERMINAL NO. 11) 成田空港第1ターミナル7番バスのりば/ 第2ターミナル11バス番のりば	8:00 ~ 17:00	¥2,450	¥1,230	To Tokyo DisneySea: 85 mins. To Tokyo Disneyland: 80 mins. Runs daily, every 60 mins. No reservations required.

Disney Resort Monorail Line ディズニー・リゾート線

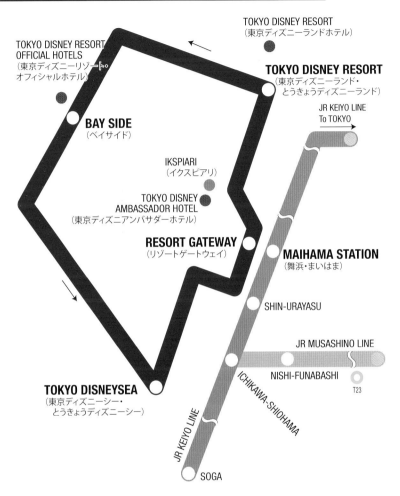

TOKYO DISNEY RESORT
(東京ディズニーランドホテル)

TOKYO DISNEY RESORT
(東京ディズニーランド・
とうきょうディズニーランド)

TOKYO DISNEY RESORT
OFFICIAL HOTELS
(東京ディズニーリゾート・
オフィシャルホテル)

JR KEIYO LINE
To TOKYO

BAY SIDE
(ベイサイド)

IKSPIARI
(イクスピアリ)

TOKYO DISNEY
AMBASSADOR HOTEL
(東京ディズニアンバサダーホテル)

RESORT GATEWAY
(リゾートゲートウェイ)

MAIHAMA STATION
(舞浜・まいはま)

SHIN-URAYASU

JR MUSASHINO LINE

NISHI-FUNABASHI

ICHIKAWA-SHIOHAMA

T23

TOKYO DISNEYSEA
(東京ディズニーシー・
とうきょうディズニーシー)

JR KEIYO LINE

SOGA

Tokyo Disney Resort Partner Hotels

The Tokyo Disney Resort Partner Hotels Program is made up of five hotels located in the Shin-Urayasu area next to the resort. All of these hotels are within a kilometer or two of JR Shin-Urayasu Station, from which Maihama is the first stop in the direction of Tokyo Station. The hotels also have a complimentary shuttle service that runs to and from the Disneyland park entrance.

Hotel Emion Tokyo Bay, 1-1-1 Hinode Urayasu-shi. 81-047-304-2727.

Mitsui Garden Hotel Prana Tokyo Bay, Akemi Urayasu. 6-2-1. 81-047-382-3331

Oriental Hotel Tokyo Bay, 1-8-2 Mihama Urayasu. 81-047-350-8111

Palm & Fountain Terrace Hotel, 7-1-1 Akemi Urayasu-shi. 81-047-353-1234

Urayasu Brighton Hotel, 1-9 Mihama Urayasu-shi. 81-047-355-7777

Yokohama: Japan's Port to the World!

Most visitors to Japan do not have Yokohama on their itinerary, but by skipping this great port city they miss a big slice of both historical and contemporary Japan. Yokohama, about 30–40 train minutes southwest of Tokyo, is the capital of Kanagawa Prefecture, the second largest city in Japan, a major commercial hub in the region, and has its own unique character and personality.

When Japan opened its doors to the outside world in 1854, the Shogunate government initially agreed that the nearby bustling town of Kanagawa-Juku would be one of the ports opened to foreign ships and foreign residents.

But there was so much resistance to having foreigners that close to the capital of Edo [Tokyo] that the government decided to build port facilities in the tiny fishing village of Yokohama on the opposite side of the inlet. In 1859 the Government renamed it the "Port of Yokohama."

By 1860 the newly christened Port of Yokohama had become Japan's primary portal to the outside world, instantly replacing Nagasaki, which had played that role since the early 1600s. Foreign traders and entrepreneurs who flocked to Yokohama attracted Japanese from all over the country, adding to the amazing atmosphere of the port and dramatically increasing the speed of its growth.

In addition to its extraordinary historical attractions [which include one of the largest Chinatowns in the world, the tallest lighthouse in the world, etc.], Yokohama also boasts some of the most futuristic and impressive business, dining, entertainment and shopping districts in the world, including the Landmark Tower complex, one of the tallest buildings in Japan.

Large numbers of Tokyoites, seeking a respite from the hustle and bustle of the capital city, make dining, shopping and recreational trips to Yokohama. Visitors to Japan who have Kamakura and/or Hakone on their agenda should consider a stopover in Yokohama.

Train and Subway Access to Yokohama

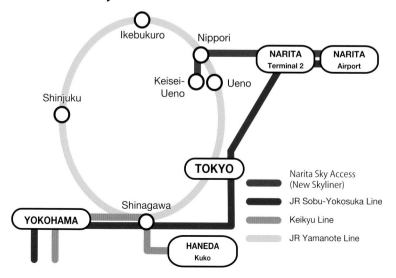

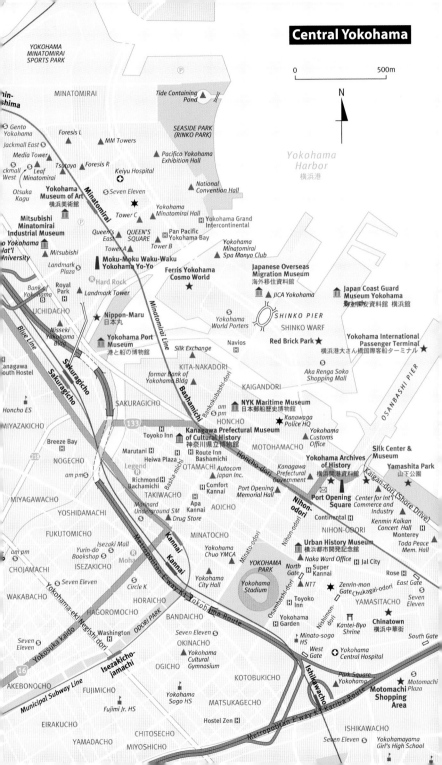

Yokohama Chinatown

Yokohama is Japan's second largest city and its largest port. Its Minato Mirai 21 town is full of high-rise buildings, with Landmark Tower and Queen's Square being the most famous. It is considered a mega-shopping town with its many shopping malls and amusement arcades. The lovely night view of this district has Yokohama Cosmo World with one of the world's largest ferris wheels illuminated.

Near Sakuragi-cho Station, the attraction lies in the Nogeyama-koen Park with its Nogeyama Zoo (this zoo has more than 100 types of animals), and Yokohama Nigiwai-za which houses Japanese entertainments. Its numerous theaters and playhouses are usually crowded.

Yokohama's Chinatown, which has 10 spectacular gates at various locations, is a major attraction for many visitors to Japan. Within the Chinatown area can be found various types of Chinese restaurants and stores for Chinese ingredients and pharmaceutical goods. Major festivals like the Chinese New Year's are held here each year.

Yokohama's upscale Yamate area is known for its hill-top foreign residences and churches, and for the Motomachi shopping district at the base of the hill, where there are dozens of shops featuring high-end fashion goods and accessories. Motomachi attracts crowds of visitors with stores that specialize in original clothes and other accessories. The Minato-no Mieru-oka-koen park has a rose garden and is a favorite strolling place for local residents as well as visitors.

The central Kannai District is the main district where government offices are found. Yokohama's famous Yamashita Koen ["Bottom-of-the-Mountain Park"], which overlooks the harbor and provides views of passing ships, is one of the most attractive and most visited areas in the city. One of Japan's most famous pre-World War II passenger liners, the Hikawa Maru [once known as the Pacific Queen], is permanently anchored alongside the park as a historical site open to visitors.

The gateway to the Port of Yokohama [known as Osanbashi / Oh-sahn-bah-she], where passenger ships and freighters dock, adjoins the southern end of the Park. It is also the homeport of restaurant-ferryboats that take passengers on cruises around the harbor bay.

Yokohama's famous **Sankei Garden**, a short distance south of the park, is the home of a 15th-century pagoda and other cultural buildings that have been moved there from different parts of Japan. Among the regular activities at the garden: flower-viewing parties, flower displays and competitions.

Getting to Yokohama from Narita Airport

There are two direct ways of getting from Narita Airport to Yokohama:

1) Limousines buses that leave from the front of the Arrival Lobbies of the two terminals every few minutes and go to the Yokohama City Air Terminal (YCAT) in downtown Yokohama. See page 33.
2) The JR Narita Express train, which leaves from boarding platforms beneath the two Narita Airport terminals. Access to the platforms is via escalators in the center areas of the Arrival Lobbies, and are identified by overhead signs. See page 21.

Getting to Yokohama from Haneda Airport

There are three ways of getting from Tokyo's Haneda Airport to Yokohama:

1) Keikyu Limousine buses that leave every 5–10 minutes from the front door of the Arrival Lobbies and go to the Yokohama City Air Terminal (YCAT) in the downtown area. Tickets are available at Limousine Bus counters in the arrival area. See page 33.
2) Keihin Kyuko Line train (Keihin Limited Express), which goes to Yokohama Station and takes 20 minutes and costs ¥470.
3) Tokyo Monorail, which goes from Haneda Airport to Hamamatsu-cho Station, where it connects with the JR Keihin Tohoku Line that goes to Yokohama Station. Travel time from Haneda to Hamamatsu-cho is 23 minutes. From there to Yokohama via the Keihin Tohoku line is 35 minutes. As of 2010 the Tokyo Monorail has a station in Haneda Airport's New International Terminal, making it especially convenient for international travelers, coming and going.

Getting to Yokohama from Tokyo

There are seven railway lines connecting Tokyo with Yokohama, of which four are from Tokyo Station and other stations on lines that go through Tokyo Station, bisecting the city from north to south, and three more lines that originate from major districts on the west, southwest and south sides of Tokyo:

The **JR Tokaido Line**, which starts at Tokyo Station and makes one stop at Shinagawa Station. Total travel time: about 45 minutes.

JR Yokosuka Line, which starts at Tokyo Station, and makes a stop at Shinagawa Station enroute to Yokohama Station and beyond. Travel time to Yokohama Station: about 45 minutes.

JR Keihin Tohoku Line, which begins on the northern outskirts of Tokyo and bisects the city from north to south, stopping at major as well as local stations. Travel time from Tokyo Station to Yokohama Station: about 40 minutes.

JR Tokaido Shinkansen Line. This is one of Japan's famous "bullet train" lines, which has several categories of trains, all of which stop at Tokyo Station and some of which (Kodama, Hikari and Nozomi class trains) stop at Shin-Yokohama Station which is about 10–12 minutes from the Yokohama Station. Travel time from Tokyo Station to Shin-Yokohama Station on these high-speed trains is about 15 minutes.

The **JR Shonan Shinjuku Line** provides service between Shinjuku (the huge business and hotel center on Tokyo's west side) and Yokohama. Travel time from Shinjuku Station to Yokohama Station: 30 minutes.

Tokyu Toyoko Line. This line connects Shibuya, the popular shopping and entertainment district on Tokyo's southwest side, with Yokohama Station, and continues on the Minato Mirai Line to the famous Motomachi dining and shopping district and Yokohama's Chinatown. It has local, limited express and express trains. Express trains make the trip in 25 minutes.

Keikyu (Keihin Kyuko) Line. This is the line that connects Shinagawa Station and Yokohama Station with Haneda Airport. It has both local and rapid limited express trains. Travel time from Shinagawa to Yokohama: 20 minutes.

Getting Around within Yokohama

Yokohama has three subway lines, Line 1, Line 3 and Line 4, although Lines 1 and 3 are operated as a single line. Lines 1 and 3 are called Blue Lines [B], and Line 4 is called the Green Line [G]. (Refer to pages 148–149)

The two Blue Lines run from Shonandai Station to Azamino Station, serving a combined total of 32 stations. The Green Line (Line 4) runs from Nakayama Station to Hiyoshi Station, with ten stops in between.

The Blue and Green Lines intersect at Center Kita (Center North) and Center Minami (Center South). Both Blue and Green lines connect with Yokohama Station and Shin-Yokohama Station (which serves the famous "bullet trains").

The three combined lines connect with all of the city's major business, entertainment and shopping areas, and are being extended to connect with other important areas in the city.

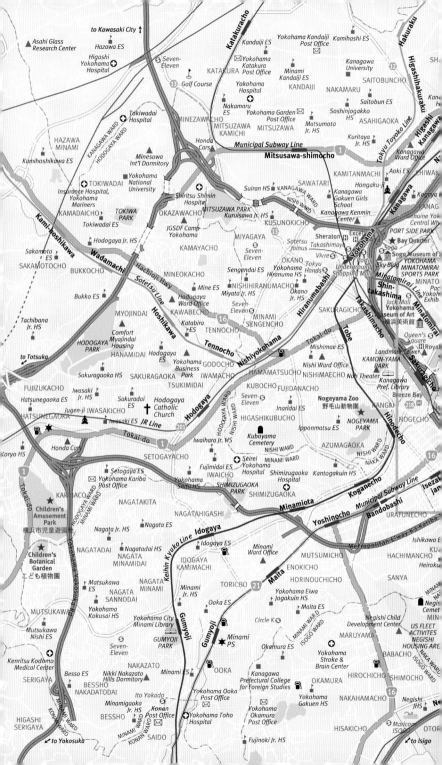

Yokohama Area

Oguchi
111
n-Eleven
SHINKOYASU
to
Kawasaki
City
Shinshibaura

Koyasu
Kelkyu-Shinkoyasu
Daiichi-Keihin Route
Toshiba
Keihin
Work

chi
Koyasu
Line
K-1
Yokohane Route
KANAGAWA Rd
Umishibaura

JR Line
MORIYACHO
Nissan Motor
Plant Area 1
Institute

EBISUCHO
TAKARACHO
Nissan Motor
Plant Area 3

Showadenko
Nissan Motor
Plant Area 2
Tsurumi
Recycle
Plaza

IZUTACHO

Tepko Yokohama
Termal Power Station

to Haneda
Airport

NORTH DOCK

MIZUHOCHO

OUCHI
SUZUSHIGECHO

Tsurumi Tsubasa
Bridge

Mizuho
Pier

DAIKOKU PIER

SEE CENTRAL YOKOHAMA MAP

PARK
RK)
DAIKOKUFUTO

on Hall
a Grand
ntinental
Yokohama
Harbor
横浜港
DAIKOKU PIER
CENTRAL PARK

kohama Cosmo World
コスモワールド

apanese Overseas Migration Museum
海外移住資料館
Yokohama Port
International Cargo
Center (Y-CC)

NKO WHARF
S
Yokohama International
Passenger Terminal
横浜港大さん橋国際客船ターミナル
DAIKOKU PIER

Brick Park
OSANBASHI
PIER

AMACHO
awa Prefectural
Office
Yamashita Park
山下公園
YAMASHITA
PIER
SHIN-YAMASHITA

Continental
Monterey
Hikawa Maru
Ocean Liner
HONMOKU
PIER A

MA
New Grand
Marine Tower

a YAMASITACHO
Motomachi
Chukagai
HONMOKU
PIER B

Chinatown
横浜中華街
HONMOKU
PIER C

MOTOMACHI
Harbor View Park

Yokohama
Foreign General
Cemetery
YAMATECHO
HONMOKUFUTO

Sacred Heart
Cathedral Yamate
山手教会
KITAGATACHO
HONMOKU
PIER D

hamakyoritsu
en HS
Yokohama Futaba
ES, JHS & SHS

ASHIWABA
HONGOCHO

NOMARU
NISHINOYACHO
HONMOKUCHO

oto
Fishing
Pier

AKAODAI
Otori ES
HONMOKU
SANCHO PARK
Park City
Honmoku
Tokyo Bay

dai JHS
Honmoku
ES

ko Gakuin HS
Yokohama Country
& Athletic Club
Yokohama City
Naka Library
Otori
Jr. HS

AKINOUE
Yokohama
Tatsuno HS
HONMOKU
HARA
Nissan Motor
Honmoku Pier

HONMOKU
MAKADO
Honmoku
Hospital

Yokohama
Makado ES
Mitsubishi Heavy Industries
Yokohama Dockyard &
Machinery Works Honmoku Plant

Nippon
Petroleum
Refining
SANKEIEN
GARDEN
HONMOKU
MINAMI ES
HONMOKU
OSATO

N

CIDORICHO
Nippon
Petroleum
Refining
KAMOMECHO
0   1km

Minami-Honmoku Final
Waste Disposal Site

357

Sakuragi-cho, the next station after Yokohama Station, is one of the main connecting stations for the above areas.

Yokohama's famous Chinatown [Yokohama Chukagai] is a short walk from Motomachi-Chukagai Station, the terminal station of the [Blue] Minato Mirai Line which connects with Yokohama Station. It is also a short walk from Ishikawacho Station on the JR Keihin Tohoku Line.

Bus Services in Yokohama

Bus transportation is popular in Yokohama for both residents and visitors, in part because city buses run on natural gas and have low barrier-free floors for ease in boarding and exiting. There are two main bus terminals in Yokohama, one adjoining the east exit of Yokohama Station and the other one next to Sakuragi-cho Station [the next station after Yokohama Station on the Yokosuka Line], the two main railway stations in the city.

Your best bet is to buy a **Minato Burari Ticket**, a discounted pass that allows you to ride all day on the city's subway and buses. *Minato* means "port," and *burari* means something like "sightseeing by leisurely strolling about."

Buses departing from the two stations go to all of the major dining, shopping and sightseeing districts in the city, including Yamate, Isezakicho, Chinatown and the area around Yamashita Park.

There are two sightseeing excursion bus services designed for visitors: the **Akai Kutsu** [Ah-kie Koot-sue] and the **Minato Mirai 100 Yen Bus**. The retro-styled **Akai Kutsu** [which means Red Shoes] buses start at Sakuragi-cho Station, tour the port area, Chinatown, Yamashita Park and the

Mieruoka Park weekdays and weekends. Fare is ¥100 for adults, ¥50 for children. (Please refer to page 158.)

There is a bus every 15 minutes. It is available on Saturdays and Sundays and public holidays, from 10 am to 8 pm. A complete loop takes 20 minutes, but may take longer because of road conditions. No reservation is required.

The so-called one-coin **Minato Mirai 100 yen buses** operate on weekends and on national holidays. These buses cover two routes, one starting from Sakuragi-cho Station and one from Hinode-cho Station. They cruise around the port area of the city, taking in historic buildings and other sites of interest.

The following bus routes take the tourists through tourist spots and other places of interest in Yokohama:

Yokohama Bayside Liner Bus

Other highlights of the Yokohama Bayside Sightseeing Bus Line tours include the "View Floor" of Sky Garden on the 69th floor of the Yokohama Landmark Tower [this is the highest "view floor" in Japan], the Yokohama Landmark Plaza [170 specialty shops], a lunch stop-over in Yokohama's picturesque Chinatown, and a visit to a cemetery in Port Hill Park where famous early foreign residents are buried. This stop also includes a visit to a Western-style house that was built just before the end of Japan's samurai Shogunate system of government in 1867.

The view of the Yokohama harbor area from Sky Garden in the Yokohama Landmark Tower is spectacular, and by itself worth the trip.

There are four different tours available—an all-day tour, a morning tour, and two evening

The Port of Yokohama

USEFUL PASSES AND TICKETS

The **"Minato Burari"** Ticket is a convenient one-day pass that offers you unlimited rides on the subway and city buses. Use it to visit the areas near the port where popular tourist sites are, to visit the Minato Mirai 21 area, Chinatown, and Yamashita Park. **Fare:** Adult: ¥500 Child: ¥250. **Fare:** Adult: ¥500 Child: ¥250

The **"Minato Burari wide Ticket"** enables you to get on and off at municipal subway Shin-Yokohama Station. **Fare:** Adult: ¥550 Child: ¥280

A **One-Day Ticket** by Minatomirai Line offers you unlimited rides on the Minatomirai Line for a whole day. Use it for city sightseeing and business. Special discounts and services are available to ticket holders at certain tourist spots. **Fare:** Adult: ¥460 Child: ¥230

The **Seaside Line One-Day Pass** allows the holder to have unlimited rides on the Seaside Line for a whole day. It comes in useful as a pass to visit the Yokohama South area, where

Yokohama Hakkeijima Sea Paradise and other sightseeing facilities are located. **Fare:** Adult: ¥670 Child: ¥340

The **Bus One-Day Pass** offers you unlimited rides on the buses for a whole day including rides on the Akaikutsu bus route. **Fare:** Adult: ¥ 600 Child: ¥300

The **Subway & Bus One-Day Pass:** also offers you unlimited rides on the subway and buses for a whole day including rides on the Akaikutsu bus route. **Fare:** Adult: ¥830 Child: ¥420

Yokohama Minatomirai Pass: This one-day pass allows unlimited travel on local and JR East trains (non-reserved seats) on the Negishi Line between Yokohama and Shin-Sugita Stations, and on the Yokohama Minatomirai Line. It can also be used for sightseeing and shopping benefits in the Yokohama area. The English version of the Pass is now available. **Fare:** Adult: ¥520 Child: ¥260

tours. The starting and ending point of all tours is at Yokohama Station, East Exit. [Tourists can be picked up at designated hotels at the start of the tours.] A Japanese guide is on board to give a commentary on the history of the places and buildings passed by, but travelers can request for an English commentary on an earphone guide. Reservations for the tours must be made in advance (in English or Japanese). Tickets are available one month before the actual day of tour from all JR Travel Centers, Yokohama Station (East Exit) Information Center, select tour agents and hotels in Yokohama.

Yokohama Half-Day Tour (page 159)– This tour runs from 9:45 am to 1:40 pm. Travelers are then taken to such famous at-tractions as the Landmark Tower where they ascend to the 69th floor for a fantastic view of the city and harbor, and then on to Red Brick Warehouse, Three Towers of Yokohama, Port Hill Park, Yokohama Bay Bridge, Marine Tower, Yamashita Park, and Chinatown [lunch or shopping] in half a day. (Several attractions will be seen from a car window.)

Fare is ¥2,900 (adult), ¥1,450 (child) and ¥2,660 (for 65 years and above). The fare includes entrance fees, but the cost of lunch in Chinatown is not included. You can reserve a special lunch in Chinatown (optional). It costs ¥5,000 to ¥7,000 per person.

Nostalgic Yokohama Tour (page 159)– This tour runs from 2:05 pm to 5:40 pm, and its first sight is also the Yokohama Bay Bridge, followed by visits to the noted Sankeien Gardens. Next is Yamate Western Residences, Marine Tower, Yamashita Park and the Red Brick Warehouse shopping emporium. (Several attractions will be seen from a car window.)

Fare is ¥2,900 (adult), ¥1,250 (child) and ¥2,690 (for 65 years and above).

Yokohama Bay Cruises

Royal Wing, a luxurious pleasure ship, oper-ates three types of cruise along the Yokohama Bay. The lunch cruise starts at 12 noon and ends at 1.50 pm. It costs ¥2,000 (adult) and ¥1,000 (child, 6–12 years). The tea cruise starts at 2.45 pm and ends at 4.15 pm [¥1,500 (adult); ¥750 (child, 6–12 years)]. The dinner cruise has two slots: 5.00 pm to 6.50 pm or 7.30 pm to 9.20 pm [¥2,500 (adult); ¥1,250 (child, 6–12 years)]. All cruis-es have an option for Chinese meals whose prices vary, according to the choice of meal selected.

The cruises depart from the Yokohama International Passenger's Terminal, and cover the Yokohama harbor area. They pass important landmarks such as the Yokohama Bay Bridge, the Yamashita Park, the Red

Brick Warehouse, among other places of interest.

The Romance of the Tokaido Line

The Tokaido [Tohh-kie-dohh] Line takes its name from the historically famous road that connected the Kansai region (Kyoto, Osaka) with the Kanto region (then Edo, now Tokyo). Tokaido means "Eastern Sea Road," and refers to the fact that the route skirted the eastern seaboard of Japan's main island of Honshu, connecting the major population centers between the Imperial capital of Kyoto and the Shogunate capital of Edo—the latter founded in 1603.

The Tokaido Road itself goes back to ancient times when what is now the Tokyo area was still inhabited by indigenous Caucasoid Ainu tribes—the first settlers of the Japanese islands who long ago came down from the northeastern regions of Siberia.

The road and the name played a major role in the history of Japan—none more spectacular and glorious than the days of the Tokugawa Shogunate era from 1603 to 1867, when it was traveled by religious pilgrims, salesmen, sumo wrestlers on tour, geisha, professional gamblers, and feudal lords—the latter required by the Shogun to travel to Edo every other year with large entourages of attendants and samurai warriors.

To accommodate these *Daimyo Gyoretsu* [Die-m'yoh G'yoh-rate-sue], or "Processions of the Lords," the Shogunate ordered the construction of hundreds of upscale and ordinary inns one day's march apart along the entire length of the Tokaido—making Japan the first country in the world to have a national network of inns.

The first railway line between the Tokyo and Kyoto-Osaka regions was completed in 1889. In 1906, all privately-run main lines were nationalized under the newly created Japan Imperial Railway [later changed to Japan National Railway and now popularly known as JR].

By the early 1950's the Tokaido Line had become the main railway artery of Japan. Although it was only 3 percent of the railway system by length, it carried 24 percent of JNR's passenger traffic and 23 percent of its freight.

The Tokaido Line in Greater Tokyo Today

The Tokaido Main Line in the Greater Tokyo Area today shares both the railway lines and the names of several other lines. Its rapid services are called Rapid Acty [*Kaisoku akutī/*

Kie-so-kuu ah-kuu-tee] and Commuter Rapid.

It runs on dedicated tracks parallel to the Yamanote Line in central Tokyo, the Keihin-Tohoku Line between Tokyo and Yokohama, and the Yokosuka-Sobu Line between Tokyo and Ofuna. Some Shonan-Shinjuku Line trains share the segment south of Yokohama to Ofuna and Odawara Stations. The Ueno-Tokyo Line—a project by JR East—officially started in March 2015. This line facilitates travel from Tokyo to the northern prefectures of Fukushima, Tochigi and Gunma, by linking the Tokaido Line with the Joban, Tohoku and Takashi Lines. Important stations such as Shingawa and Ueno Stations are served by this new line.

This combination of lines and tracks makes it possible for passengers to reach major Greater Tokyo area destinations from both Narita Airport and Haneda Airport by transferring at the three primary hub stations—Tokyo Central, Shinagawa and Yokohama.

Finding the Right Boarding Platform

There are boarding platforms for 14 interconnected lines at Tokyo Central Station, with an underground passageway to Otemachi Station where four subway lines [Chiyoda, Hanzomon, Mita and Tozai lines] converge.

Boarding platforms for Tokaido Line connections are on different levels of the station, depending on your next destination. Tokaido Line Shinkansen "Bullet Train" platforms, for example, are on the ground floor on the east [Yaesu Guchi] side of the station. Other line platforms are on 1st, 2nd, 3rd, 4th and 5th levels underground and reached via escalators and/or moving sidewalks.

The two Yokosuka-Sobu Line platforms are five stories below ground level on the west side of Tokyo Station. The two Keiyo Line platforms are four stories below ground level some two blocks south of the main station and reached via a moving sidewalk.

It is therefore important that you know in advance the name of the line you want to transfer to at Tokyo Station and what level it is on.

There are four connecting commuter train lines at Shinagawa Station and six at Yokohama Station, all of them far easier to find by following the overhead signs. The map on pages 148–149 shows the six lines you can transfer to at Yokohama Station—reachable direct from Narita Airport via the Yokosuka/Sobu Rapid Line, with stops at Shimbashi and Shinagawa Stations.

JR Train Lines to/from Yokohama

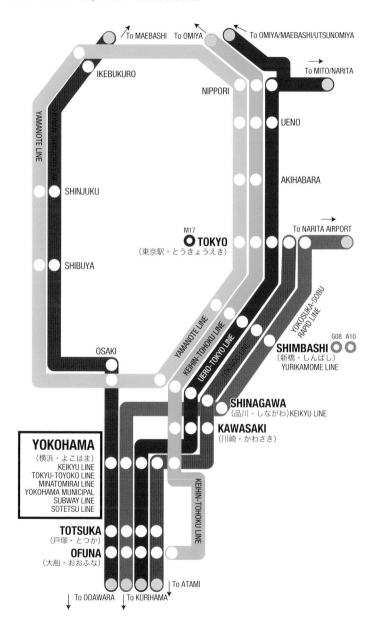

Yokohama Municipal Subway Lines 横浜市営地下鉄

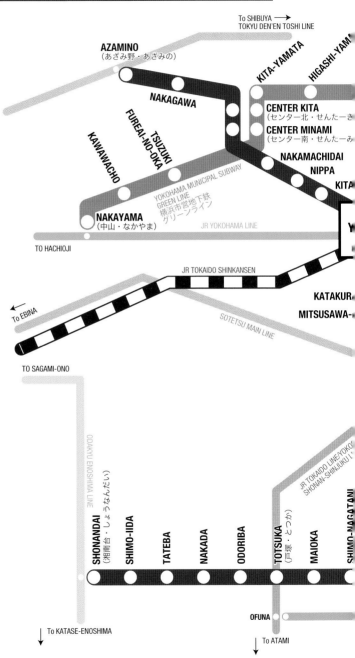

To SHIBUYA ⟶
TOKYU DEN'EN TOSHI LINE

AZAMINO
（あざみ野・あざみの）

KITA-YAMATA

HIGASHI-YAM

NAKAGAWA

CENTER KITA
（センター北・せんたーき

CENTER MINAMI
（センター南・せんたーみ

TSUZUKI
FUREAI-NO-OKA

KAWAWACHO

NAKAMACHIDAI

NIPPA

KITA

YOKOHAMA MUNICIPAL SUBWAY
GREEN LINE
横浜市営地下鉄
グリーンライン

NAKAYAMA
（中山・なかやま）

JR YOKOHAMA LINE

Y

TO HACHIOJI

JR TOKAIDO SHINKANSEN

← To EBINA

KATAKUR

MITSUSAWA-

SOTETSU MAIN LINE

TO SAGAMI-ONO

ODAKYU ENOSHIMA LINE

JR TOKAIDO LINE/YOKO
SHONAN-SHINJUKU L

SHONANDAI
（湘南台・しょうなんだい）

SHIMO-IIDA

TATEBA

NAKADA

ODORIBA

TOTSUKA
（戸塚・とつか）

MAIOKA

SHIMO-NAGATANI

OFUNA

↓ To KATASE-ENOSHIMA

↓ To ATAMI

JR Yokohama Line　JR 横浜線

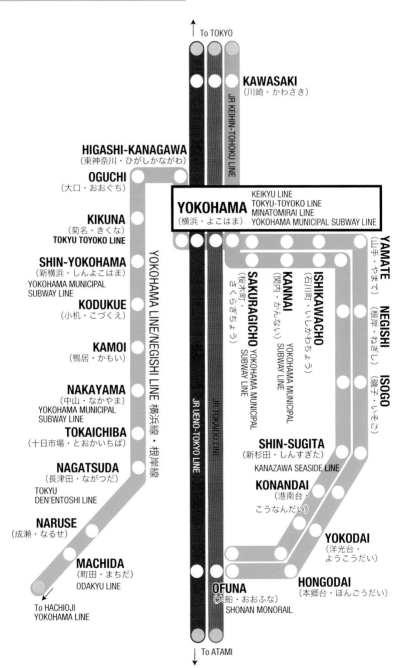

↑ To TOKYO

KAWASAKI
（川崎・かわさき）

JR KEIHIN-TOHOKU LINE

HIGASHI-KANAGAWA
（東神奈川・ひがしかながわ）

OGUCHI
（大口・おおぐち）

YOKOHAMA
（横浜・よこはま）
KEIKYU LINE
TOKYU-TOYOKO LINE
MINATOMIRAI LINE
YOKOHAMA MUNICIPAL SUBWAY LINE

KIKUNA
（菊名・きくな）
TOKYU TOYOKO LINE

SHIN-YOKOHAMA
（新横浜・しんよこはま）
YOKOHAMA MUNICIPAL
SUBWAY LINE

YOKOHAMA LINE/NEGISHI LINE 横浜線・根岸線

KODUKUE
（小机・こづくえ）

KAMOI
（鴨居・かもい）

NAKAYAMA
（中山・なかやま）
YOKOHAMA MUNICIPAL
SUBWAY LINE

TOKAICHIBA
（十日市場・とおかいちば）

NAGATSUDA
（長津田・ながつだ）
TOKYU
DEN'ENTOSHI LINE

NARUSE
（成瀬・なるせ）

MACHIDA
（町田・まちだ）
ODAKYU LINE

To HACHIOJI
YOKOHAMA LINE

JR UENO-TOKYO LINE

JR TOKAIDO LINE

SAKURAGICHO
（桜木町・さくらぎちょう）
YOKOHAMA MUNICIPAL
SUBWAY LINE

KANNAI
（関内・かんない）
YOKOHAMA MUNICIPAL
SUBWAY LINE

ISHIKAWACHO
（石川町・いしかわちょう）

YAMATE
（山手・やまて）

NEGISHI
（根岸・ねぎし）

ISOGO
（磯子・いそご）

SHIN-SUGITA
（新杉田・しんすぎた）
KANAZAWA SEASIDE LINE

KONANDAI
（港南台・
こうなんだい）

YOKODAI
（洋光台・
ようこうだい）

HONGODAI
（本郷台・ほんごうだい）

OFUNA
（大船・おおふな）
SHONAN MONORAIL

↓ To ATAMI

Yokohama Minatomirai Railway 横浜みなとみらい線

↑ To IKEBUKURO
FUKUTOSHIN LINE

SHIBUYA
(渋谷・しぶや)
Z01　G01　F16
KEIO INOKASHIRA LINE

MUSASHI-KOSUGI
(武蔵小杉・むさしこすぎ)

HIYOSHI
(日吉・ひよし)
YOKOHAMA MUNICIPAL
SUBWAY LINE

KIKUNA
(菊名・きくな)
JR YOKOHAMA LINE

YOKOHAMA JR SOTETSU LINE
(横浜・よこはま)　KEIKYU LINE
YOKOHAMA MUNICIPAL SUBWAY LINE

SHIN-TAKASHIMA
(新高島・しんたかしま)

MINATOMIRAI
(みなとみらい)

BASHAMICHI
(馬車道・ばしゃみち)

NIHONODORI
(日本大通り・にほんおおどおり)

MOTOMACHI-CHUKAGAI
(元町・中華街・もとまちちゅうかがい)

TOKYU TOYOKO LINE 東急東横線

MINATOMIRAI LINE みなとみらい線

Tokyu Electric Railway 東急電鉄

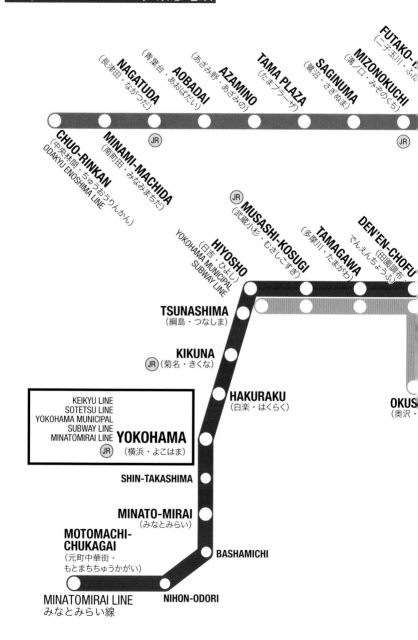

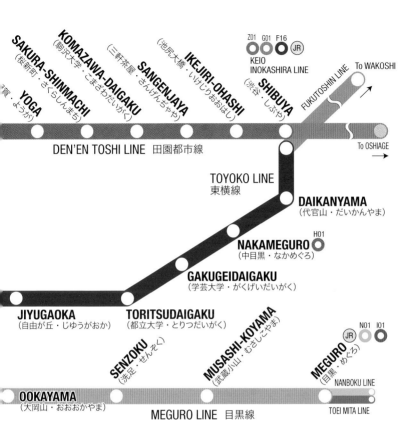

Yokohama Municipal Subway Blue and Green Lines
横浜市営地下鉄ブルーライン, グリーンライン

Kanazawa Seaside Line　金沢シーサイドライン

JR Yokosuka–Sobu Rapid Line 横須賀線・総武線快速

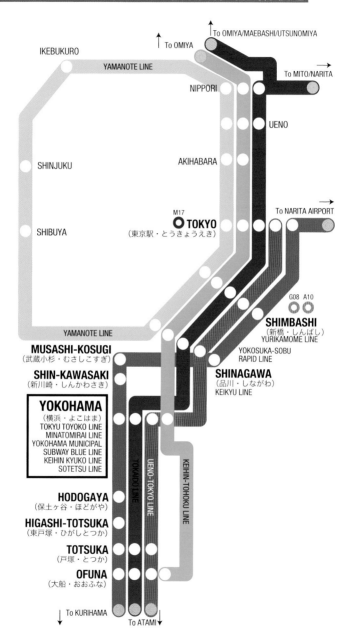

To OMIYA/MAEBASHI/UTSUNOMIYA

To OMIYA

IKEBUKURO

YAMANOTE LINE

To MITO/NARITA

NIPPORI

UENO

SHINJUKU

AKIHABARA

M17

TOKYO
（東京駅・とうきょうえき）

To NARITA AIRPORT

SHIBUYA

YAMANOTE LINE

G08 A10

SHIMBASHI
（新橋・しんばし）
YURIKAMOME LINE

MUSASHI-KOSUGI
（武蔵小杉・むさしこすぎ）

YOKOSUKA-SOBU
RAPID LINE

SHIN-KAWASAKI
（新川崎・しんかわさき）

SHINAGAWA
（品川・しながわ）
KEIKYU LINE

YOKOHAMA
（横浜・よこはま）
TOKYU TOYOKO LINE
MINATOMIRAI LINE
YOKOHAMA MUNICIPAL
SUBWAY BLUE LINE
KEIHIN KYUKO LINE
SOTETSU LINE

TOKAIDO LINE

UENO-TOKYO LINE

KEIHIN-TOHOKU LINE

HODOGAYA
（保土ヶ谷・ほどがや）

HIGASHI-TOTSUKA
（東戸塚・ひがしとつか）

TOTSUKA
（戸塚・とつか）

OFUNA
（大船・おおふな）

To KURIHAMA

To ATAMI

Yokohama Municipal Bus Routes 横浜市営バス

ROUTE NUMBER	START	VIA	DESTINATION	FARE (ADULT)
8	YOKOHAMA STATION (EAST EXIT)	TAKASHIMA-CHO, SAKURAGI-CHO CHUKAGAI, SANKEIEN	HONMOKU SHAKO	¥220
148	YOKOHAMA STATION (EAST EXIT)	TAKASHIMA-CHO, SAKURAGI-CHO CHUKAGAI, SANKEIEN	HONMOKU SHAKO	¥220
26	YOKOHAMA STATION (EAST EXIT)	SAKURAGI-CHO, OSANBASHI, YAMASHITA PARK	UMIZURI-SANBASHI, YOKOHAMAKO SYMBOL TOWER	¥220

Routes 8, 148 & 26

8 148 26

YOKOHAMA STATION (EAST EXIT)
(横浜駅・よこはまえき)

TAKASHIMA-CHO (near Minato-Mirai 21 Area)
(高島町・たかしまちょう)

SAKURAGICHO-MAE STATION (near Landmark Tower)
(桜木町駅前・さくらぎちょうえきまえ)

BASHAMICHI-MAE STATION
(馬車道駅前・ばしゃみちえきまえ)

OSANBASHI (near Yokohama International Passenger's Terminal)
(大桟橋・おおさんばし)

CHUKAGAI ENTRANCE (near Chinatown)
(中華街入口・ちゅうかがいいりぐち)

YAMASHITA PARK FRONT (near Yamashita Koen Park)
(山下公園前・やましたこうえんまえ)

YAMASHITA-CHO (near Motomachi Shopping District)
(山下町・やましたちょう)

MARINE TOWER-MAE (near Marine Tower)
(マリンタワー前・まりんたわーまえ)

YAMASHITA PIER EXIT
(山下埠頭入口・やましたふとういりぐち)

KOMINATOBASHI
(小港橋・こみなとばし)

HONMOKU PIER EXIT
(本牧埠頭入口・ほんもくふとういりぐち)

UMIZURI SANBASHI
(海づり桟橋・うみづりさんばし)

YOKOHAMA-KO SYMBOL TOWER
(横浜港シンボルタワー・
よこはまこうしんぼるたわー)

HONMOKU
(本牧・ほんもく)

HONMOKU SANKEIEN KOEN-MAE (near Sankeien Garden)
(本牧三渓園前・ほんもくさんけいえんまえ)

HONMOKU SHAKO-MAE
(本牧車庫前・ほんもくしゃこまえ)

ROUTE NUMBER	START	VIA	DESTINATION	FARE (ADULT)
156/292	SAKURAGICHO STATION FRONT	QUEEN'S SQUARE, PACIFICO YOKOHAMA	SAKURAGICHO STATION FRONT	¥220
Akaikutsu	SAKURAGICHO STATION FRONT	AKARENGA-SOKO, CHUKAGAI, YAMASHITA-KOEN PARK	SAKURAGICHO STATION FRONT	¥100

YOKOHAMA MUNICIPAL BUS
ROUTES: 156/292/ Akaikutsu

SAKURAGICHO EKI-MAE (near Landmark Tower)
（桜木町駅前・さくらぎちょうえきまえ）

MINATO-MIRAI-ODORI (near Minato-Mirai 21 Area)
（みなとみらい大通り・みなとみらいおおどおり）

ANPANMAN MUSEUM EXIT
（アンパンマンミュージアム入口・
あんぱんまんみゅーじあむいりぐち）

SHIN-TAKASHIMA EKI-MAE
（新高島駅前・しんたかしまえきまえ）

MARINOS TOWN-MAE
（マリノスタウン前・まりのすたうんまえ）

YOKOHAMA ART MUSEUM
（横浜美術館・よこはまびじゅつかん）

KEIYU HOSPITAL （けいゆ病院・けいゆうびょういん）

QUEEN'S SQUARE (near Queen's Square Shopping Mall)
（クイーンズスクエア・くいーんずすくえあ）

TENJI HALL （展示ホール・てんじほーる）

PACIFICO YOKOHAMA (near Pacifico Yokohama Convention Hall)
（パシフィコ横浜・ぱしふぃこよこはま）

WORLD PORTERS (near World Porters Shopping Mall)
（ワールドポーターズ・わーるどぽーたーず）

RED BRICK WAREHOUSE (near Red Brick Shopping Mall)
（赤レンガ倉庫・あかれんがそうこ）

SHIN-KENCHO-MAE
（新県庁前・しんけんちょうまえ）

NIHON-ODORI
（日本大通り・にほんおおどおり）

CHUKAGAI (near Chinatown)
（中華街・ちゅうかがい）

MOTOMACHI ENTRANCE
（元町入口・もとまちいりぐち）
(near Motomachi Shopping District)

MARINE TOWER-MAE
（マリンタワー前・まりんたわーまえ）

YAMASHITA KOEN-MAE (near Yamashita Koen Park)
（山下公園前・やましたこうえんまえ）

BASHAMICHI-MAE STATION
（馬車道駅前・ばしゃみちえきまえ）

**OSANBASHI KYAKUSEN
TERMINAL** （大桟橋客船ターミナル・
おおさんばしきゃくせんたーみなる）
(near Yokohama International
Passenger's Terminal)

OSANBASHI （大桟橋・おおさんばし）

Yokohama Bayside Sightseeing Bus 横浜ベイサイドライン

YOKOHAMA HALF-DAY TOUR (All-day Roundtrip)

- **YOKOHAMA STATION (EAST EXIT)** (横浜駅: 東口)
- **VIEW FLOOR "SKY GARDEN" IN THE YOKOHAMA LANDMARK TOWER 69F** (横浜ランドマークタワー69F展望台スカイガーデン) Free time
- **RED BRICK WAREHOUSE** (赤レンガ倉庫)*
- **THREE TOWERS OF YOKOHAMA** (横浜三塔)*
- **PORT HILL PARK** (横浜外国人墓地、港の見える丘公園ほか) Free time
- **YOKOHAMA BAY BRIDGE** (横浜ベイブリッジ)*
- **MARINE TOWER, YAMASHITA PARK etc.** (マリンタワー、山下公園ほか)*
- **YOKOHAMA INTERNATIONAL PASSENGER'S TERMINAL** (大さん橋国際客船ターミナル) Free time
- **YOKOHAMA CHINATOWN** (横浜中華街) Lunch or free time
- **MINATO MIRAI 21 AREA** (みなとみらい21地区)*
- **YOKOHAMA STATION (EAST EXIT)** (横浜駅: 東口)

*View from the window
Daily, from 9.45 am to 1.40 pm. Ticket costs ¥2,900 (adult), ¥1,450 (child) and ¥2,660 (senior (over 65 years). Entrance fee is included and the cost of lunch at Chinatown is excluded. Tickets will be available one month prior to your trip. For reservations and inquiries: +81 (45) 465 2077 (available in English).

NOSTALGIC YOKOHAMA (Half-day Roundtrip)

- **YOKOHAMA STATION (EAST EXIT)** (横浜駅: 東口)
- **YOKOHAMA BAY BRIDGE, DAIKOKU PIER EAST AREA** (横浜ベイブリッジ、大黒ふ頭)*
- **SANKEIEN GARDEN** (三渓園) Free time
- **YAMATE WESTERN RESIDENCE, YOKOHAMA FOREIGN GENERAL CEMETERY etc.** (山手西洋館、横浜外国人墓地ほか)*
- **MARINE TOWER, YAMASHITA PARK etc.** (マリンタワー、山下公園ほか)*
- **MEMORIAL SQUARE OF THE YOKOHAMA PORT** (開港記念広場)*
- **RED BRICK WAREHOUSE etc.** (赤レンガ倉庫)*
- **MINATO MIRAI 21 AREA** (みなとみらい21地区)*
- **YOKOHAMA STATION (EAST EXIT)** (横浜駅: 東口)

*View from the window
Daily, from 2:05 pm to 5.40 pm. Ticket costs ¥2,900 (adult) and ¥1,250 (child), ¥2,690 (senior). Entrance fee is included. Tickets will be available one month prior to your trip. For reservations and inquiries: +81 (45) 465 2077 (available in English). .

Part 10: VISITING THE KAMAKURA AREA

Kamakura: The Original Capital of Japan's Shoguns

Kamakura, one of the most popular side-trips from Tokyo and Yokohama, owes its special prominence to the fact that it was the birthplace of Japan's famous shogunate system of government. The country was ruled from Kamakura for over 400 years, and its historical artifacts are among the primary treasures of the country.

About one hour by train southwest of Tokyo on the shore of Sagami Bay, this now small, quiet city entered the pages of Japan's history in 1192 when clan leader Minamoto Yoritomo became Japan's supreme military commander by defeating the Taira clan and prevailing upon the reigning but powerless emperor in Kyoto to appoint him shogun—an ancient title that may be translated as generalissimo. This, in effect, made Minamoto the military dictator of the country.

Minamoto chose Kamakura—at that time a tiny fishing village—as his military headquarters because it was a natural fortress, surrounded on three sides by rough mountains and on the fourth side by the ocean—and because it was far away from the intrigues and decadence of the imperial capital in Kyoto.

Getting to Kamakura from Tokyo

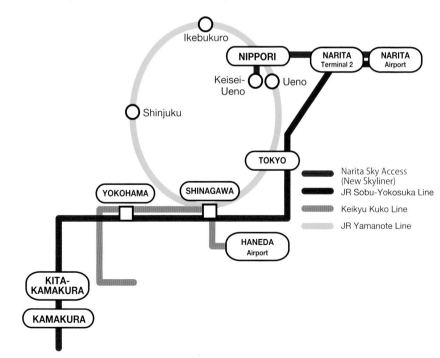

The history of Kamakura from 1192 until 1603 is a saga of epic proportions, including the construction of an astounding array of shrines and temples, the development of samurai warriors into an hereditary class that was to continue to rule Japan until 1867, dealing with two 13th-century invasions by the Mongols (who ruled China at that time), the introduction of Nichiren Buddhism and Zen Buddhism in Japan, and the development of arts, crafts, and architecture that was to distinguish Japanese culture down to modern times.

However, the reign of the Minamoto family itself was to be short-lived. Yoritomo died in 1199 and was succeeded as shogun by his first son, Yoriie. By 1202 real power was in the hands of Yoriie's grandfather, Hōjō Tokimasa, who was in fact distantly related to the Taira clan that Yoritomo had defeated in 1192.

In 1204 Yoriie was assassinated by the Hōjō. Yoritomo's second son, Minamoto Sanetomo, became the third Kamakura shogun. But in 1219 the Hōjōs had Sanetomo assassinated as well—beneath a huge ginkgo tree that still stands today—thus ending the reign of the Minamotos and bringing the Hōjō Regency to the forefront.

It was during the Hōjō Regency that Kamakura experienced an astounding period of growth that was to make it one of the most exciting cities in the country, eclipsing the reputation and position of Kyoto—a unique situation that was to last until 1333, when the Hōjōs were defeated by Nitta Yoshisada, a clan leader loyal to the emperor in Kyoto.

When it became obvious in 1333 that the Nitta forces were going to capture Kamakura, the Hōjō family and over 900 of their samurai warriors committed mass suicide at their family temple. History notes that an estimated 6,000 ordinary residents also killed themselves on that day. The Nitta forces then proceeded to sack and burn much of the city.

The next shogun, Ashikaga Takauji, installed in 1335, took up residence in Yoritomo's Kamakura mansion. A year later he moved to Kyoto, leaving a deputy in charge. Over the next 100 years Kamakura regained some of its affluence and prestige, but following a destructive attack in 1454 by still another clan lord, most of its residents moved further down the coast to Odawara.

The final blow to Kamakura came in 1603 when the newly victorious Tokugawa Ieyasu became shogun and moved his headquarters

The Great Buddha (Kamakura *Daibutsu*)

to Edo (Tokyo), then a small fishing village at the head of a large bay some 50 kilometers to the northeast. The Tokugawa shogunate was to rule Japan from Edo until 1867.

A civil war initiated in the 1860s by southern clans that favored the imperial system of government brought the Tokugawa Shogunate to an end in 1867. Shortly thereafter, the young emperor and imperial court in Kyoto were brought to Edo, which was then renamed Tokyo (Eastern Capital).

The Attractions of Kamakura

Kamakura languished as a backwater town for the next century, with a small population that did, however, include a few famous scholars, writers and artists. Then, after Japan's economic renaissance began following the end of World War II, Kamakura began to attract more and more attention, first among the Japanese themselves and then among foreign visitors.

Most of the great shrines and temples built during the Hōjō Regency had survived, and the quiet town by the sea once again became a cultural mecca that now has more than a million visitors each year. Kamakura's attractions include a giant bronze image of Buddha, 65 Buddhist temples, and 19 Shinto shrines. The history associated with these temples and shrines is a powerful drawing card for both Japanese and foreigners alike. The famous sites sponsor annual festivals, so there is

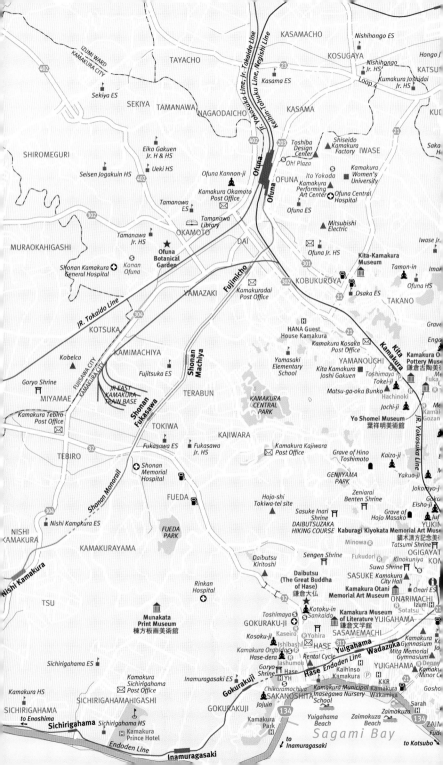

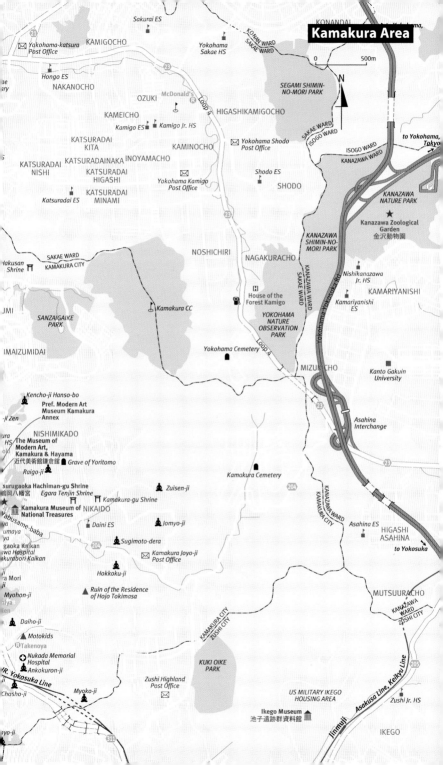

Kamakura Area

something going on in Kamakura virtually every month of the year.

Details of some of the main attractions are provided below.

Daibutsu (The Great Buddha of Hase)

Located in western Kamakura near Hase Station, the Daibutsu is Kamakura's most famous sight. It is considered the second largest statue in Japan. The giant bronze statue, cast in 1252, is 11.4 meters tall, is seated and has a serene countenance. Originally housed in a large hall that was washed away by a tsunami in 1495, today the Daibutsu sits outdoors surrounded by a stand of trees. The inside of the statue can be accessed by climbing in through a ladder at the back of the statue.

To reach this temple, take the Enoden train from Kamakura Station to Hase Station, then walk for about 15 minutes. Alternatively from Kamakura Station take a bus to Daibutsu-mae bus stop.

Hase-dera A few minutes' walk north of Hase Station near the Daibutsu, Hase-dera is a large temple sitting on a hillside, with excellent views of the city and ocean beyond. It houses an impressive 11-face Kannon statue and a small treasure hall. Each face of the Kannon has a distinct facial expression.

Engaku-ji A 10-minutes' walk from Kita-Kamakura Station, Engaku-ji, the largest of Kamakura's Zen Buddhist temple complexes, was built in 1282 to honor victims of the two unsuccessful Mongol invasions and to serve as a center for the study of Zen. There are 18 sub-temples on the site, set behind an impressive main gate within a tranquil glade of tall trees. The Shari-den, closed to visitors, is reputed to contain one of Buddha's teeth. Most of the structures of the current temple are reproductions of the original temple; only the original two-story sanmon gate from 1780 still stands.

Kencho-ji Temple Surrounded by majestic cedar trees, Kencho-ji, located in northern Kamakura near Engaku-ji and several other major temples, was built in 1253 and is the oldest training monastery in Japan. Many of the temple's original buildings were destroyed by fire, but 10 sub-temples remain, including several that were moved to the site from Kyoto and Tokyo. The original temple

bell, cast in 1255, hangs next to the towering entrance gate.

The nearest station is Kita-Kamakura Station, approximately 600 meters away.

Tsurugaoka Hachiman-gu Shrine This large shrine was built by Minamoto Yoritomo in 1063 next to the ocean, and was enlarged and moved to its present location near Kamakura Station in 1191. It can be reached from the station by a 10 minutes' walk through the busy Komachi-dori shopping area or the Dankazura pedestrian path, which is lined by cherry trees as well as shops. The front entrance to the shrine is marked by a magnificent torii (gate). The shrine contains a variety of buildings painted a bright red, most of which date from the early 19th century. But the main attraction is the grounds, which include a park with lotus ponds and arched bridges. Nearby is the **Kamakura National Treasure House Museum**, also well worth a visit. This museum houses collections of temple treasures and wonderful Buddhist pieces of art.

Other activities that can be enjoyed include shopping for traditional crafts, enjoying the beaches at Yuigahama and Inamuragasaki, and hiking.

GETTING TO KAMAKURA FROM TOKYO

The quickest way is to get on the JR Yokosuka Line train from Tokyo Station—it is an hour journey and costs ¥920, via Yokohama Station (a 25-minute ride at ¥340).

Another way is to use the JR Kamakura-Enoshima Excursion Ticket—this is a 2-consecutive day roundtrip ticket from Tokyo/Yokohama to Kamakura, good for local JR trains (non-reserved seats) only and unlimited rides on the Enoshima Electric Railway or Shonan Monorail in the Kamakura/Enoshima region (direct routes only). The cost is ¥1,110/¥1,180 if purchased from Tokyo Station, and ¥600/¥620 if purchased from Yokohama Station.

A cheaper alternative is to buy the Enoshima-Kamakura Free Pass—this costs ¥1,470 for a roundtrip from Shinjuku to Fujisawa (limited to one roundtrip), and one day's unlimited use on the Enoden train.

JR Yokosuka Line 横須賀線

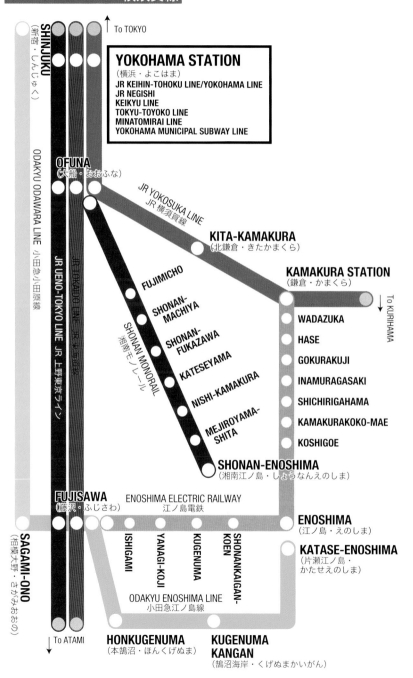

SHINJUKU
（新宿・しんじゅく）

To TOKYO

YOKOHAMA STATION
（横浜・よこはま）
JR KEIHIN-TOHOKU LINE/YOKOHAMA LINE
JR NEGISHI
KEIKYU LINE
TOKYU-TOYOKO LINE
MINATOMIRAI LINE
YOKOHAMA MUNICIPAL SUBWAY LINE

ODAKYU ODAWARA LINE 小田急小田原線

OFUNA
（大船・おおふな）

JR YOKOSUKA LINE
JR 横須賀線

KITA-KAMAKURA
（北鎌倉・きたかまくら）

KAMAKURA STATION
（鎌倉・かまくら）

To KURIHAMA

JR UENO-TOKYO LINE JR 上野東京ライン

JR TOKAIDO LINE JR 東海道線

FUJIMICHO

SHONAN-MACHIYA

SHONAN-FUKAZAWA

KATESEYAMA

NISHI-KAMAKURA

MEJIROYAMA-SHITA

SHONAN MONORAIL
湘南モノレール

WADAZUKA

HASE

GOKURAKUJI

INAMURAGASAKI

SHICHIRIGAHAMA

KAMAKURAKOKO-MAE

KOSHIGOE

SHONAN-ENOSHIMA
（湘南江ノ島・しょうなんえのしま）

FUJISAWA
（藤沢・ふじさわ）

ENOSHIMA ELECTRIC RAILWAY
江ノ島電鉄

ENOSHIMA
（江ノ島・えのしま）

ISHIGAMI

YANAGI-KOJI

KUGENUMA

SHONANKAIGAN-KOEN

KATASE-ENOSHIMA
（片瀬江ノ島・
かたせえのしま）

SAGAMI-ONO
（相模大野・さがみおおの）

ODAKYU ENOSHIMA LINE
小田急江ノ島線

To ATAMI

HONKUGENUMA
（本鵠沼・ほんくげぬま）

KUGENUMA
KANGAN
（鵠沼海岸・くげぬまかいがん）

Enoshima Electric Railway 江ノ島電鉄

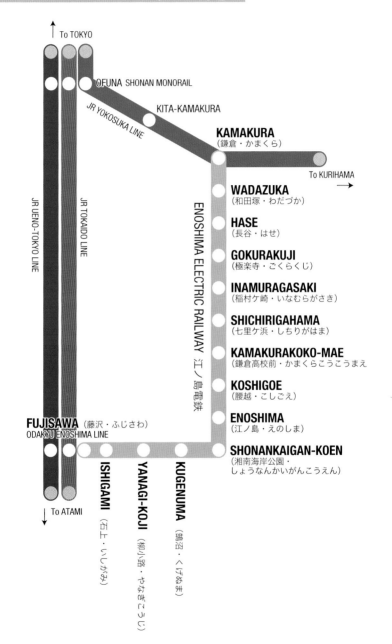

Shonan Monorail 湘南モノレール

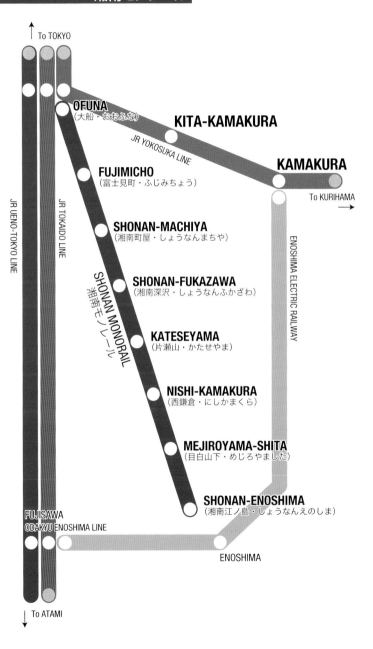

To TOKYO

OFUNA
(大船・おおふな)

KITA-KAMAKURA

JR YOKOSUKA LINE

KAMAKURA

FUJIMICHO
(富士見町・ふじみちょう)

To KURIHAMA

JR UENO-TOKYO LINE

JR TOKAIDO LINE

SHONAN-MACHIYA
(湘南町屋・しょうなんまちや)

ENOSHIMA ELECTRIC RAILWAY

SHONAN-FUKAZAWA
(湘南深沢・しょうなんふかざわ)

SHONAN MONORAIL
湘南モノレール

KATESEYAMA
(片瀬山・かたせやま)

NISHI-KAMAKURA
(西鎌倉・にしかまくら)

MEJIROYAMA-SHITA
(目白山下・めじろやました)

SHONAN-ENOSHIMA
(湘南江ノ島・しょうなんえのしま)

FUJISAWA
ODAKYU ENOSHIMA LINE

ENOSHIMA

To ATAMI

Kamakura and Enoshima Bus Routes

While there are city and tour buses that go to the major attractions in Kamakura it can also be seen on foot or by bicycle if you are into riding bikes, because its main attractions are concentrated in three areas: the vicinity of Kamakura Station, Kita-Kamakura Station, and Hase Station. [There is a bike rental shop next to Kamakura Station.]

The great Hachimangu Shrine is near Kamakura Station. The two leading Zen temples, Engakuji and Kenchoji, are near Kita-Kamakura Station, and the Great Buddha and Hase-dera near Hase Station on the Enoden Line.

There is a network of city buses that take in the more isolated attractions like Zeniarai Benten and Zuisenji. Some visitors who are determined to see these historically famous places opt for taxis.

Most of Kamakura's city bus service starts at Kamakura Station. When you exit the station you will see colorful buses lined up next to the station. If you do not already have the information you can get brochures showing which buses go to what attractions at the ticket windows.

The Enoden sightseeing bus is highly popular as it passes through many of the tourist spots that first-time visitors are likely to go to. There are three different tours:

From **Yoritomo-go**: The tour starts and ends at Kamakura Station. It is from 1 pm to 4 pm, and covers the tourist stops at Kencho-ji, Turugaoka Hachimangu Shrine, Kamakura-gu Shrine, Hase Kannon Temple, The Great Buddha (Kamakura Daibutsu) in that order. The fare is ¥2,250 (adult) and ¥1,320 (child), and includes admission fees to the temples and the bus fare. Reservation of seats is required.

From **Nagomi-go**: The tour starts and ends at Kamakura Station. The tour is from 10:30 am to 4:00 pm, and covers the tourist stops at Hase Kannon Temple, The Great Buddha (Kamakura Daibutsu), Engaku-ji, Turugaoka Hachimangu Shine in that order. The fare is ¥2,900 (adult) and ¥1,550 (child), and includes admission fees to the temples and the bus fare. Reservation of seats is required.

From **Shizuka-go**: The tour starts from Kamakura Station and ends at Enoshima Kaigan. It is from 10:20 am to 3:50 pm, and covers the tourist stops at Kencho-ji, Turugaoka Hachimangu Shrine, Kamakura-gu Shrine, Hase Kannon Temple, the Great Buddha (Kamakura Daibutsu), Enoshima in that order. The fare is ¥4,400 (adult) and ¥3,350 (child), and includes admission fees to the temples and the bus fare, and a lunch at Miyokawa Restaurant near Kamakura-gu Shrine. Reservation of seats is required.

Contact the Reservation Center of Enoden Bus Company on the following number: +81 (0) 466-24-5006. Reservations can be made three months in advance of the day of intended tour.

Keikyu Tourist Bus

Route No.	Departure	Via	Destination	Fare
2	JR Kamakura Station	→ Hasekannon	→ Daibutsumae	¥180
2	JR Kamakura Station	→ Daibutsu-mae	→ Kajiwara	¥240**
3	JR Kamakura Station	→ Daibutsu-mae	→ JR Kamakura	¥200**
4	JR Kamakura Station	→ Daibutsu-mae	→ Kamakurayama	¥200**
5	JR Kamakura Station	→ Daibutsu-mae	→ Suwagaya	¥250**
6	JR Kamakura Station	→ Enoshima Aquarium	→ Enoshima	¥310***
6	JR Ofuna Station	→ Enoshima Beach	→ Enoshima	¥310***

** These fares are fares from Kamakura Station to the Daibutsu.
*** These fares are fares from the station to Enoshima..

Enoden Tourist Bus

Departure	Main Via	Destination	Fare (Adult)
JR Fujisawa Station	→ Enoshima Beach, Enoshima Aquarium	→ Tsujido	¥290 (to Enoshima Beach, Enoshima Aquarium)
JR Kamakura Station	→ Hasekannon, Daibutsu-mae	→ Fujisawa Station	¥200 (to Daibutsu-mae)
JR Kamakura Station	→ Kitakamakura	→ JR Ofuna Station	¥240 (to Kitakamakura)
JR Ofuna Station	→ Enoshima Beach	→ Enoshima	¥300***

Keikyu Bus Routes 京急バス #1, #2, #3, #4, #5, #6

Enoden Bus Routes 江の電バス #102, #140, #1301, #601

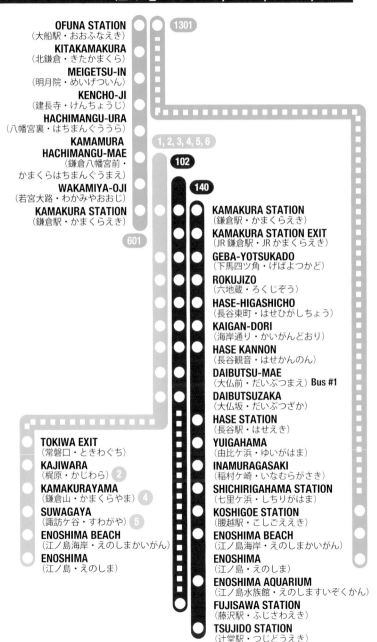

OFUNA STATION
（大船駅・おおふなえき）

KITAKAMAKURA
（北鎌倉・きたかまくら）

MEIGETSU-IN
（明月院・めいげついん）

KENCHO-JI
（建長寺・けんちょうじ）

HACHIMANGU-URA
（八幡宮裏・はちまんぐううら）

KAMAMURA
HACHIMANGU-MAE
（鎌倉八幡宮前・
かまくらはちまんぐうまえ）

WAKAMIYA-OJI
（若宮大路・わかみやおおじ）

KAMAKURA STATION
（鎌倉駅・かまくらえき）

1301

1, 2, 3, 4, 5, 6

102

140

601

KAMAKURA STATION
（鎌倉駅・かまくらえき）

KAMAKURA STATION EXIT
（JR鎌倉駅・JRかまくらえき）

GEBA-YOTSUKADO
（下馬四ツ角・げばよつかど）

ROKUJIZO
（六地蔵・ろくじぞう）

HASE-HIGASHICHO
（長谷東町・はせひがしちょう）

KAIGAN-DORI
（海岸通り・かいがんどおり）

HASE KANNON
（長谷観音・はせかんのん）

DAIBUTSU-MAE
（大仏前・だいぶつまえ）**Bus #1**

DAIBUTSUZAKA
（大仏坂・だいぶつざか）

HASE STATION
（長谷駅・はせえき）

YUIGAHAMA
（由比ケ浜・ゆいがはま）

INAMURAGASAKI
（稲村ケ崎・いなむらがさき）

SHICHIRIGAHAMA STATION
（七里ケ浜・しちりがはま）

KOSHIGOE STATION
（腰越駅・こしごええき）

ENOSHIMA BEACH
（江ノ島海岸・えのしまかいがん）

ENOSHIMA
（江ノ島・えのしま）

ENOSHIMA AQUARIUM
（江ノ島水族館・えのしますいぞくかん）

FUJISAWA STATION
（藤沢駅・ふじさわえき）

TSUJIDO STATION
（辻堂駅・つじどうえき）

TOKIWA EXIT
（常磐口・ときわぐち）

KAJIWARA
（梶原・かじわら）2

KAMAKURAYAMA
（鎌倉山・かまくらやま）4

SUWAGAYA
（諏訪ケ谷・すわがや）5

ENOSHIMA BEACH
（江ノ島海岸・えのしまかいがん）

ENOSHIMA
（江ノ島・えのしま）

Visiting Zushi and Hayama

Zushi

Zushi, about 50 train minutes southwest of Tokyo, is best known as a residential city for successful business people and writers who prefer its quiet atmosphere to the hustle and bustle of Tokyo and Yokohama, and for its beaches, its wind-surfing, and a large yacht harbor that is patronized by the well-to-do, including famous movie and TV stars. Numerous private landscaped gardens add to its bucolic beauty.

Zushi Marina is a popular beach resort with beautiful parks and classy restaurants. Because of its exotic atmosphere with palm trees, yachts and motorboats, it is frequently used as a location site for television media and fashion magazines. The peak of snow-covered Mt. Fuji can be seen from the city, adding to its special ambiance.

The classic Yanagiya Ryokan [Inn] in the Sakurayama area of Zushi is a popular place for visitors to stay. Sakurayama means "Cherry Blossom Mountain."

Hayama

Hayama, also on the west side of Miura Peninsula, facing Sagami Bay with scenic mountains in the background is approximately 50 kilometers southwest of Tokyo. Its scenic beauty and mild climate has made it a favorite residential area for people working in Yokohama and Tokyo, and it is the site of the Imperial family's vacation villa. It is noted for its long beaches and panoramic views of the ocean, the bay and the surrounding mountain chains.

Getting to Hayama from Tokyo

Railway Route
From Haneda Station: take a Keikyu Line to Shin-Zushi Station. From Narita Station: take a JR Sobu-Yokosuka Line to Zushi Station.

Keikyu bus provides a regular bus route in the town.

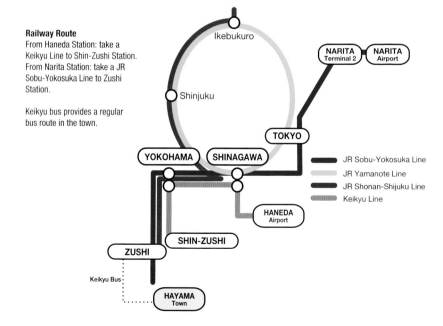

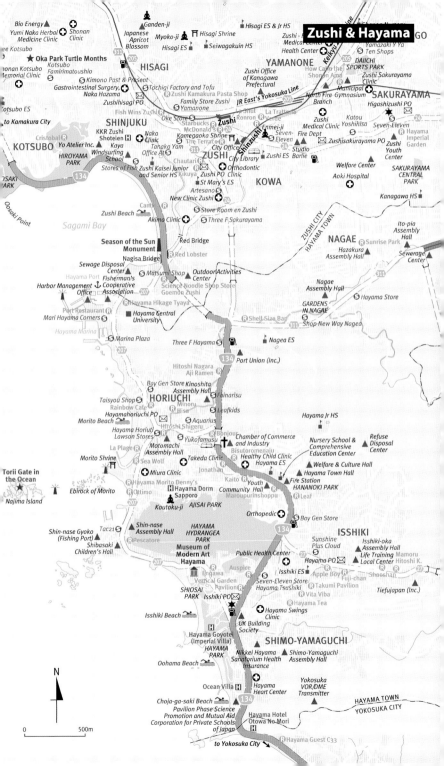

Getting to Camp Zama

Camp Zama is a United States Army post located about 40 km (25 mi) southwest of Tokyo. It is home to the U.S. Army Japan (USARJ)/I Corps (Forward), the United Nations Command (Rear), the 78th Aviation Battalion "Ninjas" (Provisional), the 500th Military Intelligence Brigade, the Japan Engineer District (U.S. Army Corps of Engineers), the 78th Signal Battalion and the 3rd Engineer Group of the Japan Ground Self-Defense Force.

The camp itself is in the Zama city limits while the two housing areas, Sagami Depot and Sagamihara Family Housing Area (SFHA), are located in the adjacent Sagamihara City. Once considered rural, this area has transformed into an urban area. New housing developments and communities along with shopping centers have increased the population and made traffic extremely congested.

There is no direct public transportation to Camp Zama from either Narita Airport or Haneda Airport. The only train access is via the Odakyu Line from Shinjuku Station on Tokyo's west side. The closest train station to the camp is the Odakyu Line's Sobudai-mae Station.

If you are traveling from Narita Airport take the Narita Sky Express to Nippori Station and transfer there to the Yamanote Line to go on to Shinjuku Station. Or take a limousine bus from the airport directly to Shinjuku Station. The limousine bus is ¥3,100; the train is ¥1,440. From Haneda Airport you take the Keikyu Line to Shinagawa Station and there transfer to the Yamanote Line that encircles central Tokyo, making sure you board a train going toward Gotanda and Osaki Stations instead of Tokyo Station…which is the long way around.

Going from Tokyo and other outlying U.S. military installations to Camp Zama takes from 1.5 to 3 hours, depending on the time of day.

Prior and during World War II Camp Zama was the Imperial Japanese Army Academy. Route 51, a road that goes to the Camp Zama from Tokyo, was specifically built in order for the Emperor of Japan to travel to review the graduating classes. The Emperor Hirohito visited the Camp Zama in 1937. Camp Zama also houses an emergency shelter for the Emperor, and to this day, it has been maintained by the U.S. Army Garrison Japan (17th ASG). The Camp Zama theater workshop is the only building remaining from the pre-occupation era. It is a large hall that was used for ceremonies by the Imperial Japanese Army.

Getting to Camp Zama from Tokyo

By Train
Take a Odakyu Line to Sobudai-mae Station, a 42-min trip from Shinjuku Station.

By Bus & Taxi
5 min from Sobudai-mae Station and get off the bus (or taxi) at the Zama Camp-mae stop.

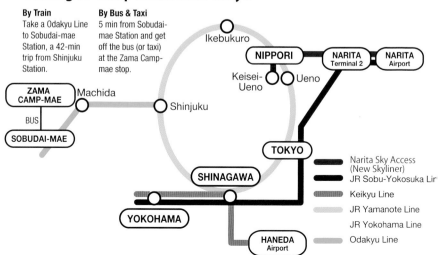

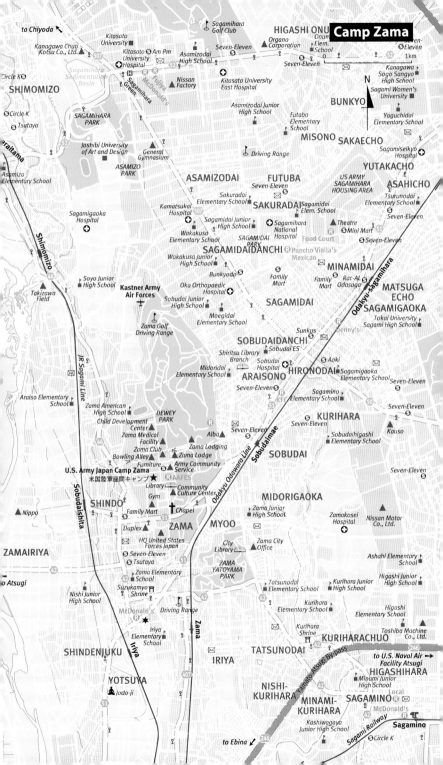

Getting to Atsugi Naval Air Facility

Naval **Air Facility Atsugi** [NAF Atsugi] is a naval air base located in the cities of Yamato and Abase in Kanagawa Prefecture, Japan. It is the largest United States Navy air base in the Pacific area and houses the squadrons of Carrier Air Wing 5, which deploys the aircraft carrier USS *George Washington* (CVN-73).

The U.S.'s CVW-5 shares the base with the Japan Maritime Self-Defense Force. NAF Atsugi is also home to Helicopter Antisubmarine Squadron (Light) 51 (HSL-51), which provides detachments of SH-60B LAMPS Mk III helicopters to forward deployed U.S. Navy guided missile cruisers, guided missile destroyers and frigates home-ported at nearby Naval Base Yokosuka.

Despite its name, the base is 4 nautical miles (7.4 km; 4.6 mi) northeast of the city of Atsugi, and is not adjacent to the city.

The Imperial Japanese Navy constructed the base in 1938 to house the Japanese 302 Naval Aviation Corps, one of Japan's most formidable fighter squadrons during World War II. Aircraft based at Atsugi shot down more than 300 American bombers during the fire bombings of 1945. After Japan's surrender, many of Atsugi's pilots refused to follow the Emperor's order to lay down their arms,

and took to the skies to drop leaflets on Tokyo and Yokohama urging locals to resist the Americans. Eventually, these pilots gave up and left Atsugi.

The U.S.'s General Douglas MacArthur arrived at Atsugi on August 30 to accept Japan's surrender and become the Supreme Allied Commander during the occupation of Japan.

NAF Atsugi was a major air base during the Korean and Vietnam Wars, serving fighters, bombers, and transport aircraft. One of the aircraft based at Atsugi was the U-2 spy plane piloted by Gary Powers, which provoked an international incident when it was downed over the Soviet Union.

In 1972, the U.S. and Japanese governments agreed to share ownership of the base. Lee Harvey Oswald, the accused assassin of President John F. Kennedy, was stationed at Atsugi for part of 1957 and 1958 as a Marine radar operator.

To go to the naval station from both Narita and Haneda Airports, take the JR Sobu-Yokosuka Line to Yokohama, and transfer to the Sagami Railway Main Line for Sagamino Station. From that station go by bus or taxi to the Hikojo-Seimonmae bus stop. The JR Sobu-Yokosuka Line can also be boarded at Tokyo Station and Shinagawa Station.

Getting to Atsugi Naval Air Facility from Tokyo

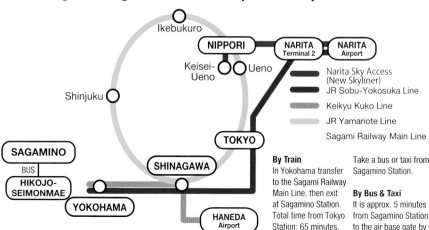

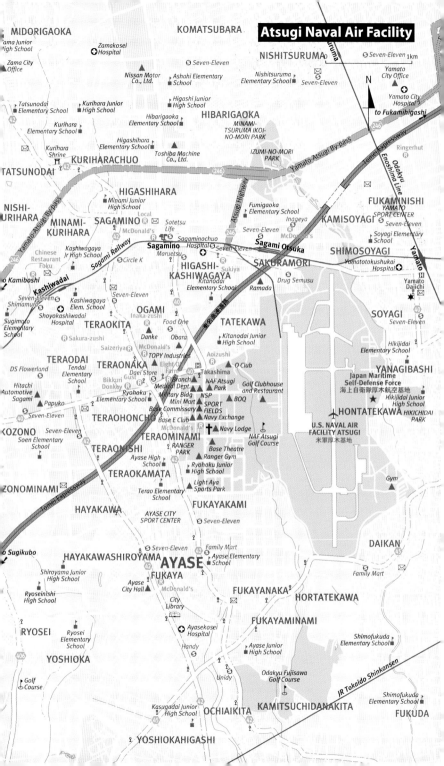

Atsugi Naval Air Facility

Getting to Yokota Air Base

Yokota Air Base, headquarters for United States Forces Japan [USFJ], is located near the city of Fussa 45 km [28 mi] northwest of central Tokyo. The base is currently used for airlift missions throughout East Asia, and is home to C-130 Hercules. The base houses 14,000 personnel, occupies a total area of 136,413 m² and has a 3,350-m runway.

The air base was originally constructed by the Imperial Japanese Army in 1940 as Tama Airfield, and used as a flight test center. It was taken over by U.S. Forces on September 4, 1945 and later expanded, reaching its current size around 1960.

YOKOTA/NARITA AIRPORT DAILY SHUTTLE BUS SERVICE: If traveling from Narita Airport and arriving at Terminal 2, take the free airport shuttle bus that goes to Terminal 1 to board the next shuttle. You must have military orders and SOFA status to use the shuttle.

YOKOTA AMC PASSENGER TERMINAL: Yokota Air Base's newly renovated AMC Passenger Terminal is located on the main part of the base next to the flight line. It is a 5-7 minute walk from the Kanto Lodge. If you arrive at Yokota Pax Terminal, either walk, take a taxi, or the free base shuttle to your destination.

HOTELS, LODGING & AIRPORT TRANSPORTATION: The Kanto Lodge is one of PACAF's largest hotel operations. Transportation to and from Narita Airport is provided by bus from the Kanto Lodge.

Dialing for Information
U.S. to Yokota: When calling from United States dial 011-81-31175 , then the last 5 digits of the DSN number. **Off-Base to Yokota:** When calling from Off-Base to Yokota Air Base use (042) 552-2510 to get the Yokota Air Base Directory then last 5 digits of the DSN number. **Yokota to U.S.:** When calling from Yokota to the U.S. dial 98-001-1+ area code and number.

Friendship Festival
Each year in August, Yokota Air Base opens its gates to the Japanese community for its annual Friendship Festival. For two days between 9 am and 8 pm local residents can tour the base. Food and events are provided for all ages. Roughly 200,000 visitors show up each year.

Getting to Yokota Air Force from Tokyo

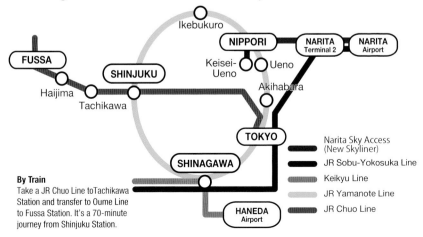

By Train
Take a JR Chuo Line toTachikawa Station and transfer to Oume Line to Fussa Station. It's a 70-minute journey from Shinjuku Station.

Yokota Air Base

500m

N

Minamidaira
to Iruma
to Mizuho
Mizuho Bypass
Walker Blvd

Hamurasankei Hospital
Hamuradaisan Jr. High School
Musashino Elem. School
Nishi-Tama Hospital
Seven-Eleven

FUTABACHO

KISHI

NAKAHARA

WEST HOUSING AREA
Cafeteria / Coffee Shop
Shoppette
Yokota West Elem. School
Yokota Passenger Terminal

YOKOTA KICHINAI
Extra
Commissary
Meijirodaini Hospital

MUSASHINODAI KOEN
Musashinodai Library
Fussa City Gymnasium
Welcia
Marufuji

MUSASHINODAI

Tokyo Ring Rd
Walker Blvd

YOKOTA AIR BASE

KISHI

O'Club Barber Shop
Kanto Lodge
Mini Mall
Yokota Chapel
Crabb
Airlift Avenue
Davis St

FUSSA
Taisei Hospital
Interior Matsumoto
Higashi-Fussa
Friendship Blvd
Art & Craft
Barrack, Bldg 413
Community Bank
Burger King
Yokota Community Center
Bowling Center
Turner St
Box Office Video
Yokota Library
Samurai Fitness Center

East Gym
EAST HOUSING AREA

Seven-Eleven

YOKOTAKICHINAI

George S. Arnold Dr.
JR Hachiko Line
Tokyo Ring Rd

Loundry/Dry Cleaning
Theatre
Base Hospital

Base Ball Field

McGuire Avenue

Fussadaisan Elem. School
Baigo
Ozam Value
Ushihama

USHIHAMA
FUSSANOMIYA
City Chuo Library
KUMAGAWA NINOMIYA
Fussadaiichi Jr. High School

Seven-Eleven

Shin Okutama Hwy
Okutama Hwy
Fussadaisan Jr. High School

James Ave
Earhart Ave

NISHISUNACHO

NAMIDENEN
Kumagawa Shrine
Mori-no-Bijutsukan Museum
杜の美術館
Fussadaigo Elem. School
Mutsumi-bashi-dori

Okutama Hwy

AAFES Administration
Furniture Mart
Hajima Driving School
Yokota Par-3 Driving Range

Yokota Par-3 Golf Course
Itsukaichi Road
Fussa City Recycle Center

Nishisuna Elem. School

FUTTO ATHLETIC GROUND

Seibu Haijima Line

MIHORICHO

Hajimadaini Elem. School

Tokyo Ring Rd
Haijima

KUMAGAWA
Spa Yura-no-Sato

MATSUBARACHO

to Akishima

Haijimadaidan Elem. School

Hajimadaini Elem. School

Seiyu

Showa-no-mori Golf Course

Forest Inn Showakan

SHOWA AIRCRAFT INDUSTRY, AKISHIMA FACTORY

Getting to Yokosuka Naval Base

Yokosuka is America's most important naval facility in the Western Pacific, and the largest, most strategically important overseas US Naval installation in the world. The centerpiece of the Pacific Fleet forward presence mission is the Forward-Deployed Naval Forces (FDNF) in Japan. The 17 ships in Japan make up the KITTY HAWK aircraft carrier battle group in Yokosuka and the BELLEAU WOOD amphibious ready group in Sasebo.

Yokosuka boasts the largest and best of everything the Navy has to offer, with 23,000 military and civilian personnel. The base comprises 568 acres and is located at the entrance of Tokyo Bay, 69 km [43 mi] south of Tokyo and approximately 29 km [18 mi] south of Yokohama on the Miura peninsula.

A new Fleet Activities Center was constructed as part of the Japanese facilities improvement program, under which the Japanese government provides support for the maintenance of U.S. forces to assist in the defense of Japan. The new Fleet Activities Center boasts a wide variety of services, including a mini-mart, barber shop, full service gymnasium, Fleet Lounge, roller skating rink, overseas telephone service center, internet surf shop cybercafe, bowling and indoor games, and more.

At the 300,000 sq. ft Fleet Recreation Center, located a short walk from the waterfront, is a huge gym, several racquetball courts, a state-of-the-art weight room, outdoor gear and an internet café.

Yokosuka has long played a part in Japan's history. America's Commodore Matthew Perry's landing in the area in 1853 initiated the end of country's feudal shogunate period and the beginning of its modernization. During World War II the base was spared from heavy bombing because the U.S. military had already chosen it as a post-war base location.

Annually in early August the base sponsors a "Friendship Day," inviting local residents to tour ships docked at the base and check out vendor stalls set up for the occasion. Visitors are also welcomed for on-base fireworks displays and Halloween parties.

Also in August Yokosuka City hosts an annual *Kaikoku Matsuri* [Kie-koe-kuu Motsue-ree], or "Opening of the Country Festival," marking the opening of the country to the outside world. This event is attended by up to 400,000 people from the Greater Tokyo and Yokohama areas.

Getting to Yokosuka Naval Base from Tokyo

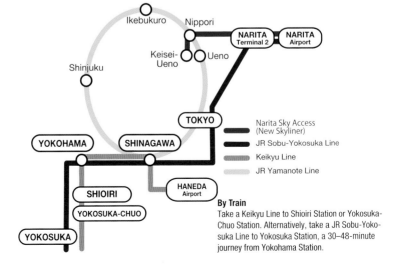

By Train
Take a Keikyu Line to Shioiri Station or Yokosuka-Chuo Station. Alternatively, take a JR Sobu-Yokosuka Line to Yokosuka Station, a 30–48-minute journey from Yokohama Station.

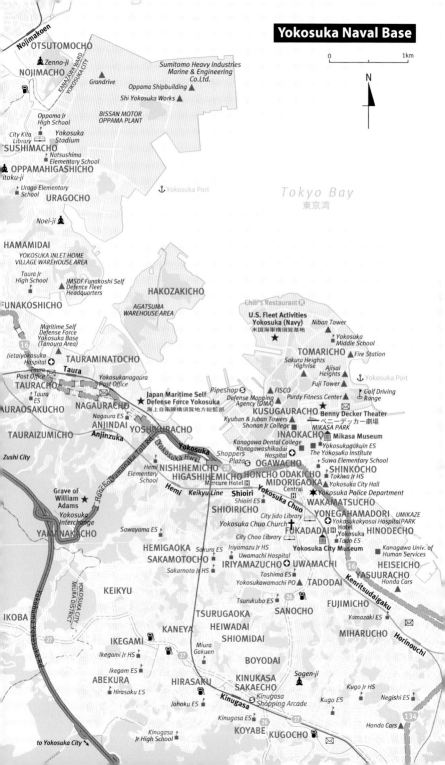

Yokosuka Naval Base

0   1km

N

Nojimakoen
OTSUTOMOCHO

Zenno-ji
NOJIMACHO

Grandrive

Sumitomo Heavy Industries
Marine & Engineering
Co.Ltd.

KANAZAWA WARD
YOKOSUKA CITY

Oppama Shipbuilding
Shi Yokosuka Works

Oppama Jr
High School
BISSAN MOTOR
OPPAMA PLANT

City Kita
Library

Yokosuka
Stadium

SUSHIMACHO

Natsushima
Elementary School

OPPAMAHIGASHICHO

itoku-ji

Urago Elementary
School
URAGOCHO

Yokosuka Port

T o k y o   B a y
東京湾

Noei-ji

HAMAMIDAI

YOKOSUKA INLET HOME
VILLAGE WAREHOUSE AREA

Taura Jr
High School

JMSDF Funakoshi Self
Defence Fleet
Headquarters

HAKOZAKICHO

Chili's Restaurant

FUNAKOSHICHO

AGATSUMA
WAREHOUSE AREA

U.S. Fleet Activities
Yokosuka (Navy)
米国海軍横須賀基地

Niban Tower

Maritime Self
Defense Force
Yokosuka Base
(Tanoura Area)

Yokosuka
Middle School

Fire Station

Jietaiyokosuka
Hospital

TAURAMINATOCHO

TOMARICHO

Sakura Heights
Highrise

Ajisai
Heights

Yokosuka Port

Taura
Post Office

Taura

Yokosukanagaura
Post Office

Pipeshop

FISCO

Fuji Tower

Golf Driving
Range

TAURACHO

Taura
ES

Defense Mapping
Agency (DMA)

KUSUGAURACHO

Purdy Fitness Center

Benny Decker Theater
ベニーデッカー劇場

TAURAOSAKUCHO

NAGAURACHO

Japan Maritime Self
Defense Force Yokosuka
海上自衛隊横須賀地方総監部

Kyuban & Juban Towers

MIKASA PARK

ANJINDAI

Nagaura ES

YOSHIKURACHO

Shonan Jr College

INAOKACHO

Mikasa Museum

TAURAIZUMICHO

Anjinzuka

Kanagawa Dental College

Yokosukagakuin ES
The Yokosuka Institute

Zushi City

Yokosuka Hwy.

Shoppers
Plaza

Kanagawashikadai
Hospital

Suwa Elementary School

SHINKOCHO

Hemi
Elementary
School

NISHIHEMICHO

OGAWACHO

Tokiwa Jr HS

Grave of
William
Adams

HIGASHIHEMICHO

HONCHO ODAKICHO
MIDORIGAOKA

Yokosuka City Hall

Yokosuka
Interchange

Hemi

Keikyu Line

Mercure Hotel

Shioiri

Central

Yokosuka Police Department

YAKATACHO

Shioiri ES

WAKAMATSUCHO

SHIOIRICHO

Yokosuka Chuo

YONEGAHAMADORI

UMIKAZE
Yokosukakyosai Hospital PARK

Sawayama ES

City Jido Library
Yokosuka Chuo Church

FUKADADAI

Yokosuka
Hotel

HINODECHO

HEMIGAOKA

Sakura ES

Iriyamazu Jr HS

City Choo Library

Tado ES

SAKAMOTOCHO

Sakarnoto Jr HS

Uwamachi Hospital

Yokosuka City Museum

HEISEICHO

IRIYAMAZUCHO

UWAMACHI

Kanagawa Univ. of
Human Services

Toshima ES

TADODAI

YASUURACHO

Yokosukawamachi PO

Honda Cars

Tsurukubo ES

FUJIMICHO

IKOBA

TSURUGAOKA

SANOCHO

Yamazaki ES

KANEYA

HEIWADAI

MIHARUCHO

Horinouchi

IKEGAMI

Miura
Gakuen

SHIOMIDAI

Ikegami Jr HS

BOYODAI

Ikegami ES

KINUKASA

Sogen-ji

Kugo Jr HS

ABEKURA

HIRASAKU

SAKAECHO

Hirasaku ES

Johoku ES

Kinugasa

Kinugasa
Shopping Arcade

Kugo ES

Negishi ES

Honda Cars

Kinugasa ES

to Yokosuka City

Kinugasa
Jr High School

KOYABE

KUGOCHO

Yokosuka has a number of extraordinary attractions the draw visitors the year around. These include the *The Perry Landing Park* which marks the place where the U.S. Navy's Commodore Perry came ashore from his squadron of "black ships" anchored in Tokyo Bay, forcing the Tokugawa Shogunate to sign a treaty of peace and friendship with the United States, thus opening the country to the world after 250 years of isolation. The park is located in Kurihama, a short distance from Yokosuka Station, by either the Keikyu or JR train line.

Another famous site in Kurihama is the burial grounds in a hilltop park dedicated to Japan's most famous early foreign resident… an English ship's pilot and boat carpenter whose damaged ship showed up in Kyushu in 1600. Eventually taken to Edo, which became the headquarters of the new Tokugawa Shogunate in 1603, Adams was retained by Shogun Ieyasu Tokugawa for his knowledge of European affairs, European weapons and shipbuilding. Awarded with a fief in Miura near Yokosuka, Adams played a significant role in Japan until his patron's death in 1616. His life was the inspiration for the Richard Chamberlain character in the famous book and film *Shogun*.

The hilltop park where Adams' tomb is located is known *Anjinzuka Park*, or "Pilot's Park." The park contains 10,000 cherry trees. It is about 1.6 km (1 mile) from Anjinzuka Station on the Keikyu Line, a few minutes from Yokosuka Station.

Also on the list of things to see in Yokosuka is the Battleship Mikasa, the flagship of Admiral Togo during the Russo-Japanese war [1904–1905] when the Japanese fleet annihilated the Russian naval forces in the battle of Tsushima.

Going to Yokosuka from Narita Airport

There are several ways to get to Yokosuka from Narita Airport. Regular JR commuter trains depart from Narita Airport for JR Yokosuka Station hourly. Some of the trains go all the way to JR Yokosuka Station. Others require a transfer wherever that particular train terminates to the next train bound for Yokosuka or Kurihama (about 3 hours, ¥2,590). These trains offer a ¥2,060 Green Car seating upgrade. Green Cars feature more comfortable seats and a drink and snack service. You can avoid having to transfer by making sure that the JR train you board at Narita goes all the way to Yokosuka.

If the JR train you board terminates at Tokyo Station you can reboard a train on the same platform that is bound for Yokosuka. (The JR Yokosuka Line platforms are on the lower level of Tokyo Station.) The trip from Tokyo Station to JR Yokosuka Station, which is about 2.5 kilometers from the more centrally-located Yokosuka-Chuo Keikyu station, takes 75 minutes.

If you use the JR Yokosuka Line from Tokyo Station or Shinagawa Station be sure to take a train bound for Yokosuka or Kurihama (and note that the front 4 cars of the train are removed at Zushi when Yokosuka-bound, so ask if you are not sure where to sit). Local buses connect Yokosuka-Chuo and JR Yokosuka stations on a frequent basis (¥180).

One of the simplest ways to go from Narita Airport to Yokosuka is to take the **Narita Sky Access** train to Sengakuji Station and change there to a Keikyu Limited Express train for Yokosuka-Chuo Station (2½ hours, ¥2,090). You may also board a Keikyu Limited Express at Shinagawa Station in Tokyo. The trip from there to Yokosuka-Chuo Station takes 43 minutes (¥640).

Another choice is to take the Narita Express train to Shinagawa Station, transfer to the Keikyu Line train that goes to Yokosuka-Chuo Station (¥2,130) — a 2-hour trip. If you have a JR Pass the cost is only ¥640 (for the Keikyu Line portion). From Yokosuka Station there are buses that go to the base; or you can go by taxi. IDs are needed for admission to the base.

From Haneda Airport to Yokosuka Naval Base

From Haneda Airport, take any Keikyu Line local or express train and change at Keikyu-Kamata Station to a limited express that is headed towards Yokohama. The trip to Yokosuka-Chuo Station takes 50–60 minutes and costs ¥810. From the station go by bus or taxi.

Sailors Hangout

Yokosuka's best-known off-base sailor-oriented entertainment district is known as The Honch, a half-block from the CFAY Naval Base Main Gate. The Honch is home to dozens of different bars, eateries and nightclubs. Most take both U.S. dollars and Japanese yen, but use a 1:100 exchange rate (1 U.S. cent = 1 Japanese yen). These establishments range from traditional Japanese-style bars to American-oriented hangouts that cater primarily to American sailors. Additionally, there are several "buy-me-a-drink" bars located in the area, typically staffed by Filipina women.

JR Yokosuka, Sobu Line Rapid Service JR横須賀線総武線 [快速]

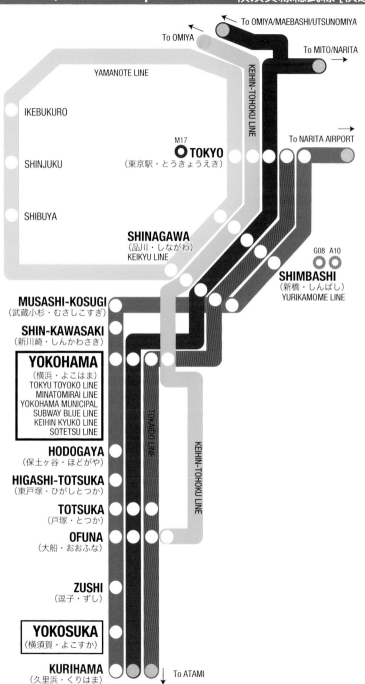

To OMIYA/MAEBASHI/UTSUNOMIYA

To OMIYA

To MITO/NARITA

YAMANOTE LINE

IKEBUKURO

KEIHIN-TOHOKU LINE

M17
TOKYO
（東京駅・とうきょうえき）

To NARITA AIRPORT

SHINJUKU

SHIBUYA

SHINAGAWA
（品川・しながわ）
KEIKYU LINE

G08 A10
SHIMBASHI
（新橋・しんばし）
YURIKAMOME LINE

MUSASHI-KOSUGI
（武蔵小杉・むさしこすぎ）

SHIN-KAWASAKI
（新川崎・しんかわさき）

YOKOHAMA
（横浜・よこはま）
TOKYU TOYOKO LINE
MINATOMIRAI LINE
YOKOHAMA MUNICIPAL
SUBWAY BLUE LINE
KEIHIN KYUKO LINE
SOTETSU LINE

TOKAIDO LINE

KEIHIN-TOHOKU LINE

HODOGAYA
（保土ヶ谷・ほどがや）

HIGASHI-TOTSUKA
（東戸塚・ひがしとつか）

TOTSUKA
（戸塚・とつか）

OFUNA
（大船・おおふな）

ZUSHI
（逗子・ずし）

YOKOSUKA
（横須賀・よこすか）

KURIHAMA
（久里浜・くりはま）

To ATAMI

Visiting the Highland Paradise and the Sacred Volcano

During the long Tokugawa Shogunate period in Japan's history [1603–1867] Hakone was a key location on the famous Tokaido road by which the country's clan lords traveled from their fiefs to Edo [Tokyo] in elaborate processions every other year to perform courtier duties at the shogun's court. They had to keep their families in Edo at all times as a control measure to avoid insurrections.

From 1618 to 1878 the shogunate maintained a barrier or check-point in Hakone to control people going to and from Edo, to prevent military arms from being smuggled into Edo and to prevent the families of the lords from leaving the shogunate capital. In the fall of each year one of these famous processions of the lords is reenacted along the shores of Lake Hakone, with the lord, his attendants and samurai warriors in authentic costumes. There is also a museum in Hakone that commemorates this extraordinary shogunate policy.

There are several popular one-day trips from Tokyo that are unique and unforgettable, with Nikko, north of Tokyo being one of the best-known. But Hakone, approximately two train or bus hours southwest of Tokyo, is in a class by itself.

The municipality of Hakone is located in the high Hakone Mountains on the edge of a large lake that was formed in the caldera of an immense volcano which collapsed after its last eruption some 3,000 years ago.

The caldera is so large that most people are surprised when they find out what it is, and began to fully appreciate it only after they discover that the outer ring of the caldera is marked by a series of hot springs that have been developed as spas and in use for many centuries.

But it is the spectacular lake, the incredible view of Mt. Fuji from the lake area, the ring of hot spring spas around the lake, and the cool summer temperatures that attract most people to this mountain resort.

Getting to Hakone from Tokyo

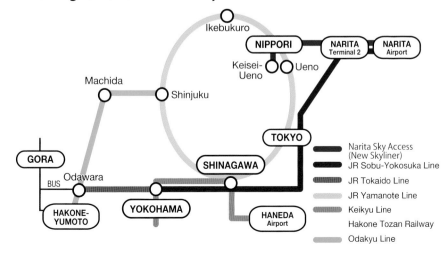

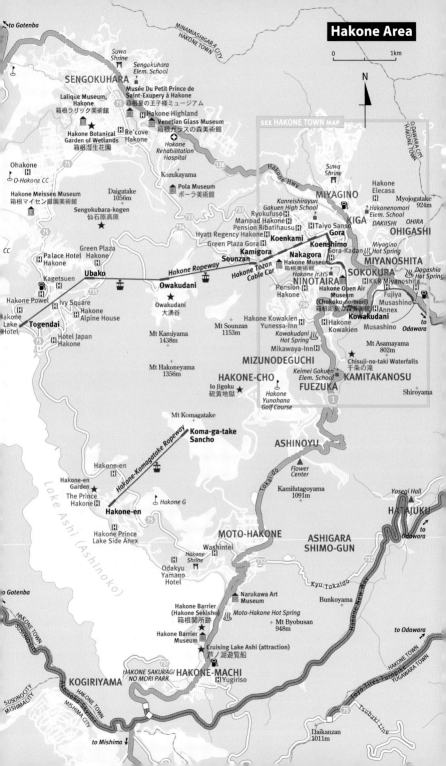

Odakyu Electric Railway 小田急電鉄

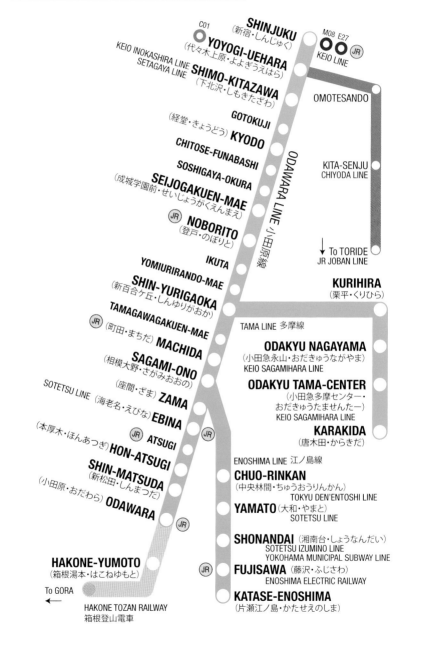

SHINJUKU （新宿・しんじゅく）

C01 YOYOGI-UEHARA （代々木上原・よよぎうえはら）

M08 E27 KEIO LINE JR

KEIO INOKASHIRA LINE
SETAGAYA LINE

SHIMO-KITAZAWA （下北沢・しもきたざわ）

OMOTESANDO

GOTOKUJI

KYODO （経堂・きょうどう）

CHITOSE-FUNABASHI

KITA-SENJU
CHIYODA LINE

SOSHIGAYA-OKURA

SEIJOGAKUEN-MAE （成城学園前・せいじょうがくえんまえ）

JR NOBORITO （登戸・のぼりと）

↓ To TORIDE
JR JOBAN LINE

IKUTA

YOMIURIRANDO-MAE

KURIHIRA （栗平・くりひら）

SHIN-YURIGAOKA （新百合ケ丘・しんゆりがおか）

TAMAGAWAGAKUEN-MAE

TAMA LINE 多摩線

JR MACHIDA （町田・まちだ）

ODAKYU NAGAYAMA
（小田急永山・おだきゅうながやま）
KEIO SAGAMIHARA LINE

SAGAMI-ONO （相模大野・さがみおおの）

ZAMA （座間・ざま）

ODAKYU TAMA-CENTER
（小田急多摩センター・
おだきゅうたませんたー）
KEIO SAGAMIHARA LINE

SOTETSU LINE

EBINA （海老名・えびな）

KARAKIDA （唐木田・からきだ）

JR ATSUGI

JR

HON-ATSUGI （本厚木・ほんあつぎ）

ENOSHIMA LINE 江ノ島線

SHIN-MATSUDA （新松田・しんまつだ）

CHUO-RINKAN
（中央林間・ちゅうおうりんかん）
TOKYU DEN'ENTOSHI LINE

ODAWARA （小田原・おだわら）

YAMATO （大和・やまと）
SOTETSU LINE

JR

SHONANDAI （湘南台・しょうなんだい）
SOTETSU IZUMINO LINE
YOKOHAMA MUNICIPAL SUBWAY LINE

HAKONE-YUMOTO
（箱根湯本・はこねゆもと）

JR FUJISAWA （藤沢・ふじさわ）
ENOSHIMA ELECTRIC RAILWAY

To GORA
←
HAKONE TOZAN RAILWAY
箱根登山電車

KATASE-ENOSHIMA
（片瀬江ノ島・かたせえのしま）

ODAWARA LINE 小田原線

Scenic Hakone

Regular cruises are available on the lake all year-around, but visitors are advised that the dramatic view of Mt. Fuji and the surrounding area may be hidden by clouds during the summer months, with the best views in the early morning and late evening.

In addition to its fleet of sightseeing boats, the Hakone area also boasts a number of cable cars and ropeways that ascend to the heights of the steam-emitting ring of the caldera and to some of the spas.

Getting to Hakone from Tokyo

Hakone is well-served by bus and train lines not only from Tokyo but also from other cities around the huge base of Mt. Fuji and the Izu Peninsula range of mountains where it is located. These transportation systems include:

Odakyu Railways: This operates direct trains between Tokyo's Shinjuku Station and Hakone-Yumoto Station, the most popular of which is the famous "Romance Car" limited express, which takes about 85 minutes one way [limited in this case means it makes few stops in between], and costs ¥2,080. A semi-express train ride from Shinjuku to Odawara, with a transfer to Hakone-Yumoto Station, takes approximately 1¾ hours and costs ¥1,190.

Odakyu also offers the Hakone Free Pass [page 186 for details] which includes the round-trip from Shinjuku to Hakone and unlimited use of selected trains, cable cars, ropeways, boats and buses in the Hakone area.

Japan Railways (JR) JR trains from Tokyo Station take you to Odawara at the foot of

Hakone Mountains, where you have to transfer to other trains or buses. [The above mentioned Hakone Free Pass can also be used from Odawara Station if you arrive there aboard a JR train.]

Local and rapid trains on the JR Tokaido Main Line, which stop at Tokyo, Shimbashi and Shinagawa Stations, make the trip to Odawara in 70–90 minutes. The JR Shonan Shinjuku Line, with stops at Ikebukuro, Shinjuku and Shibuya Stations, also provides service to Odawara. Each trip costs ¥1,490. A transfer to Hakone-Yumoto Station is required—this ride is free if one has the Hazone Free Pass.

The JR Tokaido Shinkansen goes from Tokyo and Shinagawa to Odawara in about 30 minutes. [Note that all Kodama Shinkansen but only some Hikari Shinkansen stop at Odawara Station.] The cost is ¥4,500.

From Odawara and Hakone-Yumoto

There are frequent bus services between Odawara and the Hakone area. The one-way journey from Odawara takes about 50 minutes.

A slow and scenic way of reaching Hakone from Odawara or Hakone-Yumoto is to take the Hakone Tozan Railway to Gora, followed by a cable car and ropeway ride to Togendai at the northern end of of the lake. From there continue on by boat to Hakone town. The whole journey is covered by the Hakone Free Pass.

The **Odakyu-Hakone Highway Bus** is an express highway bus with scheduled services to Hakone and Gotemba, via Shinjuku every 30 minutes. The journey takes about 2¼ hours. The Hakone Free Pass can be used but a separate ticket is needed for the Shinjuku-Gotemba portion of the trip.

Transportation within the Hakone Area

The Hakone Tozan Bus Company provides scheduled tours to the various attractions within Hakone itself as well as to the surrounding communities of Odawara, Yumoto, Gotemba and Numazu. Gotemba, on the southeast edge of Mt. Fuji, is a major gateway for hundreds of thousands of people who climb the mountain each year during the July-August season.

Sightseeing Tours to Hakone

The Japan Travel Bureau [JTB], O-Tours Hakone and several other tour companies provide daily tours from Tokyo to Hakone, with hotel pick-ups. Your hotel Information Desk can make reservations for you. Go to the following websites: www.jtb-sunrisetours.jp, and www.odakyu.jp for more information in advance.

Things to do in Hakone

One of the more popular things for visitors to do in Hakone is take a ride on the Hakone Tozan Railway, which leaves from a station at the gateway of Hakone, winds around and ascends one of the steepest slopes in Japan to the village of Gora 550 m above sea level. You can get off the train at its various stops or stay on until it reaches the end of the line. The breathtaking ride up the steep slope provides panoramic views of the huge volcanic caldera and Lake Hakone.

In Gora you can board a cable car that takes you to Owakudani, a hot spring spa resort, and there board the Hakone Ropeway, for a 33-minute gondola ride to the top of Mt. Sounzan. This ride takes you over the spectacular Owakudani Gorge and offers views of sulfurous gases rising out of the valley floor.

Among the attractions at the station are public parks, the Hakone Museum of Art, and a number of landscaped gardens. The museum features Japanese ceramics and sponsors regular exhibitions for visitors.

For your return trip on the Hakone Ropeway you can descend to the town of Togendai on the shore of Hakone Lake [known in Japanese as Ashinoko or Lake Ashi] where you can transfer to a sightseeing ship that cruises around the lake. Seven of these cruise ships are made up like pirate ships, making for some great photographs.

Some visitors "do" Hakone on one-day tours. Others choose to stay overnight or longer in one of the amazing hot spring spa resorts that are perched on the rim of the huge caldera. Among the oldest and most popular of the hot spring resorts are Hakone-Yumoto and Miyanoshita—two of the seven hot spring spa towns spread around the rim of Hakone Lake.

The Hakone-Yumoto resort area has a number of hot springs spas, some of which have been in use for over a thousand years. [The most famous one is Yumoto Spa—reputed to be 1,000 years old.] To go directly to Hakone-Yumoto take the Hakone Tozan Railway Line from Odawara Station—a 15-minute ride.

Miyanoshita [which translates as "Below a Shrine] is similar to Hakone-Yumoto but on a smaller scale, and was the first of the Hakone hot spring areas to become popular with foreign visitors and residents of Tokyo and Yokohama. It has maintained its original 1890s appearance and provides a nostalgic experience.

One of the seven hot spring towns in Hakone, the Hakone Kowakien Yunessun is styled as a theme-park, and has one pool where guests can bathe with swimsuits on.

HAKONE FREE PASS

This pass can be purchased from the Odakyu Sightseeing Service Center, Odakyu Line at Shinjuku Station, West Exit F.

Fares vary, depending on the departure station used, and cost between ¥4,000 to ¥5,140 (adults) for a 2-day pass, and ¥4,500 to ¥5,640 for a 3-day pass. (The equivalent fares for a child's pass will be ¥1,000 to ¥1,500 for a 2-day pass, and ¥1,250 to ¥1,750 for a 3-day pass.)

The pass can be used for unlimited rides on Hakone Tozan Line*, Hakone Tozan Bus**, Hakone Tozan Cable Car, Hakone Ropeway, Hakone Sightseeing Cruise, Odakyu Hakone Highway Bus**, Numazu Tozan Tokai bus**, and Tourist Facility Circle Route Bus (Hakone Tozan Bus).
*Valid for one round trip on Odakyu Line portions; however unlimited boardings along this line is allowed.
**For specified portions. Beyond specified portions, additional tickets may be required.

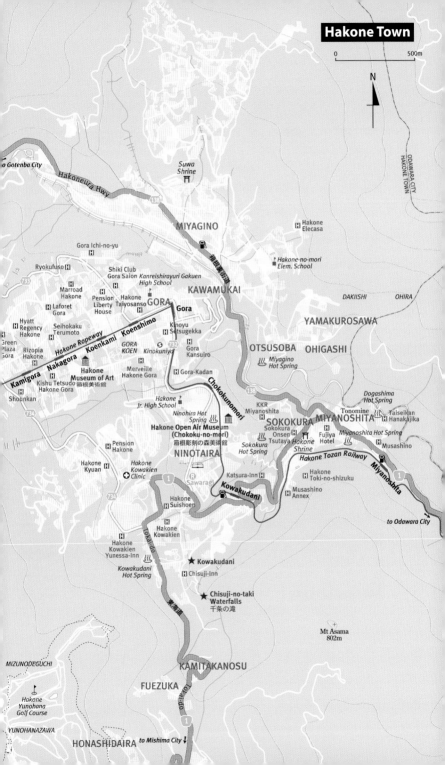

Hakone Tozan Railway Line

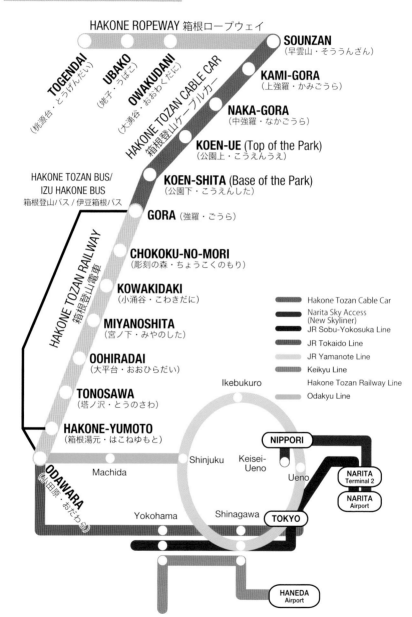

HAKONE ROPEWAY 箱根ロープウェイ

SOUNZAN
(早雲山・そううんざん)

TOGENDAI
(桃源台・とうげんだい)

UBAKO
(姥子・うばこ)

OWAKUDANI
(大涌谷・おおわくだに)

HAKONE TOZAN CABLE CAR
箱根登山ケーブルカー

KAMI-GORA
(上強羅・かみごうら)

NAKA-GORA
(中強羅・なかごうら)

KOEN-UE (Top of the Park)
(公園上・こうえんうえ)

HAKONE TOZAN BUS/
IZU HAKONE BUS
箱根登山バス / 伊豆箱根バス

KOEN-SHITA (Base of the Park)
(公園下・こうえんした)

GORA (強羅・ごうら)

CHOKOKU-NO-MORI
(彫刻の森・ちょうこくのもり)

HAKONE TOZAN RAILWAY
箱根登山電車

KOWAKIDAKI
(小涌谷・こわきだに)

MIYANOSHITA
(宮ノ下・みやのした)

OOHIRADAI
(大平台・おおひらだい)

TONOSAWA
(塔ノ沢・とうのさわ)

Ikebukuro

HAKONE-YUMOTO
(箱根湯元・はこねゆもと)

NIPPORI

ODAWARA
(小田原・おだわら)

Machida

Shinjuku

Keisei-
Ueno

Ueno

NARITA
Terminal 2

NARITA
Airport

Yokohama

Shinagawa

TOKYO

HANEDA
Airport

Hakone Tozan Cable Car
Narita Sky Access
(New Skyliner)
JR Sobu-Yokosuka Line
JR Tokaido Line
JR Yamanote Line
Keikyu Line
Hakone Tozan Railway Line
Odakyu Line

Hakone Tozan Bus 箱根登山バス

ROUTE 1	ROUTE 2	
		ODAWARA — HAKONECHO (HAKONE-EN) 小田原－箱根町
		ODAWARA — KOJIEI — HAKONECHO (HAKONE-EN) 小田原－湖尻－箱根町
		BUS STOPS
○	○	**ODAWARA STATION** 小田原駅
○	○	**YUMOTO STATION** 湯本駅
○	○	**OHIRADAI** 大平台
○	○	**MIYANOSHITA** 宮の下
○	○	**KOWAKIEN** 小涌園
○		**YUNOHANA HOTEL** 湯の花ホテル
○		**MOTO-HAKONE** 元箱根
○		**SEKISHO-ATO** 関所跡
○		**HAKONECHO** 箱根町
	○	**SOUNZAN STATION** 早雲山駅
	○	**OWAKUDANI** 大涌谷
	○	**UBAKO** 姥子
	○	**KOJIRI** 湖尻
○	○	**HAKONE-EN** 箱根園

Odakyu Hakone Highway Bus 小田急箱根高速バス

	SHINJUKU-EKI — GOTEMBA — YAMA NO HOTEL 新宿駅－御殿場駅－山のホテル
	BUS STOPS
○	**SHINJUKU STATION** 新宿駅
○	**GOTENBA STATION** 御殿場駅
○	**HAKONE GARASU-NO-MORI** 箱根ガラスの森
○	**HAKONE SENGOKU INFORMATION CENTER** 箱根仙石案内所
○	**SENGOKU-KOGEN** 仙石高原
○	**HAKONE TOGENDAI** 箱根桃源台
○	**HAKONE-EN** 箱根園
○	**HAKONE ODAKYU YAMA NO HOTEL** 箱根小田急山のホテル

Marugoto Hakone-go まるごと箱根号

SERVICE: Daily
DEPARTURE: 10:00
FARE: ¥4,980 [Adult] ¥2,480 [Child]
LANGUAGE: Japanese
REMARKS: all fares and admission charges are included. 6 hours trip.
　　　　Reservation required

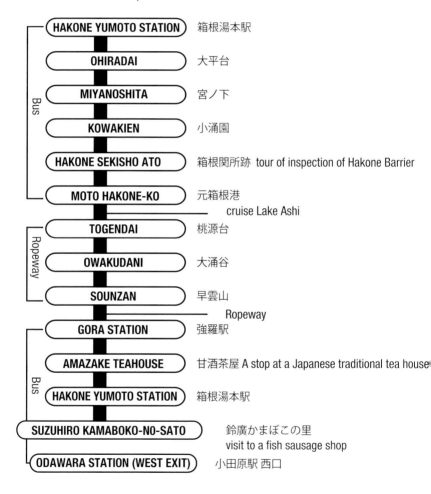

HAKONE YUMOTO STATION	箱根湯本駅	
OHIRADAI	大平台	
MIYANOSHITA	宮ノ下	
KOWAKIEN	小涌園	
HAKONE SEKISHO ATO	箱根関所跡	tour of inspection of Hakone Barrier
MOTO HAKONE-KO	元箱根港	cruise Lake Ashi
TOGENDAI	桃源台	
OWAKUDANI	大涌谷	
SOUNZAN	早雲山	Ropeway
GORA STATION	強羅駅	
AMAZAKE TEAHOUSE	甘酒茶屋	A stop at a Japanese traditional tea house
HAKONE YUMOTO STATION	箱根湯本駅	
SUZUHIRO KAMABOKO-NO-SATO	鈴廣かまぼこの里 visit to a fish sausage shop	
ODAWARA STATION (WEST EXIT)	小田原駅 西口	

Bus · Ropeway · Bus

Hakone Tozan Bus 箱根登山バス

Route descriptions:
- ROUTE 1: ODAWARA STATION – HAKONECHO 小田原駅–箱根町
- ROUTE 2: ODAWARA STATION – KYU KAIDO – UEHATASHUKU 小田原駅–旧街道–上畑宿
- ROUTE 3: ODAWARA STATION – KOJIRI 小田原駅–湖尻
- ROUTE 4: ODAWARA STATION – TOGENDAI 小田原駅–桃源台
- ROUTE 5: ODAWARA STATION – SENGOKU 小田原駅–仙石

BUS STOP	ROUTE 1	ROUTE 2	ROUTE 3	ROUTE 4	ROUTE 5
ODAWARA STATION 小田原駅	●	●	●	●	●
YUMOTO STATION 湯本駅	●	●	●	●	●
TONOSAWA 塔ノ沢	●		●	●	●
OHIRADAI STATION 大平台駅	●		●	●	●
OHIRADAI 大平台	●		●	●	●
MIYANOSHITA 宮ノ下	●		●	●	●
MIYANOSHITA ONSEN 宮ノ下温泉	●		●	●	
KOWAKIDANI STATION 小涌谷駅	●		●	●	●
KOWAKIEN 小涌園	●				
MOTO-HAKONE 元箱根	●				
HAKONE SEKISHO ATO 箱根関所跡	●				
HAKONECHO 箱根町	●				
MIYAGINO 宮城野			●	●	●
HAKONE GARASU-NO-MORI-MAE 箱根ガラスの森前			●	●	●
HAKONE HIGHLAND HOTEL 箱根ハイランドホテル			●	●	●
SENGOKU INFORMATION CENTRE 仙石案内所前			●	●	●
KAWAMUKAI (HOSHI NO OJISAMA) 川向（星の王子さま）			●	●	
SENNGOKU KOGEN 仙石高原			●	●	
HAKONE LAKE HOTEL 箱根レイクホテル前			●	●	
TOGENDAI 桃源台			●	●	
KOJIRI 湖尻			●		

Visiting Mt. Fuji

The towering volcanic cone known as Mt. Fuji is the highest mountain in Japan, and is visible from within a radius of some 780 km [300 mi] in all directions, including from arriving planes. Geologists estimate the mountain was created 600,000 years ago during the Pleistocene era. It last erupted in 1707, and is now dormant.

Mt. Fuji is named for the Buddhist fire goddess Fuchi and is sacred to the Shinto goddess Sengen-Sama, whose shrine is found at the summit. Located in the Fuji-Hakone-Izu National Park, Mt. Fuji is surrounded by five lakes around its waist: Lake Kawaguchiko, Lake Yamanakako, Lake Saiko, Lake Motosuko and Lake Shojiko. The awesome cone's dimensions: 3,776 m [12,388 ft] high; 125.5 km [78 mi] in circumference and 40–48 km [25–30 mi] in diameter around the base; topped with a crater spanning 488 km [1,600 ft] in diameter. Long before you get to the top it is like being on top of the world.

The official climbing season is two months long (July and August), during which time most of the snow has melted except inside the recesses of the cone at the top. Every season, several hundred thousand people, including tourists, climb to the summit, many of them hiking throughout the night to witness the sunrise from the summit.

Getting to Mt. Fuji from Tokyo

Note: Gotemba Station—one of the five stations on Mt Fuji— is 1,400 m above sea level. It has a small shop with toilets and parking lots. There is a bus stop at this station.

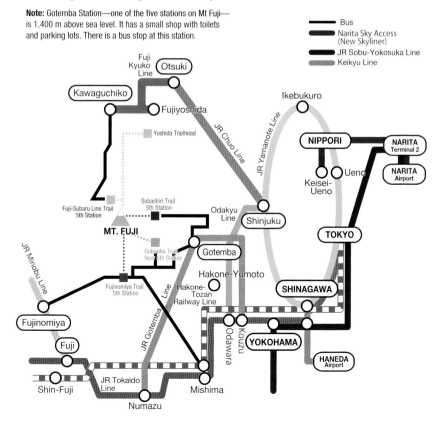

There are 10 stations and over a dozen sub-stations on the way up, the first at the foot of the mountain, where some really serious climbers start, and the 10th at the summit. These include simple huts for resting as well as other basic amenities.

There are four Station 5s located on different sides of the mountain. The most popular is Kawaguchiko on the Tokyo side, to which most climbers go by train from Shinjuku and then by bus to Station 5.

The paths up Mt. Fuji are steep and it takes about 8 hours from Station 5. Most people are moving slow on the last several hundred feet, and it pays to be in pretty good shape before you start.

Access to Mt. Fuji and Fuji-Goko (Five Lakes)

Train/Bus Service

The best way to go to Mt. Fuji from Tokyo is by the Chuo Line train from Shinjuku Station to Otsuki Station where you transfer to the Fuji Kyuko Line. The Fuji Kyuko Line train stops at Fujiyoshida Station, then goes on to Kawaguchiko, the end of the line. There you take a bus to Station 5, where most climbers start.

You can go direct to Station 5 by taking a Keio bus or a Fujikyu bus from the Shinjuku-Highway Bus Terminal next to Shinjuku Train Station in Tokyo. Buses take 2 to 2½ hours and cost ¥2,700. To buy a ticket and board a bus, take the route at the West Exit of Shinjuku Station, then follow the circle of bus stops to the left. The bus building is on the corner near Stop 26, right across from the Yodobashi Camera Shop. Buses going to Mt. Fuji first stop at Station 3 on the waist of Mt. Fuji [for dedicated climbers] before reaching Station 5, so stay on the bus unless you want a really long hike.

Bus service to the four other lakes on the waist of Mt. Fuji—all popular recreation destinations—can also be taken from the Shinjuku-Highway Bus Terminal in Shinjuku.

| DESTINATION | DEPARTURE POINTS | BUS STOPS | FARE | | TIME REQUIRED |
			ADULT (ROUND TRIP)	CHILD (ROUND TRIP)	
FUJI GOKO FIVE LAKES	SHINJUKU-HIGHWAY BUS TERMINAL (新宿高速バスターミナル) FUJIKYU BUS/ KEIO BUSU	FUJIKYU HIGHLAND (富士急ハイランド)	¥1,750	¥880	1 hr 40 min
		KAWAGUCHI LAKE (河口湖)			1 hr 45 min
		YAMANAKA LAKE (山中湖)	¥2,050	¥1,030	2 hr 15 min
		MOTOSU LAKE (本栖湖)			2 hr 30 min
	JR TOKYO STATION BUS TERMINAL (JRハイウェイバスのりば) JR BUS/FUJIKYU BUS	YAMANAKA LAKESIDE (山中湖畔)	¥1,750	¥880	2 hr 20 min
		FUJIKYU HIGHLAND (富士急ハイランド)			2 hr 30 min
		KAWAGUCHI LAKE STATION (河口湖駅)			2 hr 40 min
MT. FUJI	SHINJUKU-HIGHWAY BUS TERMINAL (新宿高速バスターミナル) FUJIKYU BUS/ KEIO BUSU	MT. FUJI SANGO-ME (⅓ of the way to MT. FUJI) (富士山三合目)	¥2,300	¥1,150	2 hr 05 min
		MT. FUJI GOGO-ME (Halfway to MT. FUJI) (富士山五合目)	¥2,700	¥1,350	2 hr 25 min
	KAWAGUCHI-KO STATION (河口湖駅)	MT. FUJI GOGO-ME YOSHIDA-GUCHI (Halfway to MT. FUJI) (富士山五合目吉田口)	¥1,540 (¥2,100)	¥770 (¥1,050)	50 min
	GOTEMBA STATION (御殿場駅)	MT. FUJI SHIN-GOGO-ME SUBASHIRI-GUCHI (Halfway to MT. FUJI) (富士山新五合目須走口)	¥1,540 (¥2,060)	¥770 (¥1,030)	60 min